SOCIAL
RESEARCH
METHODS

Dennis P. Forcese
Carleton University, Ottawa

Stephen Richer
Carleton University, Ottawa

PRENTICE-HALL, INC., ENGLEWOOD CLIFFS, NEW JERSEY

Library of Congress Cataloging in Publication Data

FORCESE, DENNIS P.
    Social research methods.

    Bibliography: p.
        1. Social science research.   2. Sociology—Methodology.   3. Social   sciences—Method-
ology.   Richer, Stephen, joint author.   II. Title.
H62.F62   301.072   73-39062
ISBN   0-13-8

PRENTICE-HALL SOCIOLOGY SERIES

Neil J. Smelser, Editor

10 9 8 7 6 5 4 3 2 1

PRINTED IN THE UNITED STATES OF AMERICA

PRENTICE-HALL INTERNATIONAL, INC., *London*
PRENTICE-HALL OF AUSTRALIA PTY. LTD., *Sydney*
PRENTICE-HALL OF CANADA, LTD., *Toronto*
PRENTICE-HALL OF INDIA PRIVATE LIMITED, *New Delhi*
PRENTICE-HALL OF JAPAN, INC., *Tokyo*

Contents

iii

iv   Contents

Preface

If you are beginning your studies in sociology, we hope that this text will be of assistance. It is our view that an overview of social research methods can only enhance your appreciation of any area of study in sociology. Ideally, this text will begin to provide a basis for your critical analysis of the substantive material which you study and are asked to accept in your other courses.

It is our express wish, therefore, that this text not be used simply as an isolated attempt to grasp some understanding of research techniques. Instead, it should be a means of reinforcing your broader studies.

Similarly, other material in sociology should make the contents of this book more meaningful. As you become familiar with actual examples of social research, whether in deviance, politics, urban studies, or any of the substantive areas, discussion of research methods will become progressively less abstract. In this sense, the book is only a preliminary means to formal training in the conduct of social research.

We would be foolish to believe that this or any other methods text may serve as a complete learning experience in research methods. Especially it cannot serve as a substitute for the actual *experience* of research. However, we do believe that there is value in the pre-knowledge and suggestions to be found in a text. Accordingly, we intend that this book be used by you as a guide. It is an introduction to the meaning and context of social research, and the options in research approach and technique. It will not enable you to avoid all errors as you attempt a research project, but it should enable you to avoid many.

We have presented the conduct of research as a series of interrelated decisions and have attempted to make clear the options available to researchers in research design or format and in data collection tools or techniques. The appropriateness and implications of decisions for given research problems are identified. There is obviously some sequence in research decisions—some problems must necessarily be overcome before others. And, as each decision is made, such as the kind of data generated, subsequent options are narrowed, such as the statistical tests appropriately employed. There are thus chains of dependence. We of course concede that this view of the research process is somewhat of a distortion insofar as there is not a perfectly linear sequence of decision and action. In point of fact, there is an interaction, with a researcher necessarily anticipating contingencies and possibilities. Nor are research designs perfectly discrete, or data collection tools mutually exclusive; rather they are supplementary with mixed design and data collection normally advisable. But for purposes of exposition, we believe it valuable to present the materials in a manner which emphasizes stages of dependency. You should be aware, therefore, that our discussion—in particular our discussion of research formats—is ideal-typical.

We must also acknowledge our explicit emphasis upon a causal orientation—a characteristic of the text which some sociologists will undoubtedly find intellectually offensive. Yet, it is this orientation which we believe characterizes Western science, and which now manifests itself quite visibly in the social sciences in the efforts devoted to formal causal modeling.

The attempt to study phenomena scientifically is obviously

premised, whether explicitly or not, upon some conception of causality. In that we attempt to explain phenomena—account for the variation in one variable by virtue of its association with variation in another variable—we are assuming connections among such factors which one might as well identify as causal.

We tend to take causal thinking very much in stride. Our ordered, industrialized, change-oriented culture takes for granted the existence of cause and effect—a knowable and controllable universe. Anthropologists tell us, however, that not all peoples think causally. For example, present-oriented peasant cultures, lacking a temporal reference to the past, will in large part lack the causal attitude of our culture. Dorothy Lee, an anthropologist, has written of "lineal and nonlineal codifications of reality," the latter lack the sequential-temporal attitude to phenomena which we take for granted. So, for example, Lee discusses the Trobriand Islanders, who do not think in terms of causal chains, but of present happenings—an orientation reflected in the Trobriand language. (Dorothy Lee, "Lineal and Nonlineal Codification of Reality," *Psychosomatic Medicine* XII: (1950) 89–97.)

The causal orientation of Western civilization, therefore, is not in any sense a human universal. But it is an orientation which has permitted the realization of that unique enterprise, science. Today many scientists choose to avoid the word "cause" for, in their view, it denotes a rigidity, a precise determinism which they believe science never realizes. Whatever the euphemism one adopts for "cause," it seems clear that any scientist has causation in mind as he conducts his enquiry.

However, *no scientist can ever prove causation.* It is always a matter of inference. A sociologist, for example, may establish a statistical relationship among variables—a relationship sufficient to account for a good deal of the variance in variable X by reference to variable Y. But he cannot ever conclude definitively that X causes Y, or that Y causes X. He can only infer such possibilities on the bases of supporting theory or information.

Although the object of this text is to present research procedure, we also emphasize that research is not to be viewed as something independent of the substantive interests of a science. It should be understood that such abstraction from substantive content is only a device in any methods text in order that the several procedures of data collection and analysis are more clearly illuminated.

So as to minimize the abstraction of research technique from research context, we have taken care to emphasize the inextricable connection between the conduct of research and the environmental context and theoretical derivation and import of research. Although intent upon describing "techniques" of data collection and management, we believed it necessary to emphasize the essential narrowness of that activity, insofar as it is only a fragment of action derived from a societal context. Thus, public and personal values and interests influence the prescientific question of what is to be researched. And they also affect how it is to be researched and if and how the results of the research are used. So, in this sense at least, we do not subscribe to the "myth of value-free sociology." This is not an utter rejection of the objectivity in replicable procedures of investigation once a research problem has been determined.

In sum, we view the scientific approach as a peculiar ideology. Social science is a way of approaching the world of which it is itself a part. And while there is no final truth, no ultimate proof, science has at least offered useful truth claims. For this reason at least, we believe that it is inevitable that social science will persist even if it often lacks the drama and emotional appeal of short-cut answers to the questions which trouble contemporary man.

PART ONE

Some Men Call It Science

chapter one

SCIENTIFIC ENQUIRY

It is almost impossible to state when the scientific mode of enquiry assumed dominant importance in human intellectual history. One can refer to names such as Copernicus, Galileo, Bacon, and Newton and still be rather arbitrary in designating a "scientific revolution." There really was no revolution in the sense of a sudden achievement, but rather an accretion of achievements that reinforced the "rationalist" economics of Post-Reformation Europeans.

Science as a mode of enquiry had established itself firmly in Western civilization with the Industrial Revolution. By the nineteenth century in England, science had attained the stature that magic enjoyed in other cultures. In some part its prestige was derived from the social class from which many scientific vocations were drawn, for science had become the intellectual pastime of

3

gentlemen. But the prestige of science also derived in large part from its payoff; its findings were utilizable in the expanding industrial colossus. It was thereby acceptable to the middle class as well as to the aristocracy.

Little wonder, then, that in the nineteenth century the scientific study of man began to attract attention. The physical sciences constituted the model, literally, with frequent analogy to the subject matter of the physical scientists. The analogy of society consisting of similar structure and function to biological organisms influenced the work of almost every nineteenth-century sociologist. For example in France, Auguste Comte, the conventionally designated "father of sociology," adopted a biological referent and advocated sociology as the queen of sciences—the ultimate achievement of rational society.

Yet in the eyes of many, sociology and the other social sciences have not as yet produced the "payoff" that is expected of the scientific method and that was optimistically predicted by nineteenth-century sociologists such as Comte. Contemplating the applications derived from the physical sciences, many observers have suggested that the social sciences suffer from a superabundance of trivia and essentially useless speculation and petty findings. A sociologist, Alan Mazur, has argued that the distinguishing feature of science is profundity (Mazur, 1968). Sociology, when assessed against this criterion, proves to be less than science proper, in Mazur's view, for its findings are readily comprehensible by the layman, and often little more than restatements of common sense.

Serious as this charge is, it appears to be an overstatement. The literature in social science abounds with research findings that fly in the face of common sense as it may have been perceived at a given time and place. For example, one might use Berelson and Steiner's inventory of more than a thousand empirical statements as a checklist of social science findings (Berelson and Steiner, 1964). Consider as specific examples the following popular beliefs cited by Dean and Valdes (Dean and Valdes, 1967). Each of them has been demonstrated to be false on the basis of social science research.

"Fuller knowledge about other nations promotes international good will."

"Murderers are among the worst risks of all law violators on parole."

"In mate selection, it is true that 'opposites attract'."

These statements are all plausible and still widely believed, yet research findings do not support them. But even given such correction of common-sense knowledge as an indication of sociological output, there would seem to be a danger in overemphasizing tangible results such as measured against those apparently derivative of the physical sciences. Particularly is this so if we consider that many of these results have produced unintended and often undesirable social consequences. Many of the problems now being researched by social scientists are precisely those derived from the rapid social change associated with scientific-industrial innovations.

Similarly, it is doubtful that we should value in itself the esoteric expression of scientific findings. Difficulty in comprehension or access for the layman does not guarantee profundity or significance. Rather, the success of the scientific method is in large part attributable to its rigorous method, including the collective scrutiny and constant reexamination of findings by some community of scientists. That is to say, canons of verification which render supposition and common sense conceptions of reality into fact—that which is proven to be—are the basic characteristics of the scientific method. Consider further that such systematic verification requires that scientists—whether physicists, chemists, biologists, psychologists, or sociologists, to mention but a few—are necessarily concerned with apparently undramatic trivia. Most scientists are persons picking away, contributing, and building upon rather modest observations. Infrequently is such labor blessed with the spectacular drama of the genius and his great intuitive mental leap and discovery. Perhaps this has happened, as our folk myths would have us believe, but if so, these mental leaps were preceded by, made possible by, or followed by the work of less conspicuous researchers than the Galileos, the Newtons, and the Einsteins (Kuhn, 1962).

Science may "rest on the shoulders of giants," but the giants are themselves supported by mere mortals. Perhaps science is after all nearer the entertaining but deflating speculation of an infinite number of monkeys set loose upon an infinite number of typewriters. Max Gluckman has observed, "a science is any discipline in which the fool of this generation can go beyond the point reached by the genius of the last generation" (Gluckman, 1965). A science, then, is a cumulative thing—the product of the efforts of many and not just the lucky or intuitive few. What in fact are the distinguishing features of this practice called science?

Imagine for a moment that you are faced with a situation in which it is necessary to respond to an examiner's demands to summarize the critical assumptions, characteristics, and goals of science. Imagine further that this very unreasonable examiner requires that your response be limited to a maximum of six words, and that your reply be equally applicable to sociology, psychology, chemistry, physics, astronomy, or any other area of scientific enquiry. However disagreeable a chap he might be, the examiner would be bound to concede your mastery were you to utter these six associated words: explanation, prediction, pattern, repetition, replication, and quantification. The goals of explanation and prediction, the assumption of patterned and repetitious phenomena, and enquiry characterized by quantification and replication are inextricably intertwined and summarize the essence of any science.

Explanation and Prediction

It is commonly argued that the objects of scientific enquiry are explanation and prediction. *By prediction we mean the ability to anticipate some given outcome.* This anticipation is predicated upon appreciation of some relationship between phenomena such that knowledge or control of one phenomenon will permit prediction of the second. Thus, for example, we might infer from past experience that whenever it snows, people roast chestnuts. Accepting for purposes of illustration this implausible prediction, notice that it is knowledge of the presence of snow that enables us to anticipate the action of roasting chestnuts. We are making an inductive inference on the basis of repeated observation. *Induction* is, therefore, *a process of generalization derived from numerous observations*—what J. S. Mill called "generalization from experience." Note that in our example there is not necessarily the suggestion that the snow causes the behavior, chestnut roasting. Or, to take an actual example from sociology, from an examination of the religious composition of societies and the phenomenon of suicide, Durkheim was able to predict that Protestant nations would manifest a higher incidence of suicide than would Catholic nations (Durkheim, 1951). Although he was quite prepared to suggest an explanation, Durkheim was able to make the prediction without any attempt to suggest why the prediction would be realized, other than by reference to a pattern of prior association. Thus, as in these examples, one should be aware that *prediction is possible without explanation.* Moreover it should be noted that a prediction is typically a statement of probable outcome or stochastic relationship. That is, a predicted outcome is expected to occur within certain limits of probability as opposed to its always occurring. Thus Durkheim spoke in terms of aggregate rates of suicide rather than stating that certain specific individuals would or would not commit suicide.

When, in addition, Durkheim attempted a response to the question "Why?" he was venturing an *explanation*. He suggested that there was a difference in the extent to which Protestants and Catholics emphasized and achieved an integrated group structure, thereby influencing the occurrence of the individual decisions to commit suicide. In highly integrated Catholic communities, suicide was less apt to occur than in the relatively less integrated Protestant communities. Durkheim, speaking not in terms of the presence or absence of suicide but in terms of its extent, thereby offered an explanation of the relationship between religion and suicide. He had a factual relationship and inferred a possible basis for the relationship—that is, he suggested why the relationship might exist. *Explanation is essentially an answer to the query "Why?"* This process of *causal inference* or imputation will be dealt with in subsequent chapters. Suffice it to note here that the explanation was a matter of making sense of the relationship between phenomena. If we explain the occurrence of some given phenomenon, then we should be able to better predict the *condition* of its future occurrence—but not the precise time or place. The last will always depend upon prior knowledge of the presence of causal agents. That is, we may know that *x* causes *y*, but in order to precisely predict *y*, we must identify the presence of *x*.

Ultimately science, as a form of human intellectual enquiry, seeks to explain, to predict, and to control phenomena. This appreciation of the causes of the given behavior provides us an opportunity to control that behavior in the sense of preparing for it, adjusting for it, and perhaps altering the necessary conditions such that it does not occur, or if it is so desired, it occurs more often, or occurs only when we wish it to. Thus whatever his more superficial motives, the object of a sociologist's efforts acting as a social *scientist* is to predict, explain, and thereby potentially provide the means of greater control of human behavior. This last is a grievously serious prospect, as shall be discussed in the next chapter.

Patterned and Repetitious Phenomena

If explanation and prediction are the objects of science, then it is perfectly obvious that scientists assume that their phenomena, whether atoms or people, are capable of explanation, implying in turn the more fundamental assumption that the behavior of these phenomena is patterned. If there are no systemic properties among phenomena—if there is no order, no structure, no sequence of relations among phenomena—then anything but the grossest explanation would be impossible. If anarchy prevailed such that atoms circulated randomly or people wandered aimlessly, then it would not be possible to establish links between phenomena and aspects of phenomena, for there would be none of any enduring sort. Fleeting, idiosyncratic explanations or gross, general explanations might be offered, but these would be modest indeed. Moreover, they would not permit accurate prediction.

This would be so in that lacking pattern or order these phenomena would also lack repetition. That which occurs once and only once is simply not amenable to *verifiable* explanation. This is not to say that there may not be some rather unique events, but that however unique such events may appear, unless they share certain attributes or characteristics with other events of a similar class or set, they will not be capable of scientific explanation or prediction.

Some scientists shun the word "cause," for it implies a precision and a determinism they are hesitant to endorse. But however the word is regarded, some assumption of a causally ordered universe of phenomena is made by a scientist. Phenomena recur, and they recur in the context of some discernable relationships. Thus the physical scientist works with certain laws of physical behavior which relate, for example, mass, volume, and velocity. Accordingly, an eight-ounce apple the size of your hand will react in a predictable manner when thrown against a brick wall, as will an automobile, superficially distinct from the apple, when it encounters the same brick wall at 30 miles per hour. The sun will reappear regularly, as verified through succeeding observations, or the seasons will vary regularly and predictably. Similarly, people will report for work at a fixed time, eat their meals at a regular time, and perhaps respond aggressively in a regular and predictable manner given appropriate and specific conditions. Such *patterned* and *repetitious* behavior is that which permits the peculiar mode of enquiry known as science.

Replication

But philosophy as well as science may have as its object the explanation, and even conceivably the prediction, of behavior. Thus a philosopher or anyone else might well suggest plausible and logical explanation of some feature of his environment. But a scientist, in doing so, will specify criteria of plausibility and will offer information that will satisfy these criteria. He will deal in verified relationships and explanations. Leaving aside for the moment the means whereby a scientist would gather and measure the appropriate information for such an explanation, it is necessary to note that his explanation would be based upon repeated observations of the relationship to be explained. That is, through *replication*—the successive examination and reexamination of his own findings and those of other scientists—he will have verified a set of findings. The observations will be known to occur because they will have been discerned under comparable, if not identical, conditions by many independent observers. There will be thus some assurance of *reliable* observation. If suggested relationships are based upon the findings of one or a few individuals, then we are not dealing with a scientific fact. Replication is a distinguishing characteristic of the scientific approach to the acquisition of knowledge.

Quantification

The observations with which scientists deal in the present century are extremely precise compared to those that characterized all previous historical attempts at dealing with observable phenomena. The phenomena are carefully and finely identified such that their distinguishing characteristics and their relationships can be repeatedly identified. The scientist is not depending upon some impression of pattern and repetition, but rather upon some standardized representation of such phenomena.

Such standardization and the consequent relative precision have been associated with quantification. *Quantification* refers, in its most simple sense, to counting. That is, something is identified, and each time it occurs it is noted. More generally, then, *quantification refers to the assignment of numerical values to the phenomena under investigation.* Such counting or designation of numerical value can assume different forms of varying precision and utility, as we shall discuss in Chapter 5. But whatever its form, basically quantification permits the simplification and ordering of observations such that those features that given objects might have in common are distinguished from those that may superficially suggest the objects are different. In a very general sense, quantification has permitted the scientist to abstract from the apparent confusion of reality, to systematize the apparent plethora of observation.

In science one deals with *variables*. *A variable is literally an item that may assume more than one value.* Minimally, there will be two values, such as hot or cold, black or white. But more precisely, we can identify several values, degrees of coldness, or degrees of blackness. Quantification permits the relatively accurate designation of such values. The more developed the quantification, the finer the identification of values such that, to take up our example again, we come to deal in degrees of temperature rather than dealing merely with hotness or coldness. As we shall discuss when considering measurement, quantification permits a science to specify relationships among variables, thereby permitting in turn, explanation and prediction.

Sociology shares each of these distinguishing assumptions, goals, and procedures. As an empirical science, sociology is intent upon quantification as a means of accurately identifying aspects of human behavior so that they might be explained and predicted. The manner in which sociologists and other social scientists attempt to realize this intention is the subject of each of the subsequent chapters of this book.

CONCLUSIONS

In this chapter we have equated explanation to statements of causal deduction. That is, in our view, an answer to the question "Why?" inevitably entails reference to some causal factor(s). Whether implicitly or explicitly, relationships among variables are expressed so that the behavior of a given variable can be accounted for by reference to some other variable or variables.

This emphasis upon causal explanation is not one with which all scientists would be comfortable. Many would prefer to speak only in terms of statistical relationships among variables. This is a practical position given the state of empirical social science; it is simply too often impractical to engage in causal inference. Many given statistical relationships among variables simply do not reflect causal relationships.

But causal statements are a goal of science. They are not the only output: good description of empirical phenomena and statistical-functional relationships also are necessary products of research. However, as should become more apparent in subsequent discussion, especially in Chapters 4, 6, 7, 14, and 15, it is our view that causal statements should ultimately be realized.

REFERENCES

BERELSON, B. AND G. STEINER, *Human Behavior: An Inventory of Scientific Findings.* New York: Harcourt Brace Jovanovich, 1964.

DEAN, D. AND D. VALDES, *Experiments in Sociology* (2nd ed., Student's Manual). New York: Appleton-Century-Crofts, 1967.

DURKHEIM, EMILE, *Suicide.* New York: Free Press, 1951.

GLUCKMAN, MAX, *Politics, Law and Ritual in Tribal Society.* New York: New American Library, 1965.

KUHN, THOMAS, *The Structure of Scientific Revolutions.* Chicago: University of Chicago Press, 1962.

MAZUR, ALAN, "The Littlest Science," *The American Sociologist*, Vol. 3 (August 1968), 195–200; reprinted in D. Forcese and S. Richer, eds., *Stages of Social Research: Contemporary Perspectives*, pp. 4–14. Englewood Cliffs, N.J.: Prentice-Hall, 1970.

SELECTED ADDITIONAL READINGS (ANNOTATED)

BUTTERFIELD, HERBERT, *The Origins of Modern Science* (rev. ed.). New York: Crowell Collier and Macmillan, 1962. A brief and very readable history of scientific development up to the eighteenth century.

HINKLE, R. AND G. HINKLE, *The Development of Modern Sociology.* New York: Random House, 1954. A brief work that traces the European origins of contemporary American Sociology and its quest for scientific status.

MADGE, JOHN, *The Origins of Scientific Sociology*. New York: Free Press, 1962. An examination of sociology as science by means of analysis of selected works in the discipline, including Durkheim's *Suicide*.

ROSE, ARNOLD, *Theory and Method in the Social Sciences*. Minneapolis: University of Minnesota Press, 1954. Replication in sociology often seems all too rare a thing. Rose offers a list of replicated studies.

Objectivity and Science

Given the objectives of description, explanation, and prediction of human social behavior, social science obviously cannot be viewed as divorced from its societal context. Its activities and findings are necessarily of some social import. Consequently it is imperative that before we examine the stages of research we consider some possible misconceptions regarding scientific neutrality or objectivity.

Insofar as science is concerned with verified fact, procedural criteria which maximize objectivity are critical to scientific enquiry. Yet when we pause to reflect, it is apparent that there are three closely related points in the total process of enquiry associated with some research problem at which science is influenced by "extra-scientific" factors. The first such general point of extra-objective influence precedes the actual acts of data collection and analysis. The second occurs during the course of these acts. The third follows them.

OBJECTIVITY AND PROBLEM SELECTION

In the first instance we have the several social influences that prompt a scientist or a group of scientists to select a given research problem. A popular stereotype of the scientist is that of the dedicated individual supremely indifferent to the diversions of the outside world. There are variations on this theme, with the notions of absent-mindedness and hermit-like existence often associated with this folk conception. But the meaning constantly conveyed is that of the individual totally committed to his quest for knowledge, seeking truth for truth's sake, unaffected by influences external to his scientific pursuits. In fact, many social scientists have advocated isolated commitments to enquiry that are quite similar to these stereotypes. For example, many sociologists subscribed to what they understood to be Max Weber's suggestion of role segregation: a sociologist should be ethically neutral in the capacity of researcher, whatever he may do in the capacity of the individual citizen (Weber, 1949).

However, such a role segregation does not seem to render research free from extra-scientific influence. Roles are not so conveniently distinguishable. Just as a sociologist would insist that any man is in large part the product of his environment, including his social relationships, we would have to insist that the sociologist as researcher as much as the sociologist as citizen is dependent upon a variety of social influences to which he is exposed, whether he attempts to be ethically neutral or not. Our researcher, like everyone else, will be a man in society, a citizen, bound by the constraints of his social relationships. And he will have acquired certain attitudes and beliefs—"values"—that will govern his behavioral decisions. Weber in fact was well aware of such cultural-historical influences upon a scientist's behavior, and rightly viewed them as inevitable (Weber, 1949, 77). His suggested role segregation was not intended to eliminate such influences.

Rather, it was an ethic intended to limit politics in the name of science, with persons using the mantle of objective science to propagate personal views (Weber, 1949; also Aron, 1964, 67–106).

Values will influence a scientist's selection of a researchable problem. In selecting some problem for investigation, the researcher will have been prompted by some notions of the import or significance of the research. Such criteria of significance will vary in their consciousness or explicitness. In some instances the decision may reflect very deliberate utilitarian calculations. But even where such consciousness is lacking, the individual researcher will be guided by some shared beliefs and values that will suggest research priorities. Research problems in nuclear physics, for example, were significantly defined in response to the demands of wartime. The societal inputs influencing the selection of given research problems in nuclear physics consisted of government decisions of priority and support, which largely determined what a scientist would be able to do, as well as the attitudes of the scientists themselves which prompted them to accept, and sometimes encourage, these government definitions of research scope. Similarly, looking at the history of sociology's development in the United States, public interest in the problems associated with the assimilation of immigrant peoples and expanding urban centers prompted considerable research examining deviance, such as delinquency and crime. That individual sociologists shared the view that such phenomena were undesirable in some way and worthy of amelioration prompted them to attempt to meet public demand for research related to such behavior.

At the very least, therefore, any science lacks autonomy insofar as it is dependent upon some social definition of priority or significance. Inevitably there will be societal demands that certain phenomena be investigated with a view to eventual control, such as public pressures for pollution investigation. Not only will a researcher's interests be shaped by social definitions, but some objects of enquiry will more readily realize financial support, even excessive support, while others lack such support, thereby deterring research. In this sense there is no "pure" science, for even if we could realize the ideal of the scientist interested in knowledge for its own sake, someone else is interested in its application, or at least interested in the illusion of its potential application.

Similarly, there will be societal sensibilities, often shared by a researcher, that will deter some kinds of research. Certain aspects of human behavior, such as sexuality, for example, may be socially defined as inviolate or too sensitive to be subject to scientific examination. Some aspects of behavior may be ideologically prohibited, as manifest, for example, in the frequent unwillingness of liberal social scientists to entertain hypotheses regarding significant biological variations related to race. Conversely, other liberal social scientists will be prompted to research race-related hypotheses from the conviction that racial stigmata are reprehensible and to be corrected through social awareness.

Since a scientist is not independent of his social milieu any more than anyone else, he is bound to share some public enthusiasms, some public predispositions, some public conventions, which will in some way limit the range of researchable problems from which he will select, or indeed, of which he will even conceive.

Moreover, the scientist as an individual will have personal needs and career aspirations that may significantly affect his problem selection. Too often the visibility and popularity of certain areas of research will influence a scientist's choice as he considers professional and public recognition opportunities rather than theoretically inspired criteria in selecting a research problem. The scope of research problems will be narrowed further as funding agencies apply their interests in selecting among research proposals appealing for support. Such agencies have selection biases, and often a research scientist may express a research proposal in a manner calculated to appeal to such biases.

The above influences are summarized in Figure 2–1.

These influences upon problem selection are inevitable. They do not violate any canons of scientific method, insofar as we must view science as a mode of enquiry once a research problem has been designated. These influences can be thought of, therefore, as "prescientific," in that they precede the actual conduct of research and validation procedures. As we shall discuss in a sub-

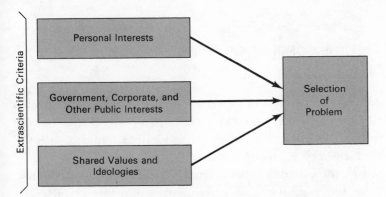

FIG. 2-1 FACTORS AFFECTING PROBLEM SELECTION

sequent chapter, these influences are in effect a prior set of criteria which guide research in addition to criteria internal to a scientific discipline itself.

It is the concession that such prescientific influences do affect research definitions that has prompted many scientists, from physicists concerned with the applications of nuclear research to sociologists concerned with urban growth, to argue that rather than pretend that such influences are nonexistent or unimportant, they should be employed more deliberately as criteria of problem selection. That is, the individual scientist should depend upon his own value position as a guide rather than that of other decision makers, thereby accepting a moral responsibility for the potential of research findings. Accordingly, a sociologist might emphasize enquiry relating to pressing social problems, and in this way achieve research of social significance (Mazur, 1968). The selection of the problem would have been made by the sociologist as a participating and concerned member of his society. Then the role of citizen would be suspended, insofar as it is possible to do so, once the research problem has been selected. From this point he would be guided by professionally shared standards of objectivity which allow for the verification of his work by others, until such time as the appropriate research activities are terminated.

MORALITY AND THE CONDUCT OF RESEARCH

In addition, however, to extra-scientific influences upon problem designation, there is a second manner in which societal values affect research. This relates to social guidelines and limitations upon techniques of scientific enquiry.

Obviously the research instruments available to scientists are affected by the magnitude of public support. Most research is supported by government agencies, corporate agencies, or "independent" granting agencies which in turn derive financial and legal status from government and corporate bases. Therefore the technology of research available to a researcher is often dependent upon decisions made by nonscientists. Similarly, the time scientists will have available to devote to given research will be related to the tangible financial support they receive. The hardware of scientific enquiry and the time devoted to the enquiry are both commodities associated with the conduct of research as well as with the prior question of designating a research problem. Whether the scientist is left to resort to tedious tabulations by hand or the liberated manipulations of computer technology will depend upon decisions external to the research enterprise. The more important research is perceived to be by funding agencies the greater the financial support for research tools.

In addition, there are moral judgments made by a public and by the researcher as a member of that public regarding the appropriateness of given research procedures. Public attitudes will affect the freedom to experiment upon human subjects in psychological research. The separation of twin infants and their isolation in carefully controlled experimental settings, for example, would be a difficult situation to fully realize, for it would not be condoned by an informed public in most societies. Similarly, the removal of infants from slum communities with a view to disrupting the poverty cycle would not presently be supported in most nations.

Not least, it must also be recognized that value judgments are inherent in the researcher's perception and interpretation of research findings. Clearly his expectations will affect whether or not he notes and responds to given research outcomes. Barber and Fox describe the manner in which the expectations of two independently operating researchers influenced response to the phenomenon of floppy ears when rabbits were injected with a given enzyme, one researcher following up on the phenomenon, and another not (Barber and Fox, 1958). The floppy ears were not anticipated by either researcher. In one instance a researcher was so preoccupied with his predefined research problem and hypotheses as to fail to follow up on the unexpected or anomalous phenomena of the floppy ears.

How we make sense of or interpret findings—the meaning we attach to them—is dependent upon theoretical and perhaps personal commitments. Such preconceptions can affect what we see, what we judge it to mean, and even what we report.

In addition, some value or moral judgment enters the assessment of research when we determine whether or not to accept some given findings. We deal with relationships between variables; these relationships are established within certain limits of confidence. Insofar as we decide that we accept some given finding and its theoretical and applied implications, we do so with some probability of error—one, two, or five chances in a hundred, for example. In doing so, as Rudner argues, we are saying that such error is important or unimportant. In Rudner's words:

Since no scientific hypothesis is ever completely verified, in accepting a hypothesis on the basis of evidence, the scientist must make the decision that the evidence is sufficiently strong and that the probability is sufficiently high to warrant the acceptance of the hypothesis. Obviously, our decision with regard to the evidence and how strong is 'strong enough' is going to be a function of the 'importance', in the typically ethnical sense, or making a mistake in accepting or rejecting the hypothesis (Rudner, 1961, 32–33).

Figure 2–2 summarizes the sources of influence upon the actual conduct of research, including the very techniques of research

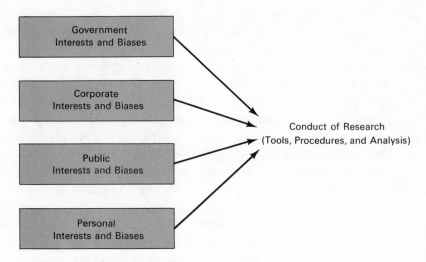

FIG. 2–2 FACTORS AFFECTING THE CONDUCT OF RESEARCH

as well as the acceptance or rejection and the interpretation of research data.

MORALITY AND RESEARCH APPLICATION

The question of the tolerability of error is related to the application of research. It suggests that the social significance of some research findings will affect a researcher's willingness to accept them. It may not be simply a matter of tolerable error.

Research findings, because of potential application, may be resisted by the researcher himself and/or by those informed of research findings. Research may suggest the necessity of disrupting slum family relations in order to destroy persisting poverty; it may suggest the need for the infusion of massive financial support to eliminate forms of deviance; it may suggest the futility of censorship and the positive functions of pornography; but these findings may also be resisted by policy makers.

Whether or not and how the findings of research are utilized is a counterpart of the prescientific factors with which we began.

Decisions regarding application are *postscientific*, distinguishable from the conduct of investigation. As the research is being conducted or after the research results are in, someone must make a decision as to the use to which the results might be put. Depending in part upon such decisions, therefore, are research applications. And, as indicated in Figure 2–3, dependent upon such application decisions are future research allocations. Moreover, applications will affect the conduct of research already underway in the sense of influencing resource commitments and the attitudes of researchers insofar as they are aware of or anticipate application decisions. In the same manner, it must be noted, if some given research is initiated with a view to some predetermined application, the conduct of research will be affected.

OBJECTIVE SUBJECTIVITY

Like prescientific influences, application decisions are not irrelevant to the individual scientist or community of scientists. In fact, most scientific bodies have some statement of ethical expectations that relates to the application potential of research as well as to the actual conduct of research.

Such pre- and postscientific factors need not be confounded with research per se. This is not to suggest that we shut our eyes and wish them away; depending upon our point of view we will necessarily cope with them in some way or another. But to point to the existence of such influences or to point to the scientists con-

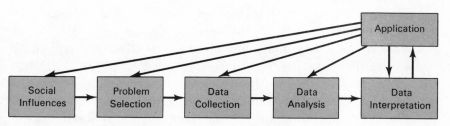

Fig. 2–3 Interaction of Factors Affecting Complete Research Process

spicuously affected by or indulging in such influences does not at the same time necessarily point to the existence of biased or subjectively contaminated research.

If a science employs some standardized techniques of enquiry, and more important, explicit canons of verification, then science may correct for extra-scientific influences relative to a given social environment. An individual scientist may attempt to be objective and honest in his work, or not. He may attempt to control or correct for his predispositions and interests, or he may not. And he may succeed in his efforts, or he may not.

Fortunately no science depends upon the findings of an individual researcher or a few researchers. Nor is any science dependent upon the research of one or a few generations or periods. Nor is any science dependent upon the research of any one nation or collectivity. As noted in the previous chapter, science is cumulative and should be based upon continual replications of findings leading to refinements, adjustments, corrections, and ultimately the growth of a fund of information.

Ultimately it is the community of scientists, not simply one or a few academic disciplines, nor one or a few nations or historical periods, which is the means to scientific objectivity. Individual introspection and control may flag, schools of enquiry may indulge in peculiar excesses. But a scientific fact is never irrevocable and never based upon individual claim. Value biases may not be eliminated through individual self-criticism, but as Nagel put it, they will be controlled "through the self-corrective mechanism of science as a social enterprise" (Nagel, 1961, 489). Objectivity, then, is derived from "critical examination by an indefinitely large community of students" (Nagel, 1961, 490). Thereby, as research persists, research findings—scientific facts—become more reliable, more nearly approximations of some ideal of truth, yet paradoxically, less inviolable, less absolute. But they remain objective findings.

As such, a researcher need not be obsessed with the view that he must abstain from public involvement in issues related to his research. Indeed, because of the very real social significance of most research, it is imperative that such intervention be undertaken. As Newman argues:

Since everything science discovers affects man's behavior and brings about changes—slight or profound, immediate or deferred—in his relation to himself, society and the physical world, it is evident that science has ethical consequences and that the notion of a 'neutral', passive science is absurd. There is no inconsistency between the proposition (which is true) that the scientist at work must not permit his preconceptions and preferences to interfere with an unbiased appraisal, and the proposition (which is equally true) that the scientist has the right, and duty, to express opinions about the social meaning of his results.

The responsible scientist is esthetically obligated to be un-neutral, to direct attention to evils when he sees them, and to press for reforms when the results of his research point the need and the proper direction; in sum, to regard special knowledge not as a disability but as a means to special good (Newman, 1961, Vol. 2, 102).

CONCLUSIONS

As we conduct research, standardized and replicable procedures should be identified and employed. They should be used with the conscious intention of systematically and honestly exploring human behavior. This done, and the findings communicated, the research will be scrutinized by a community of researchers such that findings will not be accepted on the basis of a researcher's intention, moral stance, or reputation. Rather, eventually, the criterion of acceptability will be replicability. The means to standardization of procedures such that replication may be undertaken are discussed in the following chapters.

REFERENCES

ARON, RAYMOND, *German Sociology*. New York: Free Press, 1964.
BARBER, B. AND R. FOX, "The Case of the Floppy-Eared Rabbits: An Instance of Serendipity Gained and Serendipity Lost," *The Ameri-*

can Journal of Sociology, Vol. 54 (1958), 128–36; reprinted in **D.** Forcese and S. Richer, eds., *Stages of Social Research: Contemporary Perspectives*, pp. 27–37. Englewood Cliffs, N.J.: Prentice-Hall, 1970.

MAZUR, ALAN, "The Littlest Science," *The American Sociologist*, Vol. 3 (August 1968), 195–200; reprinted in Forcese and Richer, *Stages of Social Research: Contemporary Perspectives*, pp. 4–14.

NAGEL, ERNEST, *The Structure of Science*. New York: Harcourt Brace Jovanovich, 1961.

NEWMAN, JAMES, *Science and Sensibility*, Vols. 1 and 2. New York: Simon & Schuster, 1961.

RUDNER, R., "Value Judgments in the Acceptance of Theories," in P. Frank, ed., *The Validation of Scientific Theories*, pp. 31–35. New York: Crowell-Collier and Macmillan, 1961.

WEBER, MAX, *On the Methodology of the Social Sciences*. New York: Oxford University Press, 1949.

SELECTED ADDITIONAL READINGS (ANNOTATED)

GOULDNER, ALVIN, "Anti-Minotaur: The Myth of a Value-Free Sociology," in M. Stein and A. Vidich, eds., *Sociology on Trial*, pp. 35–52. Englewood Cliffs, N.J.: Prentice-Hall, 1963. A very well-written critique of the interpretations placed by some sociologists upon Max Weber's views on science and objectivity.

LYND, ROBERT, *Knowledge for What?* Princeton: Princeton University Press, 1939. One of the earliest and best pleas for a value-committed American sociology.

MILLS, C. W., *The Sociological Imagination*. New York: Oxford University Press, 1959. A powerful polemic condemning contemporary sociology for its failure to come to grips with American social problems.

WEBER, MAX, "Science as a Vocation," in H. Gerth and C. W. Mills, eds. and translators, *From Max Weber: Essays in Sociology*, pp. 129–56. New York: Oxford University Press, 1958. The lecture in which Weber argued for a role segregation, with roles of teacher and scientist distinct from one's role activities as citizen and politician.

Conceptualization: Abstract and Operational

In the previous chapter we considered the manner in which environmental influences affect the selection of research problems, the conduct of research, and the analysis, interpretation, and application of research findings. We shall now consider another limitation upon the conduct of research, one which is inherent in human expression.

Symbols as Expressions of Reality

It has commonly been asserted that the unique characteristic of the human animal is his ability to deal in abstractions. Human beings, as all organisms, are sensory receptors. We see, we hear, we smell, and we taste, registering the multitude of stimuli we constantly encounter. However, not only do we perceive phenomena in these ways; we also describe and summarize our perceptions. We associate symbols with perceptions. Thus a dark object circumscribed by vertical and horizontal lines is called a box, and a set of similar objects are likewise known as boxes. We are thereby associating words with perceived objects, as we have been taught to do within a given cultural context. In some instances the words refer to classes of objects that someone from a different culture would perceive quite differently. Thus an Eskimo has several words for snow which serve to distinguish differences in snow that are very salient to him in his environment. Or a Trobriand Islander has several words for yams denoting different stages of the development of the vegetable—which for the Trobriander are different stages of being. Words, therefore, are symbols that summarize and then guide our perceptions of reality. As Kaplan notes, we must be aware that what we perceive depends upon what we have been sensitized to perceive by our conceptual repertoire; our perceptions are always shaped by our conceptual filter. Borrowing the expression attributed to Nietzsche, there is no such thing, therefore, as "immaculate perception" (Kaplan, 1964, 131).

These abstractions or symbols which represent phenomena come to assume a reality of their own. In this sense we can conceive of and communicate the features of the perceived object in the absence of the object. Indeed, we can manipulate—add, multiply, and so on—these symbols. Communication and the accumulation and transmission of knowledge are based upon this ability to abstract and to symbolize.

We, of course, take this process of perception–abstraction–perception for granted. It is not usually a deliberate activity. But if we require, for whatever reason, some precise designation of phenomena—of sets and subsets of phenomena—then we are necessarily obliged to engage in a very deliberate and careful association of perception and symbols.

CONCEPTUAL PRECISION

Communication varies in precision with variations in the precision of the abstractions utilized. Consequently, any human intellectual endeavour that aspires to elevate the standards or quality of knowledge necessarily seeks to maximize the precision of its conceptual apparati. Such has been the case of science. Any science has necessarily been concerned with its vocabulary or "jargon," for these symbolized representations of empirical phenomena comprise the basis of communication and of enquiry.

Inevitably, therefore, social science has sought to distinguish a precise body of abstractions to characterize its subject matter. If we consider the very considerable literature which has accumulated in the social sciences since the last century, we are apt to be overwhelmed by the sheer volume of concepts. Sociologists, if they never achieve another distinction, have at least proven to be great inventors and manipulators of words. An inventory of the discipline would reach into the thousands, including concepts both extinct and unfashionable and those which are current. Moreover, a systematic examination would likely find an alarming inconsistency and ambiguity in the meaning of any one of these concepts as used by any representative number of sociologists.

It is inevitable that an infant science will indulge in conceptual invention and refinement. Especially is this so when the science is faced with the problem of distinguishing its symbols from those popularly and freely used by the public it wishes to study. For example, a word such as prejudice will have a range of popular meaning so extensive as to render it useless unless some convention of precise designation is explicitly understood within sociology. And perhaps it would be better if some entirely different word were invented to represent that precise concept, so that there would be no confusion with the popular usage of the word. Literally, a jargon must be developed. As Hempel writes: "In the initial stages of scientific inquiry, description as well as generalization is stated in the vocabulary of everyday language. The growth of a scientific discipline, however, always brings with it the development of a system of specialized, more or less abstract, concepts and of a corresponding technical terminology" (Hempel, 1952, 1).

Given a justifiable period of conceptual exploration and creation, there necessarily comes a time when some measure of consensus regarding the meaning of critical concepts becomes vital.

A critical concept would be one referring to phenomena agreed to be of primary concern to the given science. Similarly, there comes a time when it is vital that not only the words as abstractions be collectively agreed upon but also that the empirical referents of most of these conceptual abstractions be clearly specified and accepted by the scientific community. In point of fact, lacking the latter, the former is unlikely to be adequately realized.

Inevitably we are dealing with abstractions from empirical reality, whether these abstractions are words, numbers, or some other symbolic representation. But if we agree that science, in order to achieve generalization, explanation, and prediction, must be capable of specifying replicable relationships among phenomena, then the abstractions employed to represent these phenomena must be understood by all persons intent upon such scientific investigation. Moreover, these abstractions must be associated in some consistent and plausible way with the empirical phenomena they are meant to represent. Properly put, there should be *epistemic rules* (Northrop, 1959; Dumont and Wilson, 1967) that spell out the links between the words taken to represent the phenomena, and the tangible, empirical indicators taken to represent the words and the phenomena. Simply stated, when a piece of research is undertaken, the abstractions must be operationalized.

Operations as Expressions of Symbols

When we operationalize a conceptual abstraction, we are specifying the perceivable and measurable counterparts of the phenomena or variables which the abstraction represents. That is to say, we operationalize by specifying empirical "things" which are taken to represent the meaning conveyed by the word, which in turn has been developed to represent some grossly perceived object. Thus, for example, we have a concept of "intelligence." Let us assume that within a scientific collectivity such as psychology or sociology it is understood that intelligence refers to an individual's innate mental capacity. This is the popular understanding of the concept. Given this definition, then, we might view as operational indicators of intelligence the various responses that a given individual might make to certain questions or problems. Thus, an individual is "intelligent" if he is adept with certain words and their meanings, and if he is familiar with certain arithmetic symbols and manipulations. Such indicators might be combined into a battery of demands or questions to which an individual is asked to respond; the rate of successful response will then be taken to mean "intelligence." We might call such a battery of demands an Intelligence Quotient (IQ) test.

But few behavioral scientists would hold the view that IQ tests, of whatever version, satisfactorily operationalize the concept of intelligence if that concept is understood to mean innate mental capacity. There are considerable research findings pointing to the relationship between social environment and IQ scores, with significant differences, for example, by social class. This information, coupled with the recognition that IQ tests are usually prepared by individuals with middle-class criteria of intelligent behavior, suggests a bias in the results of such tests that prevents us from viewing them as adequate or *valid* operational representations of mental capacity. Such tests may tap or partially reflect mental ability, but they also reflect social experience.

If, however, we had defined intelligence to mean the extent of individual adaptation to environment, then IQ tests might be more satisfactory operational counterparts. That is, given the debatable assumption of a middle-class-dominated North American society, an individual is adapted to this middle-class environment insofar as he is skillful in manipulating verbal and mathematical symbols such as those which constitute the demands on an IQ test. Although still an approximation of the abstract meaning of intelligence—operationalizations are always approximations—the IQ test may more nearly satisfy the adaptive definition of intelligence than it does the conception of innate mental ability.

Invariably, statements of scientific fact are statements relating operationalized concepts. Lacking operationalizations, we are left manipulating words alone, and moreover, words with vaguely indicated empirical derivations (see the discussion of Models in Chapter 4). If, having grossly identified some phenomenon, we then wish to examine it and its relationships to other factors with any degree of precision, this phenomenon must be respecified.

That is, abstractions, originating as representations of empirical phenomena, must be linked to the phenomenon. In a sense, the concept must be rendered tangible, with the full realization that the operationalization may not be altogether satisfactory.

Let us take another example, that of the familiar concept of "social class." We can begin with a conceptual definition of social class such as: "A category (stratum) of individuals along a hierarchy of differential social standing (stratification)." Our definition denotes individuals who share with some other individuals an identifiable social rank. However the definition does not specify the dimensions of this ranking, and there are many possible dimensions. For example, Marx would have defined social class by reference to 1) a shared economic position and 2) an awareness or consciousness (class consciousness) of the position. Thus if we were to operationalize the concept from this perspective, we might distinguish two classes, the bourgeoisie and the proletariat. The former are all those who own land, and the latter are all those who subsist on wages. This operationalization would at least satisfy the first part of the Marxist view of social class. In addition, we might require that the owners and the employees be aware of their objective position. Thus, when the question: "Do you perceive yourself as a "capitalist" or a "worker"? is answered, one would categorize individuals according to response.

However, our definition might also be taken to denote the additional dimension of "prestige." The deference or respect associated with one's social position, some argue, is not altogether dependent upon objective economic position; for example, a poor professor may have greater prestige and class standing than a wealthy mortician. We would therefore wish an operational indicator which combines economic standing and prestige. Accordingly, contemporary sociologists have argued that the best indicator in industrialized nations is occupation. One's occupation summarizes income and educational qualifications; and people are able to rank-order occupations in order of prestige. Thus we could operationalize social class by reference to a socioeconomic status scale (SES) that consists of rank-ordered occupations, by prestige or income and education. Examples are the North Hatt Scale in the United States (prestige), or the Blishen Scale in

Canada (income and education); similar scales exist for other industrialized nations (Miller, 1970, 179–96; Blishen, 1967). With such scales a numerical score can be associated with each occupation, and clusters of occupations taken to represent social class.

Operationalization and Validity

Operationalization always involves some measure of judgment: invariably it is difficult to satisfactorily represent a given concept empirically. To the extent that such satisfaction is achieved we speak of *validity*. But we never escape the judgment component, for essentially, a valid operationalization is perceived as such if it seems to make sense in view of what we know—an internal or face validity—and if predictions made are realized when examined using the given operationalizations (Zetterberg, 1965, 114–20).

Zetterberg suggests three possible sources of error in the process of operationalization. The first is an instance in which the concept or abstraction has a broader meaning than that represented by the operation; the second is an instance in which the operation conveys a broader range of meaning than that intended by the concept; and the third is an instance in which there is some overlap in the meaning of each, but the one does not properly represent the other (Zetterberg, 1965, 114–20).

The first error would exist if we defined social class as consisting of income level and awareness of membership in a given stratum and then operationalized this concept using only income. The second type of error would be committed if we viewed social class at the conceptual level of abstraction as a group of individuals who have the same income, and yet operationalized social class by using one of the conventional socioeconomic scales (SES) which incorporated income and educational standing. The operationalization consists of a factor additional to our limited abstract notion of class. An example of the third form of error would be an instance in which we viewed class as representing persons of similar income and operationalized class by ranking the prestige of ethnic groups. In this instance we would be taking two related (correlated) variables, income and ethnicity, and be suggesting that the relative prestige of ethnic membership in and of itself adequately summarizes class distinctions. In point of fact, knowledge of income may tell us something about ethnic prestige and vice versa, but the two are distinguishable factors, both conceptually and empirically. It is not a question of the abstraction meaning *more or less* than the operation but, rather, of meaning something *different*.

CONCLUSIONS

Generally the necessary process of operationalization consists of designating the empirical phenomena represented by a given concept. It is the first step in the direction of quantification or measurement, for *operationalization gives us something to count*. More than that, it is *the specification of what to count* or do in order to realize our abstract concept. Operationalization is a procedure which may itself introduce errors in research, for there is always the possibility of operationalizations that fail to represent adequately the abstract concepts with which a researcher begins and to which he returns in presenting his research findings. Consequently the precise and open specification of abstract conceptualization and of operational counterparts is a critical stage in the conduct of research. As we shall consider in Chapter 5, operationalization is the necessary step preceding the measurement of empirical phenomena.

REFERENCES

BLISHEN, BERNARD, "A Socio-Economic Index for Occupations in Canada," *Canadian Review of Sociology and Anthropology*, IV (February 1967), 41–53; reprinted in B. Blishen et al., eds., *Canadian Society* (3rd ed.), pp. 741–53. Toronto: Macmillan of Canada, 1961.

DUMONT, R. AND W. WILSON, "Aspects of Concept Formation, Explication, and Theory Construction in Sociology," *American Sociological Review*, 32 (1967), 985–95; reprinted in D. Forcese and S. Richer, eds., *Stages of Social Research: Contemporary Perspectives*, pp. 40–53. Englewood Cliffs, N.J.: Prentice-Hall, 1970.

HEMPEL, CARL, *Fundamentals of Concept Formation in Empirical Science*. Chicago: University of Chicago Press, 1952.

KAPLAN, ABRAHAM, *The Conduct of Inquiry*, pp. 46–83, 131–36. San Francisco: Chandler, 1964.

MILLER, DELBERT, *Handbook of Research Design and Social Measurement* (2nd ed.), pp. 169–99. New York: McKay, 1970.

NORTHROP, F. S. C., *The Logic of the Sciences and the Humanities*, pp. 119–32. New York: World Publ. Inc.–Meridian Books, Inc., 1959.

ZETTERBERG, HANS, *On Theory and Verification in Sociology* (3rd ed.), pp. 30–62, 114–23. Totowa, N.J.: Bedminister Press, 1965.

ADDITIONAL SELECTED READINGS (ANNOTATED)

BLAU, PETER, "Operationalizing a Conceptual Scheme: The Universalism-Particularism Pattern Variable," *American Sociological Review*, 27 (1962), 159–69; reprinted in Forcese and Richer, *Stages of Social Research*, pp. 54–67. An example of operationalizing a very abstract but frequently employed concept in sociology.

WARTOFSKY, M., *Conceptual Foundations in Scientific Thought*. New York: Macmillan, 1968. A thorough discussion, from the point of view of the philosophy of science, of the nature of scientific conceptualization and inquiry.

Models,
Hypotheses,
and Theory

Sociological concepts—the abstractions from reality which we discussed in the previous chapter—should not exist as isolates. Rather they are usually organized, with varying explicitness, into systems of related concepts. These systems are meant to represent the systems of phenomena in which the sociologist is interested.

As we rummage through the literature of the social sciences, we inevitably encounter several such systems of concepts, often presented under different labels. For example, we might find a conceptual system referred to as a conceptual framework; or we might encounter a taxonomy, a model, or a theory.

It is possible to distinguish more or less subtle variations in meaning among these labels, not all of which are agreed upon. But they do have in common a reference to some systematic arrangement of the various concepts utilized in a given scientific discipline such as sociology. We will briefly consider the function of such conceptual systematizations in science. However, first we must indicate some ground rules by way of indicating some distinctions among the several conceptual labels.

MODELS

Basically we will distinguish between a model and a theory, for these are the two expressions most frequently used to describe conceptual organizations. Put most simply, we may view a model as a likeness of something. *A model is an imitation or an abstraction from reality that is intended to order and to simplify our view of that reality while still capturing its essential characteristics.* Thus, for example, an engineer might have a model of a machine such as an aircraft. The aircraft model is a miniature reproduction of the real aircraft, including scale representation of some of the real airplane's features—its structure—while omitting other aspects, such as, perhaps, its control instruments and engine. The model aircraft might serve to physically and visibly represent the structure and features of the aircraft. Or more than that it might be used in place of the real machine in order to test certain structural features. For example, the engineer might subject his model to the effects of a wind tunnel—itself a model or simulation of the environmental condition—to determine how a genuine aircraft might perform.

This example is illustrative of the manner in which we normally conceive of a model. But a model need not be a three-dimensional structural imitation. Often, as is the case in sociology, a model will consist of symbols rather than of physical matter. That is, the characteristics of some phenomenon, including its variable components, and the relationships among these components, will be represented in the arrangements among the words or concepts agreed upon in a discipline.

Ideally, the relationships will have been deliberately and carefully specified. But sometimes this conceptual arrangement will in large part be implicit, with a number of concepts having become associated by disciplinary convention. These are often of a descriptive nature such that the essential intention is to identify the characteristics of the phenomenon in question rather than to specify the relationships among variable components. In such instances we are dealing with models which at various times have been termed *taxonomies, conceptual frameworks,* or *typologies.* These are literally inventories of concepts relevant to some given phenomenon. They serve the function of pointing out distinctions among phenomena—identifying types. Thus, for example, Robert Redfield and others have listed several conceptual characteristics that distinguish "folk societies" from "modern" or "industrial societies" (Redfield, 1947). The former are small, simple, isolated, and homogeneous, with a slight division of labor, while the latter are large, complex, in frequent communication, heterogeneous, and so on. The characteristics of folk and urban societies are listed, without any explicit suggestion of the nature of the relationships among the several factors, but the rationale for their designation could suggest possible relationships.

Because models include some suggestion of explanatory relationships, we may speak of them as *explanation sketches* or *theory sketches* (Dumont and Wilson, 1967, 43–44). Such sketches suggest possible explanatory relationships among variables—possible relationships rather than verified relationships.

An example in our view, of a theory sketch in which the relationships are explicit rather than implied is Robert Merton's specification of the relationship between societally defined goals, societally defined means to the realization of these goals, and different forms of deviance, as indicated in Figure 4–1 (Merton, 1957).

Thus, dependent upon whether one accepts (+) or rejects (−)

Behavioral Types	Goals	Means
Conformist	+	+
Ritualist	−	+
Innovator	+	−
Retreatist	−	−
Revolutionist	− +	− +

Fig. 4–1. Merton's Paradigm

the societally defined goals and means will depend the nature of one's response. The possibility of disparity between goals and means suggests an explanation for the behavioral types.

HYPOTHESES

Merton's model, in suggesting an explanation for the behavioral types identified, provides a source of hypotheses. *An explanatory hypothesis is an untested or unproven relationship among two or more variables.* Thus, for example, we might hypothesize that: "The higher the aspirations of students, the greater the incidence of cheating among students." Thus, a relationship is being suggested between two variables—aspiration levels and cheating behavior. These variables would of course have to be adequately defined and operationalized if the hypothesis were to be tested. But our interest here is in noting that this potential relationship is deduced from Merton's model. The model suggests that, in the context of some given social system, the acceptance of goals might lead to deviant behavior in pursuit of these goals if legitimate means are in some way inadequate. Logically, then, the greater the aspirations (that is, the more difficult or elaborate the goals), the greater the probability that the legitimate means may prove inadequate and illegitimate or deviant means might be employed. Thus a student who aspires to be a pharmacist, for example, might be more likely to cheat in school than students who aspire to be ditchdiggers.

The genesis of hypotheses is the more important function of a model. Models may organize our conceptual apparatus, but they also suggest relationships among these concepts and the phenomena the concepts represent. A model may also suggest descriptive hypotheses in the sense of expectations as to what phenomena a researcher might be expected to discover without any attempt to explain these phenomena.

For example, a researcher embarking upon a study of an agrarian society in Africa would expect it to be homogeneous in ethnic and class composition and with a relatively simple division of labor, as suggested by Redfield's model of folk or rural social systems. The model suggests a descriptive hypothesis, thereby providing guidelines to research.

Earlier we discussed the manner in which various environmental influences might affect the selection of a research problem. Thus, for example, perhaps because it offends us morally, or perhaps because our employer defines it as wasteful, we might be interested in researching the causes of student cheating. This general research interest will be focused upon specific hunches or hypotheses on the basis of some prior information—information or speculation organized, in effect, in some model, whether this model be detailed, elaborate, or very vague and sparse. The model will serve to narrow down the research interest into a form amenable to investigation; to wit, hypotheses. Hypotheses, the necessary step in the design of any explanatory research, are thereby derived from preconceptions inherent in the scientific discipline. These internal preconceptions will guide research and suggest the kind of data to be collected, and to some extent, the meaning attached to these data, as indicated in Figure 4–2.

Models: Induction and Deduction

In science we often encounter the idealized distinction between induction and deduction. *Induction* has been taken to mean *the process of organizing isolated observations or facts into some set*

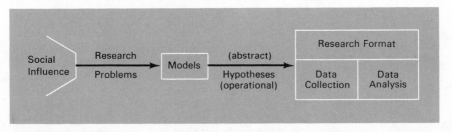

FIG. 4–2. THE SOCIAL DERIVATION OF A RESEARCH PROJECT

of ordered relationships, or generalizations. On the other hand, *deduction refers to the derivation of relationships which are unobserved from previously established generalizations.* Induction begins with a set of observations from which we infer higher order statements which seem to account for these observations, and thereby realize a plausible explanation of these observations. For example, we might have numerous observations which indicate that students who plan a professional career are more likely to cheat in school than are students aspiring to lower level occupations. These observations might suggest to us the more general statement that the higher the aspirations, the greater the probability of deviant behavior. This in turn might be recognized as a special case derivative of Merton's model dealing with means and goals. In short, the initial observations may eventually be explained by reference to a general model of which the observed phenomenon is a particular instance.

This is quite different from explanation achieved deductively. Previously we began with the Merton model and derived the hypothesis about student cheating. If the general model is valid, the hypothesis should be proved empirically correct. The hypothesis might be tested by comparing cheating behavior of professionally oriented and nonprofessionally oriented students. If there is empirical support for the hypothesis, we increase our confidence in the entire model relating goals, means, and deviant behavior. We have moved from the general, to the particular, and back to the general. When proceeding purely inductively, however, we move from the particular to the general. So doing, we will always have the illusion of explanation, since we are adding higher order statements in an ad hoc fashion. Deductive systems are therefore to be preferred because they derive previously unobserved relationships from systems of stated relationships; the unexamined relationships are literally deduced, and the deduction is *falsifiable.* Newman comments:

There is no evidence ... that a single scientific discovery ever was made by induction as conceived by Bacon. On the contrary it is quite clear that to engage in research without the stimulus and guidance of hypotheses, rules, preconceptions, anticipations, control criteria and the like is a hopeless if not indeed frivolous activity (Newman, 1961, Vol. 1, 91).

Rather than the Baconian ideal type of induction, what we find is a continual interaction between observations and the conceptual models of a science.

Thus, models serve a guiding and exploratory function. The relationships comprising the model, built up through cumulative observation and speculative logic, are relationships which might be profitably tested in the "real" world. The relationships of the model are hypotheses—sometimes stated in a general form meant to apply to a broad range of behavior, such as deviance in general rather than cheating in particular. Thus, the researcher can deduce testable relationships among variables from a conceptual model.

Generally it is the case that any model serves the inevitable role of reality filter. Because models are incomplete representations of reality, they inevitably are limiting factors in any science. As guides or lenses to scientific reality, models will lead the researcher to expect certain outcomes, to perceive certain things, and to fail to perceive other things. For example, Barber and Fox describe an instance in medical research in which two scientists perceiving the same phenomenon proceeded in different directions—the one discovering the "cause" of the phenomenon, and the other failing to even be interested in it (Barber and Fox, 1958). Models, therefore, typically become overviews of a science's subject matter. As such, there are related assumptions or beliefs that may result in the failure to isolate some specific relationship. Butterfield believes that this is what accounted for the persistence of Ptolemaic astronomy. As Butterfield writes: "The truth was that Ptolomy in ancient times had rejected the hypothesis of the movement of the earth, not because he had failed to consider it, but because it was impossible to make such a hypothesis square with Aristotelian physics. It was not until Aristotelian physics had been overthrown in other regions altogether that the hypothesis could make any serious headway . . ." (Butterfield, 1962, 45).

The thesis has been seriously advanced that any science proceeds in a dialectic fashion. At any given time, one model will dominate a scientific community. So long as that model is deemed satisfactory and research findings do not overwhelmingly refute its assumptions and specifications, it will persist. But as anomalous findings accumulate—data which do not fit the model—the point is eventually reached where the model is challenged and another substituted (Kuhn, 1962).

It is debatable whether we could view social science as progressing in this manner. Some might not agree that in sociology, for example, there is a model sufficiently dominant and broad that it governs the perceptions and the research of all or most sociologists. However, it would seem that we can discern indications of such a process through the history of sociology. The progressive refinement of the functionalist model of society as data became available from several societies was a process of response to unanticipated findings that failed to correspond to the statements and assumptions of the functionalist model. These prompted changes in the model in the manner that Merton suggests is an inevitable function of empirical research (Merton, 1948). Eventually, it may lead to the rejection of the model altogether.

A model, therefore, is an inevitable perceptual filter. It will shape research in a scientific discipline by governing the kinds of research questions which will be posed, how they are stated, and how they are examined. Thus, where we have previously noted the several extra-scientific influences upon the derivation of research problems, we would now have to include a source of predilections intrinsic to the given science, as we illustrated in Fig. 4–2.

THEORY

In addition, a researcher may deduce relationships from a theory. In some sense, *theory is a model that has been tested.* More specifically, the concepts used in the model have been operationalized and the relationships between these factors have been verified. A theory—or what Dumont and Wilson call an "explicit theory"—has "epistemic significance" and "constitutive significance" (Dumont and Wilson, 1967, 42–43). The former refers to the operationalization of the constitutive concepts such that the words or conceptual abstractions are linked to observable features of the empirical world, and linked, moreover, by explicit rules of correspondence. By "constitutive significance" is meant that the concepts comprising the theory are interlinked in that they serve to predict and explain empirically discernible behavior (Dumont and Wilson, 1967, 44). A theory, then, consists of a set of propositions that are interrelated, a proposition taken to mean a verified statement of relationship between variables.

Note that an apparently unsuccessful testing of a model may be due to four factors: 1) the model is indeed wrong and needs respecifying; or 2) the concepts have been poorly operationalized so that we are not really testing what we think we are; or 3) our deduction of hypotheses from the model is inadequate, that is, illogical; or 4) the research format employed to test the hypotheses is in some way inadequate, perhaps failing to control for confounding variables.

Of course we never really test or prove an entire model, but insofar as we are deriving hypotheses from a model, testing these hypotheses, and verifying them, these verified outputs—propositions—are the building blocks of theory. And by virtue of their derivative origin we may think of a theory as the verified counterpart of some model(s).

As used above, the relationships expressed in a theory are known as propositions. *A proposition is an established or proven relationship among variables.* This implies that the conceptual components of a theory have been previously operationalized in that the variables comprising the model have been examined empirically such that relations among them have been proven. This is unlike the case with a model, where many of the concepts which comprise it may not have been operationalized. Thus, for example, the many concepts making up Talcott Parsons's systems model have not all been operationalized, and those which have been, only tentatively (Parsons, 1951). This is consistent with a model's speculative nature. But a theory, strictly viewed, represents fact and not speculation. The relationship among hypotheses, models, propositions, and theories can be viewed as parallel continua, as in the illustration below (Figure 4–3).

A theory consists, then, of propositions. These propositions are arranged such that one can deduce lower-order propositions from higher-order propositions. That is, the propositions vary in generality or scope. A more general proposition will express the meaning or conditions represented by lower-order propositions, and then some. Moreover, the higher-order propositions will serve to explain the lower-order relationships. That is, relationships at the higher level account for relationships at the lower level; the latter are logically and empirically derivative. Thus for example, assuming verification for purposes of illustration, the proposition:

The greater the occupational aspiration, the greater the incidence of cheating

would be derivative of and explained by the more general proposition:

The greater the aspirations, the greater the incidence of deviance.

Theory, therefore, is an explanatory system. It may suggest hypotheses relating to as yet unexamined or unverified relationships. Not only models but also theories will suggest hypotheses. But at least, whether relating to extensive phenomena or not,

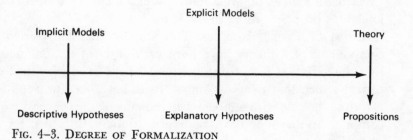

FIG. 4–3. DEGREE OF FORMALIZATION

theory is distinguished by its factual nature. It is an explanatory system, not a speculative system, although a theory might indeed incite speculation. Theory, then, is the object or goal of science, and therefore theory is the output and result of cumulative research.

As research is conducted, the findings are in a sense collated—they are gradually arranged into a theoretical system. Thereby certain orientations and assumptions will be built into every science not only because of the models utilized but also because of the theory. This is inevitably so in that it is unlikely that a theory would ever encompass all the pertinent phenomena of a given science.

A theory, therefore, is always limited. Potentially, then, it can always grow. As research continues, additions will be made to the theory. And, since there is no ultimate or perfect verification in any science because of the fallibility of conceptualization and measurement, there will inevitably be corrections and deletions made in theory. Similarly, as research proceeds, the cumulative findings and theory will necessarily affect the system of preconceptions, assumptions, and speculation which we have called models. Thus, in sociology, as in any science, there will not only be an interaction between theory and research as Merton suggested (Merton, 1948) but also an interaction between research, theory, and models.

Conceptual Isolates

We have been presenting a view that has emphasized conceptual order. The assumption from which we have operated is that the ideal of any science is the explicit theory—that is, an explanatory system. This is consistent with our earlier view that the object of social science is explanation and prediction.

It should be noted, however, that there is some considerable and necessary departure from the ideal. Not all concepts are carefully related to others. There are what Dumont and Wilson call "conceptual isolates" (Dumont and Wilson, 1967, 44). These are vaguely defined words which convey a broad range of meaning. They will have some ill-defined relationship to observable behavior from which they were derived. But they have yet to be refined, and in fact they may never be, for they may be abandoned as unsatisfactory. These conceptual isolates may be viewed as exploratory conceptualizations that may or may not eventually be incorporated into conceptual systems—that is, theory sketches or theories.

It is also the case that not all concepts are operationalized. The conceptual isolates noted above may be so vague as to defy operationalization. But there are also concepts used in explicit theories that are not operationalized (Hempel, 1952, 39–50). These are in a sense representatives of missing theoretical links —the unknown factors that permit the organization of those operationalized concepts making up the explicit theory. These unknown factors may eventually come to be operationally specified or they may eventually come to prove unnecessary. But in the meanwhile they serve a necessary function in the logic of theoretical organization.

Explicit theories, then, are a goal. And operationalization is the means to the realization of that goal. But we will not find a science in which all concepts—even all those used in an explicit theory— are operationally specified.

THEORY AND SOCIAL ENVIRONMENT

In Chapter 2 we considered that research findings will likely be applied. For example, there may be interest in the correction of some social problems, such as delinquency. Research and theory will therefore affect the environmental influences that themselves influence research. Thus there is an interaction or constant feedback among the several items we have outlined schematically in Figure 4–4.

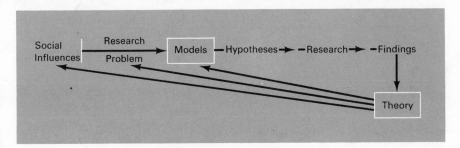

FIG. 4–4. FACTORS INFLUENCING RESEARCH

CONCLUSIONS

Social scientists do not wander about selecting research problems at random. Nor do they collect information randomly in the fond expectation that some day it will all make sense. A research problem will have been isolated by a scientist subject to numerous social influences, and guided by existing preconceptions in a given science. Ideally, the researcher will have deduced hypotheses from highly formalized conceptual systems. But whether the deduction has been explicit or not, the researcher invariably will have been influenced by models with which he is familiar.

Outlined very generally, and with reference only to the scientific discipline, the steps in research would be as follows:

General Steps	Example
Selection of problem	Cheating among students.
Selection of plausible model (theory sketch)	Mertonian outline of relationship between societal goals, means, and deviant behavior.
Deduction of hypothesis	Other factors being equal (for example, social class), professionally oriented students (higher aspirations) are more

General Steps	Example
	likely to cheat (deviant behavior) than are nonprofessionally oriented students (lower aspirations).
Operationalization of concepts	1) professional versus nonprofessional distinguished by self-reported plans; 2) cheating distinguished as copying from notes during examinations and copying from published or unpublished work of others for papers, as self-reported in anonymous questionnaires.
Analysis	Comparison of professionally oriented and nonprofessionally oriented students on frequency of cheating.
Interpretation of findings	If consistent with model you have some increased confidence in its applicability. If inconsistent with model, question model itself, your logic, operationalizations, and testing and analysis procedures.

REFERENCES

BARBER, B. AND R. FOX, "The Case of the Floppy-Eared Rabbits: An Instance of Serendipity Gained and Serendipity Lost," *American Journal of Sociology*, Vol. 54 (1958), 128–36; reprinted in D. Forcese and S. Richer, eds., *Stages of Social Research: Contemporary Perspectives*, pp. 27–37. Englewood Cliffs, N.J.: Prentice-Hall, 1970.

BUTTERFIELD, HERBERT, *The Origins of Modern Science* (rev. ed.). New York: Crowell Collier and Macmillan, 1962.

DUMONT, R. AND W. WILSON, "Aspects of Concept Formation, Explication, and Theory Construction in Sociology," *American Sociological Review*, Vol. 32 (1967), 985–95; reprinted in Forcese and Richer, *Stages of Social Research*, pp. 40–53.

HEMPEL, CARL, *Fundamentals of Concept Formation in Empirical Science*. Chicago: University of Chicago Press, 1952.

KUHN, THOMAS, *The Structure of Scientific Revolutions*. Chicago: University of Chicago Press, 1962.

MERTON, ROBERT, "The Bearing of Empirical Research Upon the Development of Social Theory," *American Sociological Review*, Vol. 5 (1948), 505–55; reprinted in Forcese and Richer, *Stages of Social Research*, pp. 14–27.

MERTON, ROBERT, *Social Theory and Social Structure* (rev. ed.), chaps. 4, 5. New York: Free Press, 1957.

NEWMAN, JAMES, *Science and Sensibility*, Vols. 1 and 2. New York: Simon & Schuster, 1961.

PARSONS, TALCOTT, *The Social System*. New York: Free Press, 1951.

REDFIELD, ROBERT, "The Folk Society," *American Journal of Sociology*, Vol. 52 (1947), 293–308.

SELECTED ADDITIONAL READINGS (ANNOTATED)

HOMANS, GEORGE, "Bringing Men Back In," *American Sociological Review*, Vol. 29 (1964), 809–18; reprinted in Forcese and Richer, *Stages of Social Research*, pp. 379–90. A famous, or infamous paper, depending upon one's point of view, in which Homans outlines what he believes theory to be.

HOMANS, GEORGE, *The Nature of Social Science*. New York: Harcourt Brace Jovanovich, 1967. A brief monograph in which Homans elaborates his view of the propositional basis of theory and its explanatory function.

WILLER, DAVID, *Scientific Sociology: Theory and Method*. Englewood Cliffs, N.J.: Prentice-Hall, 1967. A monograph attempting to distinguish among types of models and theories.

Measurement

In previous chapters we have considered operationalism, or the definition of an abstract concept in terms of observable phenomena. These observable phenomena are to be explicitly linked to the abstract conceptual definition. In addition, these observable phenomena must be distinguished as variables. That is, the several values which the observable phenomena may assume have to be recognized and recorded. Such a record is integral to what we spoke of in Chapter 1 as quantification—the procedure whereby empirical phenomena are designated by numerical symbols. When such numerical designation is achieved according to some set of rules such that it is systematic and replicable, we realize quantification or what we shall henceforth refer to as *measurement.*

Measurement consists of identifying the values which may be assumed by some variable, and representing these values by some numerical notation. The numerical notation is systematically and consistently assigned; that is, it is assigned according to some set of rules. Or, as Galtung has put it, "Measurement is the mapping of the values on a set of numbers" (Galtung, 1967). Thus, for each and every value, there is an exclusive number. Thereby, given a variable x, the numerals 1, 2, 3, and 4 may represent the variable as it assumes each of four conditions or values. Moreover, as similar phenomena are observed, each variable x_1, x_2, x_3 ... x_4 will have its values so identified that we can realize a count of the number of instances in which value 1, value 2, value 3, or value 4 obtain empirically. Thus the numerically represented variables come to represent classes or categories.

For example, we may have the abstract concept of "nonconformity," which we define as disregard for established conventions of dress. In dealing with this abstraction we recognize the variable nature of nonconformity, for the disregard for convention may assume several values—that is, it will vary in intensity, with some people departing from convention more than others. Thus we might distinguish: (1) high nonconformity, (2) moderate nonconformity, (3) moderate conformity, and (4) high conformity. Given the abstract concepts and an interest in researching nonconformity, we must operationalize the concept; that is, relate it to observable phenomena. Let us agree for purposes of illustration that a plausible empirical indicator of disregard for conventions of dress would be the nature of footwear. We could take as specific indicators, therefore, the following behavioral manifestations which correspond to the four values of our abstract concept:

1. high nonconformity indicated by bare feet;
2. moderate nonconformity indicated by shoes without socks;
3. moderate conformity indicated by unpolished shoes or boots with socks;
4. high conformity indicated by polished shoes or boots with socks.

Then, continuing with this rather facetious example, we might simply designate each of these categories with a numerical symbol—quite literally the numerical values 1, 2, 3, and 4 may be taken to represent the range in intensity of nonconformity illustrated by the four categories. The frequency of each degree of conformity would be noted by counting the instances observed and recorded in each of the four categories. In this instance, the numbers 1, 2, 3, 4 are convenient means of indicating that the categories represent degrees of "conformity," that is, more or less. We must be cautious in the use of numbers as labels in this way, for just as if we had used a, b, c, d to distinguish the categories— as we could—we cannot perform arithmetic manipulations upon these numbers. As will be explained below, we lack a genuine zero point and equal intervals. But insofar as the categorization is the product of the *systematic* and *replicable* procedures of *several* observers, we will nonetheless have achieved some primitive measurement.

The numerals in measurement, therefore, and measurement itself constitute summary designations of the state or value of some phenomena. But more than that, measurement permits the systematic identification of similarities and differences among phenomena, the number or quantity of these phenomena, and changes in these phenomena. Provided the assignment of numerical values is operationally definable, reproducible, and valid, then we are measuring phenomena. Measurement must be operationally definable; that is, we must specify the conditions of measurement and the operations performed under these conditions—the what, when, where, and how, such that the phenomena are measured. Thus measurement does not consist of the arbitrary or idiosyncratic assignment of numerical values so that one might realize the appearance of quantification. Measurement is not achieved if a researcher simply assigns numerical values on the basis of his preconceptions. For example, Lipset has compared the value structures of the United States, the United Kingdom, Canada, and Australia (Lipset, 1963, 249). Lipset provides the illusion of measurement by assigning numerical values to the positions of each of these nations along continua of pattern variables, such as egalitarianism. But the numerical representations merely represent the judgment of one individual—Lipset himself—and do not constitute measurement. Given a specification of conditions and procedures, the measurement must be reproducible; that is, the *measurement of one individual must be capable of replication by others*. Then we may speak of the *reliability* of measurement. In addition, if our measurement routine identifies and measures the phenomena which we intend to measure, then we may speak of the *validity* of measurement.

Consistent with this general view of measurement, it is conventional to distinguish four levels of measurement: (1) nominal, (2) ordinal, (3) interval, and (4) ratio.

NOMINAL MEASUREMENT

Most scientists would accept the view that measurement is minimally realized when we engage in counting. When we count, essentially we are listing and summating objects or phenomena perceived to be identical in some way. Thus one may identify all objects in the room that are black. We are thereby keying upon the one attribute or dimension of the many different objects in the room, identifying those that are similar in color; that is, those that are black. In counting these objects, we are associating numbers with the objects identified as black and thus singling out an identity or similarity among apparently diverse phenomena or objects, thereby achieving a fundamental task of all science. Such counting, however, implies more than one kind of object, even in terms of the limitations of some specified dimension. Thus, for example, in our conventional conceptual usage, black is distinguished from white, and we have at least two alternate colors, black or white, each constituting a category in which we might place objects. All those objects in the room identified as black are placed in category black, and all those identified as white are placed in category white. In so distinguishing black and white we have utilized the most rudimentary of measurement scales, known as *nominal scales*. To assign objects to categories is to measure in the fundamental sense of distinguishing likenesses or differences along some dimension. We are measuring insofar as we are indicating variability along the dimension of color. In this instance, color is a variable attribute of the objects in our room because it assumes at least two values, black or white. If we wished we could assign numerical symbols to represent our two categories;

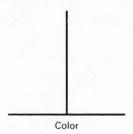

Color

FIG. 5-1

1 = black, 2 = white. Then we could assign all objects in our room manifesting the attribute of whiteness to category 2, and count them. Thereby our nominal scale consists of the two points of numerical representations—1 and 2—along the dimension of color.

We might, of course, have more than two categories—we might have black, white, red, blue, and yellow. We could then assign the objects in our room to five categories and in so doing undoubtedly be making finer and more thorough distinctions along the dimensions of color. Where previously we had but two alternatives, we now have five mutually exclusive categories and will realize a more exhaustive scale. Such categorical distinctions are sometimes referred to as *qualitative* or *discrete*, for they are viewed as rigidly distinct and exclusive categories.

Such classification into "all or nothing" categories is very common in the social sciences. Much of our data consists of responses solicited from people. Thus, we might ask a respondent a question—the question constituting a stimulus—and the response may be classified. A "yes" or "no" response to a question would constitute nominal measurement of that response. Similarly, data such as "male" or "female," "married" or "unmarried," or "separated" or "divorced" would constitute nominal level measurement.

In all such cases we are realizing a simple nonmetrical organization of observable phenomena. We are identifying classes or categories of phenomena; objects are either assigned to a category or they are not. However, even to achieve a proper nominal scale, the properties of *exclusiveness* and *exhaustiveness* must be realized. If one is categorizing for a given category x, only objects with the characteristic x are included in the category—exclusiveness. Moreover, all objects with the variable characteristics we are measuring can be placed along our scale. To take a tangible example, consider the categories "male" and "female": all males and only males are categorized as such, while all females and only females are classified as such. A nominal scale of male or female will be exhaustive in that there is a category for each and every person. Many of the data we derive from a national census are nominal in nature, consisting of the categorization of persons on the basis of certain variable attributes such as sex, religion, ethnic group, or citizenship.

Thus, the either-or nature of nominal scales serves to order or systematize observations of phenomena. This is achieved by differentiating among kinds of things; that is, more elegantly, by distinguishing objects by their attributes. In short, certain attributes serve as criteria whereby some things are treated as the same class or set, and others as different. This systematic classification of observable phenomena is the most fundamental of scientific activities. Anything more sophisticated is dependent upon an accretion of such classifications.

Constructing Nominal Measures

It is possible to distinguish two types of nominal measurement: 1) those derived from common usage, and 2) those which we must create from some kind of data base. Examples of the former are distinctions by sex or distinctions by religious affiliation. In order to classify people with reference to these variables we typically rely upon self-reported data, such as when we allow respondents to indicate male or female or, dealing with religious affiliation, Protestant, Catholic, Jewish. We do have to be certain that these categories are exhaustive and mutually exclusive. Adding the category "Other" to our three religious categories would see to exhaustiveness. Exclusiveness would be gained by avoiding subtypes of the general categories used. For example, we would violate the mutually exclusive criterion if we used both "Anglican" and "Protestant" as religious categories.

However, some nominal measures are not so readily realized.

An example, described in Chapter 10, is Bales's method of coding social interaction. Bales was interested in developing a set of behavioral categories which would make it possible to classify all verbal and nonverbal behavior emitted in a group setting. No self-evident set of categories existed, and only after a prolonged series of group observations in a laboratory setting did Bales and his co-workers produce a set of categories which appeared to be exhaustive. (Bales, 1950.)

A second example of a situation where we must essentially create a set of categories may be taken from survey research. Often we find ourselves in a position of having to make sense of responses to open-ended questions included in interviews or questionnaires (Chapter 11). We can take as an example the following question asked of 500 students who have dropped out of high school:

"What would you say was the most important reason for your leaving school?"

Given a question such as this, the researcher is likely to collect a very large number of stated reasons. The researcher is therefore left with the task of inducing a set of nominal categories which might sensibly summarize all of the different responses. In such a circumstance it is quite common to devise a set of categories by considering the degree of similarity among the various responses and the frequency of each type of response. For example, consider the hypothetical responses from a sample of fifty high-school dropouts (Table 5–1).

Given a distribution of responses such as that in Table 5–1, the researcher's task is to collapse the twenty categories without losing too much information. Examination of the responses indicates several practical combinations of response, with often the same attitude being expressed in different ways. Table 5–2 presents an alternate set of categories, consisting of combinations of those of Table 5–1.

Having collapsed the data for fifty students, the researcher may now classify the full number of 500 respondents using the combined categories.

TABLE 5-1 HYPOTHETICAL RESPONSES TO SCHOOL-LEAVING QUESTION

	% Mentioning
1. Bored with school	5
2. Found a good job	20
3. Father is ill, must work	2
4. Financial problems at home	4
5. To get married	2
6. Dislike school work	6
7. Unhappy with school	3
8. Parents want me to quit	3
9. Not sure	4
10. To make my own living	2
11. Lousy teacher	3
12. Waste of time to stay	3
13. Employment possibilities	22
14. Uselessness of school	2
15. Poor grades	4
16. Don't know	4
17. Who needs it?	2
18. No reason to continue	2
19. I want to be independent	3
20. No answer	4
	100% (N = 50)

TABLE 5-2 COMBINED HYPOTHETICAL RESPONSES TO SCHOOL-LEAVING QUESTION

	% Mentioning
1. Negative attitudes to school (1, 6, 7, 11, 12, 14, 17, 18)	26
2. Positive attitudes to job (2, 13)	42
3. Financial problems (3, 4)	6
4. Independence (10, 19)	5
5. Marriage (5)	2
6. Lack of parental support (8)	3
7. Poor academic performance (15)	4
8. Uncertain or don't know (9, 16)	8
9. No answer (20)	4
	100% (N = 50)

ORDINAL MEASUREMENT

It is clear that many attributes, such as color, need not be conceived of as discrete alternatives; either black or white. Often we speak of blackness or whiteness—literally, degrees of black or white. Such a realization suggests that, rather than deal in discrete categories, we can conceive of a plane or continuum along which we arrange several shades, degrees, or values of color. In our example we might consider the dimension to consist of the depth or intensity of color as represented by degrees of blackness, ranging from black through several degrees of blackness or whiteness to white itself. Again these points or degrees along our continuum or scale could be conveniently identified using some numerical notation. And insofar as the scale suggests more or less blackness —that is degrees of blackness—we will have realized an ordinal scale. An *ordinal scale* exists when we have some sequence of degree such that one degree, point, or value precedes the other. There is a rank order.

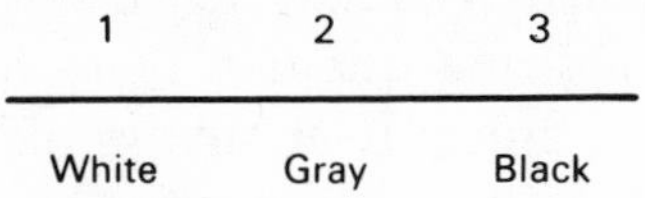

1	2	3
White	Gray	Black

Fig. 5–2

Or to take up one of our earlier examples, we may require that the respondent express his opinion not in terms of a categorical "yes" or "no" but rather in expression of the degree to which he agrees or disagrees with some statement. We may have the ordered alternatives of "strongly agree," "agree," "slightly agree," "slightly disagree," "disagree," or "strongly disagree."

The formal properties of ordinal scales are those of nominal scales—exclusiveness and exhaustiveness. But more than simply providing categories, as we have seen, ordinal scales offer a sequence or an ordering of categories or classes. Thereby, in that we are speaking of more or less, an adequate ordinal scale must possess the properties of *transitivity*, and *asymmetry*. Thus, if x is greater than y and y is greater than z, then x is greater than z—transitivity. Or similarly, if x is greater than y and y is greater than z, then z cannot be greater than x—asymmetry.

Constructing Ordinal Measures: Sociometric Scaling

More than twenty years ago the technique of sociometry was developed in order to measure the structural aspects of particular groups—that is, dyadic relationships, cliques, and leadership patterns (Moreno, 1959). The method is essentially quite simple, although with large groups the problems of processing the data obtained are quite complex.

In its simplest form, we question the individuals in a group as to whom they generally associate with or would prefer to associate with in a particular activity. Although we can allow the respondent to select any number of individuals, when the group is large (over ten), it is easier to process the data when choices are limited.

As an illustration of some of the potential measures emerging from the technique, let us assume that we are interested in studying five students who comprise a small graduate department of sociology. We decide to ask the following question of each student: Which of your fellow graduate students, if any, would you define as close friends of yours? This, then, is a general measure of friendship, not confined to a particular kind of activity or circumstance.

When the data are secured, one can arrange them in a sociometric matrix, simply a table of who chooses whom (Figure 5–3).

With this matrix as a basic working tool, one can develop various measures. These are of two kinds—group characteristics and individual characteristics. An example of a group measure is the cohesiveness index, a measure of the strength of in-group bonds. The ratio

$$\frac{\text{Number of in-group choices}}{\text{Number of possible in-group choices}}$$

Choosers	Chosen					
	A	B	C	D	E	Total Number Choices Made
A		1	1			2
B	1		1			2
C	1	1				2
D	1	1	1		1	4
E	1					1
Total Number Choices Received	4	3	3	0	1	11

Total Number Possible Choices = 20

Fig. 5–3 Matrix for Sociology Students

is one such index. In our case, this would be 11/20 or 0.55. If we found that another department (for example, psychology) yielded a ratio of 0.20, we could argue that the sociology department displayed greater cohesiveness than did the psychology department.

The number of individual level measures one could construct is quite large. First, one could rank individuals according to the number of choices received. This is an ordinal scale of popularity; in our case A and D represent the two polar values. One might also rank the subjects according to the number of choices given, perhaps a measure of social aggressiveness or extroversion. A combination of these two yields a third measure

$$\frac{\text{Number of choices received,}}{\text{Number of choices given,}}$$

which one might term a social success index. A ratio of one would indicate that the individual is holding his own socially—for every choice given he receives one in return. A score greater than one would indicate high social success, while a ratio of less than one would suggest the opposite.

As can be seen, the possibilities are quite broad. It should be emphasized, however, that one is producing only an ordinal scale. We cannot say that A is four times as popular as E, nor even that the difference in popularity between A and E is equal to that between C and D. This is because we have no rationale for assuming equal intervals.

Constructing Ordinal Measures: Guttman Scaling

Sociometric scaling as discussed above is quite straightforward. The total number of times an individual was mentioned by others in his group became his scale score. The reason this type of scaling is not too problematic is that only one item is involved. This means that tabulation of scale scores is just a matter of counting choices received or given out. Further, one need not concern himself with the problem of establishing the existence of a continuum. An ordinal scale implies that individuals can be ranked relative to one another on a given characteristic. This in turn implies that the characteristic is a reflection of an underlying continuum along which individuals can indeed be placed. In sociometric scaling, since only one item is involved simple addition of choices received would reflect higher or lower position on some continuum (putting aside for now the issue of what the continuum actually measures).

For scales other than sociometric, however, one item is hardly sufficient. To illustrate, suppose we wish to develop an ordinal scale of "radicalism among college students." We decide to ask the following question: "Have you ever participated in a protest demonstration? Yes___ No___." Few researchers, however, would agree that this item alone is a valid operational definition of the concept. The more items we have the more confidence we generally have in a measure of this kind. We might then ask these two questions as well: "Have you ever attended a student rights meeting? Yes___ No___. Have you ever read an underground newspaper? Yes___ No___." We might wish to combine the items in the following way:

Protest Demonstration

	+		−	
	Newspaper		Newspaper	
	+	−	+	−
	3	2	2	1

Rights Meeting

	2	1	1	0

FIG. 5–4

We have thus allotted one point for each "yes" and have produced a scale ranging from 0 to 3, supposedly reflecting the continuum "student radicalism." However, this is a very arbitrary procedure of assigning numbers. We do not know whether these items do in fact fall on the same continuum. For example, reading an underground paper may reflect not radicalism but, for many students, simply curiosity as to what their more activist peers are up to. In this case the dimension radicalism may be confused with that of curiosity about the phenomenon; that is, they may fall on different continua.

Guttman scaling provides a way of assigning scale scores in a logical, systematic fashion, thus removing much of the arbitrary character from scale construction (Stouffer, 1951). The reasoning is as follows: If indeed our three items fall on the same continuum, and if protest participation is the highest point on the continuum, with rights meeting and underground reading the ensuing two points, then there should only be four patterns of response extant in our data:

Scale Score	Protest Demonstration	Rights Meeting	Underground Paper
3	+	+	+
2	−	+	+
1	−	−	+
0	−	−	−

FIG. 5–5 ACCEPTABLE SCALE PATTERNS FOR THREE ITEMS

In short, no one should answer that he has attended a protest demonstration but has not read an underground paper, or that he has attended a rights meeting but has not read an underground paper. If the scale does indeed reflect a continuum, then one cannot reach the highest point on it without first having gone through the lower stages. It is a cumulative phenomenon. In passing, it might be noted that the number of acceptable scale types can be calculated by the ensuing formula:

Number of acceptable scale types = Number of items + 1 (in our case 4)

If only the above four patterns are discovered, we have a perfect scale, what is termed 100% *reproducibility*. That is, knowing only an individual's scale score, we are able to generate or reproduce his response pattern on all items. Of course, such perfection is not typically attained. We may find any or all of four *non*-acceptable scale patterns in our data (Figure 5–6).

We have, then, the possibility of finding four scale types and four nonscale types among our responses. This suggests a general formula for calculating the total number of possible patterns (both acceptable and nonacceptable ones):

Total number of scale patterns = 2^n (where n = the number of items —in our case 3)

With three items, then, there are eight possible patterns, four of these being consistent with the Guttman logic. With four items there would be sixteen possible patterns, with five of these being acceptable scale types.

Now, it is quite reasonable that the more nonscale types we have, the less confidence we have that our items do form an ordinal scale. What we wish at this point is some measure of extent of departure from the ideal patterns. The technique is conveyed in Table 5–3, which presents hypothetical data for 100 students.

Protest Demonstration	Rights Meeting	Underground Paper
+	−	+
−	+	−
+	−	−
+	+	−

FIG. 5–6 NONACCEPTABLE SCALE PATTERNS FOR THREE ITEMS

FROM **PRENTICE-HALL, INC.**
ENGLEWOOD CLIFFS, N.J. 07632

We are interested in the opinion of —

ILLINOIS BENEDICTINE COL.
LISLE IL 60532

concerning these books —

6097 4 GOVT BY PEOPLE BASIC

1 8522 7 SOCIAL RES METH

TOTAL BOOKS	C	D

C RF

1

106681 **F**

Sent with the
compliments of
your P-H
representative

D HILDEBRAND

TABLE 5–3 PROCEDURE FOR CALCULATING REPRODUCIBILITY

	Protest Demon-stration	Rights Meeting	Under-ground Paper	Errors Per Scale Type	Number of People in Each Pattern	Total Number of Errors
3 (acceptable)	+	+	+	0	5	0
unacceptable	+	+	−	1	3	3
2 (acceptable)	−	+	+	0	15	0
unacceptable	−	+	−	1	10	10
1 (acceptable)	−	−	+	0	25	0
unacceptable	+	−	+	1	7	7
0 (acceptable)	−	−	−	0	35	0
					N = 100	20

$$
\begin{aligned}
\text{Coefficient of Reproducibility} \ &= \ 1 - \frac{\text{Total errors}}{\#\ \text{items (N)}} \\
&= \ 1 - \frac{20}{300} \\
&= \ 1 - .067 \\
&= \ .933
\end{aligned}
$$

An error is thus any entry that prevents the scale type from being acceptable. The number 300 is arrived at by multiplying the number of items (in our case 3) by the total number of respondents (100), a measure of the total number of potential errors.

We find, then, that the probability of reproducing an individual's pattern by knowing his score is 0.933. The rule of thumb generally used is 0.90. Any coefficient below this is considered insufficiently large to permit the claim of a one-continuum measure. In our case, we may be confident that we do possess an ordinal scale and that the few nonacceptable types that arose are simply errors on the part of individual respondents.[1] We are, according to this reasoning, allowed to assign these error respondents to one of the acceptable types, the one chosen being the closest to the error pattern manifested.

In conclusion, ordinal scales are more desirable than nominal

---

[1] It should be pointed out that, in general, the fewer items one is working with the easier it is to attain a high coefficient of reproducibility by chance alone.

measures because of the higher level statistical usage we are permitted. Nevertheless, we are not permitted to convey the illusion of ordinality by an arbitrary assignment of numbers. The Guttman technique provides us with a rationale for assigning scale scores, a rationale consistent with the basic property of ordinality.

INTERVAL MEASUREMENT

If, in addition to indicating rank order, we are able to specify the degree or amount of variation along some dimension we are measuring such that the classes are of equal size, we have an interval scale. An *interval scale* exists if we have a fixed and constant unit of distance between each of the points along our dimension or continuum. For example, if moderately black is from modestly black as modestly black is from gray as gray is from white, then we have an interval scale. The distance between the points, representing the values, is equal.

In the social sciences, we occasionally realize interval data. For example, the scores from IQ tests are interval level, for the distance between a score of 100 and a score of 120 is equal to the distance between a score of 80 and a score of 100. Opinions or attitudes have been measured directly when a respondent is asked to respond to some stimulus—a statement or question—by assigning the statement to one of several categories which have been identified only numerically. These numerical classes are supposed to be equally spaced, and the respondent makes his decision on the basis of his hypothetical zero category.

This was the method initiated by Thurstone in his development of equal-appearing interval scales (Thurstone, 1959). Respondents might be asked to indicate the degree of favorableness or unfavor-

1	2	3	4	5
White	Gray	Modestly Black	Moderately Black	Black

Fig. 5–7

ableness toward university education of each of several statements. Favorableness or unfavorableness would vary through several intervals.

A   B   C   D   E   F   G   H   I   J   K

Unfavorable   Neutral   Favorable

Fig. 5–8

After a series of statements, say fifty, have been allocated to these eleven categories by several judges, each statement is analyzed to discover the median scale category assigned it. Items displaying the highest consensus among the judges as to scale-values are retained by the researcher and ultimately make up the final instrument. The clustered evaluations, determined by the median values, are thus taken to represent each of the points along the scale. Questions for which there was little or no consensus are discarded. The intervals between each of the points so determined are taken to be equal. The rationale is that when one has many items to begin with (i.e., 50) and a relatively large number of categories (i.e., 11), the difference between any two points will be barely discernible. It is this barely discernible unit that constitutes the equal interval between any two adjacent points.

The interval scale is a level of measurement that satisfies the properties of ordinal scales, and more. Not only does an interval scale permit statements of more or less, but statements of how *much* more or less. The interval or distance between the points of the scale are equal—the distance between point A and point B is equal to the interval between point B and point C. Thereby, in addition to the properties of exclusiveness, exhaustiveness, transitivity, and assymetry, the interval scale has the additional property of *additivity*. Additivity means that we may literally add or subtract. Thus, for example, the interval or distance between point A and point B plus the distance between point B and point C is equal to the distance between point B and point C plus the distance between point C and point D. Similarly, for any given combination of intervals on an interval scale,

$$A + B + C = D + E + F.$$

RATIO MEASUREMENT

Although we may add or subtract, we must remember that any conception of zero in an interval scale is purely imaginary, or, as in the case of our common thermometer, the zero point is simply arbitrary, without an *isomorphism* to empirical reality. By isomorphism we mean a relationship between the numbers and the empirical phenomena such that there is a one-to-one relationship —the numerical representation is consistent with observable empirical phenomena. However, if we were able to identify the utter absence of some variable—for example, the utter absence of color along our color dimension—then we might realize what is known as a ratio scale. A *ratio scale* exists when we are able to designate a zero point in our measurement—a zero point that is isomorphic or consistent with empirical reality.

The zero point, therefore, is the distinguishing characteristic of the ratio scale. It enables us to say, unlike in an interval scale, that value four is twice as great as value two, for example. Not only is the distance or interval between points equal, enabling us to add and subtract, but the empirically isomorphic zero state enables us to multiply. Literally, we can deal in ratios.

In the social sciences we are more apt to deal with ratio data than we are with interval data. The measurement of formal education or of income is ratio level. We can point to an empirical state of no education or no income, and can speak of an education of twelve years being twice as great as an education of six years. Or similarly, we may speak of an income of $20,000 as twice as great as one of $10,000, although, as with education, some persons would argue that there are differences between the two income levels that are not represented by the numerical units of our measurement.

When the social group rather than the individual is the unit of study, as occurs often in sociology, ratio scales are much more common. One typical way of characterizing such units is by the percentage of their members displaying a particular attribute. Since percentages are essentially ratio scales, such measures provide a powerful tool of analyses.

It is in the measurement of attitude or opinion that we rarely achieve ratio measures. However, S. S. Stevens's pioneering work in psychophysics suggested that respondents could make estimates of stimuli that would realize ratio level measures. Thus, by being provided with one object or stimulus in a range, with a specified value, the respondent is then required to estimate subsequent stimuli by reference to this base. For example, if the prestige of individual x is given as 100, then the prestige of other individuals will be estimated as multiples of 100. Individual A may be assigned a score of 500, individual B of 50, and so on (Stevens, 1951; Hamblin, 1967, 1971). These *magnitude estimations* have been demonstrated to yield mathematical functions satisfying conceptions of ratio measurement.

Reliability and Validity

It is imperative that measurements be reliable and valid. Failing this, science does not proceed beyond impressionist observation and comment. In subsequent chapters on observation and questionnaire and interview schedule design, we discuss both reliability and validity in a practical context. Here it should be noted that *by reliability we mean that the same measure can be used again and again by the same or different researchers, and the same results will be obtained.* The measurement is consistent rather than idiosyncratic. *By validity we mean that we are measuring what we intend to measure.* That is, when our measurement instrument is an accurate record of that variable in which we are interested rather than an unintended record of some other factor(s), we may speak of validity.

We have emphasized from the first chapter that science is dependent upon replication. If we produce findings that another scientist cannot reproduce using the same procedures, the findings and the measurement approach are called into question. The reliability of a measurement instrument is crucial to the scientific process.

Fundamentally, we can estimate an instrument's reliability by means of its reapplication to the same or similar subjects. That is, the reuse of the instrument, given identical or similar phenomena, should realize identical or similar results. Properly, a *test-retest* procedure would be used on the same population. However, we have no reassurance that the original measurement has not in some way altered that population, and thereby ensured a disparity given our subsequent remeasurement. Similarly, if we were to apply the measurement to another population that we believed to be similar or identical, we would have no assurance that any disparity in measurement result was a function of instrument error rather than population dissimilarity. Generally, we must be aware that a disparity in measurement result from one application to another may be a result of actual variation in the phenomenon rather than a weakness of the measurement instrument itself.

Ideally, if we are in a position to divide a population randomly into two groups, we can estimate reliability by correlating the results of the two independent measurement applications. The random distribution into two groups gives us assurance that they will not differ significantly, and we avoid the effect of prior measurement.

Obviously a valid measure is impossible to achieve without first realizing reliability. If our instrument does not provide us with a consistent record of the variable with which we are concerned, then we are not consistently tapping that which we wished to measure. However, it is sometimes the case that a reliable measure does not guarantee validity. We may realize a consistent or replicable measure routinely used by many researchers, and yet not be measuring that which we believe ourselves to be measuring.

We always wish to know whether we are measuring what we wish to measure, but validity is usually difficult to establish. Ideally we will have some independent measure of the phenomenon with which we are dealing and to which we can compare our measurement. But practically speaking, if such an independent measure is available, we will not be likely to undertake a measurement instrument of our own, unless it is an attempt to realize greater economy and ease of application.

Very often we are satisfied with a *face validity*. This is really an elegant way of saying that we often must be satisfied with deciding that a measurement seems to be doing what we intended. Such face validity can be increased by acquiring the judgements of experts. But it remains ultimately a matter of informed judgement.

It is always advisable, within the bounds of financial and temporal cost, to attempt more than one independent measurement approach to a given phenomenon. This could consist of modified versions of the same basic measurement instrument. A correspondence among the different approaches would be some indication of validity, while a marked disparity would require the researcher to question and to reexamine his measurements.

CONCLUSIONS

Each of the four levels of measurements are used in the social sciences. They represent, in a very real sense, stages of precision. Sciences all seem to have begun with a concentration upon the nominal level. The elaboration of taxonomies seems to be a fundamental task at the inception of sciences, and sometimes is a task of some considerable temporal duration. Guerlac has observed that such classification tasks, relating to the various substances, occupied the science of chemistry up to the nineteenth century (Guerlac, 1961, p. 66). Yet the nearer we come to ratio measurement, the more precise our measurement and the more varied and powerful the arithmetic operations we can employ upon the measured data.

In the social sciences our measurements have been extremely varied. We have developed measurement scales to cope with attitudes, opinions, behavior, and features of social structure. Much of the contemporary emphasis in the social sciences has been upon achieving measurement of such phenomena at interval, if not ratio level measurement. To the extent that this is achieved, not only are phenomena more precisely indicated but also arithmetic and statistical operations of greater power and sophistication can be performed which render the data more convenient for scrutiny and which permit scientists more accurately to express and demonstrate relationships among the phenomena studied. At the same time, some considerable attention has been devoted to developing statistical procedures appropriate to the nominal and ordinal measures that some social scientists are convinced will remain our dominant level of measurement (Coleman, 1964).

In Chapters 13 and 14 we shall indicate in more depth the relationship between levels of measurement and the various analysis procedures which are appropriate for each of the four measurement levels.

REFERENCES

BALES, ROBERT, "A Set of Categories for the Analysis of Small Group Interaction," *American Sociological Review*, Vol. 15 (1950), 257–63; reprinted in D. Forcese and S. Richer, eds., *Stages of Social Research: Contemporary Perspectives*, pp. 216–24. Englewood Cliffs, N.J.: Prentice-Hall, 1970.

COLEMAN, JAMES, *Introduction to Mathematical Sociology*. New York: Free Press, 1964.

GALTUNG, JOHAN, *Theory and Method of Social Research*. New York: Columbia University Press, 1967.

GUERLAC, HENRY, "Quantification in Chemistry," in H. Woolf, ed., *Quantification: A History of the Meaning of Measurement in the Natural and Social Sciences*, pp. 64–84. Indianapolis and New York: Bobbs-Merrill, 1961.

HAMBLIN, ROBERT, "Ratio Measurement and Sociological Theory: A Critical Analysis." Saint Louis: Washington University, mimeo, 1967.

HAMBLIN, ROBERT, "Ratio Measurement for the Social Sciences," *Social Forces*, 50 (December 1971), 191–206.

LIPSET, S. M., *The First New Nation*. New York: Basic Books, 1963.

MORENO, JACOB et al., *The Sociometry Reader.* Glencoe, Ill.: Free Press, 1959.

STEVENS, S. S., *Handbook of Experimental Psychology,* pp. 1–49. New York: John Wiley, 1951.

STOUFFER, SAMUEL A. et al., *The American Soldier.* Princeton, N.J.: Princeton University Press, 1951.

THURSTONE, L. L., *The Measurement of Values.* Chicago: University of Chicago Press, 1959.

SELECTED ADDITIONAL READINGS (ANNOTATED)

HEMPEL, CARL, *Fundamentals of Concept Formation in Empirical Science,* pp. 50–78. Chicago: University of Chicago Press, 1952. An excellent discussion of the formal properties of each of the four levels of measurement.

MILLER, DELBERT, *Handbook of Research Design and Social Measurement,* (2nd ed.). New York: McKay, 1970. This book contains examples of frequently used measurement scales.

STEVENS, S. S. "On the Theory of Scales of Measurement," *Science,* Vol. 684 (1946), 677–80; reprinted in D. Forcese and S. Richer, eds., *Stages of Social Research,* pp. 70–75. A brief but lucid paper outlining the four levels of measurement.

UPSHAW, HARRY, "Attitude Measurement," in H. Blalock, Jr. and A. Blalock, eds., *Methodology in Social Research,* pp. 60–111. New York: McGraw-Hill, 1968. An excellent and current paper examining measurement scales in the social sciences.

PART TWO

The
Research Format I:
Descriptive

When considering the actual conduct and output of research, it is possible to distinguish two basic research emphases. Social scientists are concerned with descriptive enquiry and explanatory enquiry. *Descriptive enquiry* has as its object the exploration and clarification of some phenomena where accurate information is lacking; often such research is explicitly labeled exploratory research. Such enquiry is literally intended to provide description, as thorough as possible, often with a view to providing material and guidance for subsequent research.

This subsequent investigation is usually *explanatory* in nature, permitting generalization or, at least, intending generalizations. That is, there will be more than an attempt to describe the existence and the nature of some phenomena; there will also be an attempt to account for these phenomena by specifying propositions of general tenability. There will be explicitly stated relationships among variables such that we could infer causal links among them. Properly, these relationships will have been anticipated in formally stated hypotheses prior to the conduct of the research. Although we may also speak of descriptive hypotheses insofar as a researcher may anticipate certain features of the phenomena to be investigated, such explicitly hypothesized relationships are often absent in descriptive research.

Of course the distinction between descriptive/taxonomic research and explanatory research is ideal-typical. There are frequent instances in which a researcher makes explanatory statements on the basis of descriptive data—in effect, saying more than the data properly allow. More significantly, good explanatory analysis is impossible without prior descriptive research.

This basic distinction between descriptive and explanatory enquiry provides a means of discussing the broad alternatives offered a social scientist in research formats. By research format we mean one of the three general types of research approach characteristic of work in sociology: the case study, distinguished by its exhaustive consideration of one case; the survey, less intensive but involving a large number of units of study; and the experiment, characterized by the explicit manipulation of variables by the researcher. It is possible, proceeding cautiously, to relate the descriptive-explanatory distinction to the research format. Typically, formats for describing have been associated with the *case study* format and the *survey* format. On the other hand, explanatory research has relied upon the *experiment* and the *survey* format. These are *modal* patterns of research. When sociologists carry out descriptive research we usually find them employing case studies or surveys. When they are concerned explicitly with explanation we may look for experimental and survey formats.

As we shall discuss in subsequent chapters, the case study approach or format may utilize several modes of data collection, ranging from forms of observational enquiry to the analysis of secondary sources such as letters or diaries or some combination of these. Similarly, the survey format may depend upon interviews, questionnaires, secondary analysis of available information, or some combination of these. The precise mode or tool of data collection is less important in distinguishing the nature of research than are the types of questions the researcher is interested in. Is he interested in fundamental description alone or in explanation; will he be dealing with one, a few, or many units of analysis? Decisions regarding such options influence what, how, and where specific data collection tools will be utilized.

DESCRIPTIVE RESEARCH FORMATS

In order to describe the case study format and the survey format as approaches to descriptive study, it is useful to make a simple distinction regarding the unit to be studied; that is, whether the focus of concern is the individual or the social group. A researcher's unit of investigation or analysis may be an individual or some group or collectivity such as a fraternity, corporation, or nation. With this distinction in mind, we can outline four general types of descriptive study, as indicated in Figure 6–1.

The Case Study

The case study format has frequently been employed in the study of groups (Cell D2, Figure 6–1) and in the study of individuals (Cell D1, Figure 6–1). In sociology there are frequent reported studies of community ethnic groups, such as Thomas and Znaniecki's study of the Polish peasant in America (Thomas and Znaniecki, 1918–1920); of juvenile gangs, such as Whyte's famous *Streetcorner Society* (Whyte, 1943); of total communities, such as undertaken by the Lynds in Middletown (Lynd and Lynd,

	Descriptive Studies	
	Unit of Study	
	Individual	Social Group
Case Study	D 1	D 2
Format		
Survey	D 3	D 4

FIG. 6–1

1929); or the famous study of a labor union, *Union Democracy* (Lipset, Trow and Coleman, 1956). Case studies of the individual have been traditionally associated with the psychoanalytic tradition in psychology and social psychology. Freud, of course, constructed his theory of human psychic response through the accumulation of many such intensive case studies of individuals (Breuer and Freud, 1957); or, to take another example, there is the post-Freudian work of Karen Horney, as in *The Neurotic Personality of Our Time* (Horney, 1937). Studies such as these, both of Cell D1 and Cell D2, suggest factors that might explain behavior; but they are essentially descriptive or exploratory in that the units of study are too few in number and therefore are not usually amenable to generalization. Lacking numerous replicated instances of observation, the researcher cannot make general statements of explanatory relationship. If he wishes to make general statements about some phenomena, then observation of numerous manifestations of these phenomena is required. In general, the more units of study a given statement of relationship is based upon, the more valid, ultimately, is the explanatory system (see Chapter 9 and the discussion of "sampling"). There are exceptions, such as in the case of some studies of total communities that have data permitting generalization within the given community but not permitting generalization regarding communities at large. There is also the possibility of generalization given the accumulation of numerous case studies which provide comparable and cumulative data, such as in the instance of the thousands of psychoanalytic studies or hundreds of ethnographic case studies.

The essential feature of a case study is that the unit of study, whether a group or an individual, is *studied intensively as an entity*. Thus, for example, Freud attempted to reconstruct the life histories of his patients to the extent that this was possible, learning all he could about their past and their present. Similarly, Whyte attempted a thorough familiarity with the life of the street gangs with a view to learning as much as possible about the individual members of the gang and the gang itself. Obviously, such intensive familiarity with the object of study is not realized short of several months' investigation. Given this time factor, it must be realized, therefore, that unless he is endowed with unlimited time, assistants, and financing, an extended series of case studies is virtually impossible for the researcher. Consequently, the cumulative compilation of intensive case studies that might permit some degree of generalization is rarely achieved, particularly in sociology, in which the group rather than the individual is the object of enquiry.

The Survey

Contrast this with the survey format, where essentially we are examining many individuals or groups with a view to some particular characteristics or variables. We are frequently intent upon variations in individual response within some population (Cell D3, Figure 6–1). Consequently, we gather information pertaining to the specific response from many individuals utilizing some sampling technique in order to select the individuals (to be discussed in Chapter 9). It must be pointed out, however, that we are interested in the manner in which these individual responses cluster in the sense of being representative of subgroup categories within the population. Thus, in sociology, we may derive our data in a survey from the responses of many individuals, but the information is taken to represent group distinctions insofar as we make inferences from the sum of the individual responses. So, on the basis of surveys of individuals we distinguish differences in behavior by ethnic group, by religious group, by class, and so on, as did Durkheim in his *Suicide* (Durkheim, 1951).

Polls which attempt to tap public opinion are descriptive surveys. For example, a sample of Americans might be asked whether they eat "Corny Cereal." Or, to take a less facetious example, election predictions are derived from sample surveys which solicit public reaction to alternate candidates for public office. Recently in Canada, sampling procedures were used in the census, with a representative sample of the population receiving a more elaborate questionnaire than the majority of the citizens. The data collected are, of course, descriptive insofar as they are used to draw a profile of life style and demographic characteristics of the Canadian population. There are, in addition, instances in which groups rather than individuals are surveyed (Cell D4, Figure 6–1), such as in the case of examining, for example, the structure of several corporations, fraternities, or, to take a current example, of United States employment security agencies, as undertaken by Blau (Blau, 1970).

In general, the major distinction between case study and survey is that in the latter *several* units (whether individuals or groups) are examined. They are normally examined far less intensively than in a case study of a single unit, in that certain information pertaining to the unit of study is not obtained. Rather, information is acquired pertaining to some predesignated factors the researcher is particularly interested in, such as social class, age, sex, attitudes toward authority, and so on. Here, then, the object is to make statements about some sets of individuals or groups from which we might then generalize to a larger population.

Case Study and Survey Compared

For the sociologist undertaking a descriptive study, a decision has to be made among Cells D2, D3, and D4 (Figure 6–1). As suggested above, D1 is traditionally within the realm of psychology as opposed to sociology. Whether the sociologist selects D2, D3, or D4 depends largely on the purpose of his study.

In the survey of individuals, D3, he is interested in the characteristics of a particular population. These may be attitudes, behavioral items, or simply social characteristics (for example, age composition, educational level, occupational distribution). The purpose, then, is simply to describe along several specific dimensions.

Often, however, the sociologist wishes to investigate the functioning of entire groups. Of interest are the interaction patterns, the norms and values extant in the group, as well as other aspects of social structure. Here he must choose between D2 and D4. Given that he is interested in studying a social group, does he wish to undertake a case study or a survey?

While no fully satisfactory criteria of choice exist, there are factors that will necessarily affect the choice. Financial resources and time, the nature and the size of the units to be studied, and the degree to which we wish to generalize from the findings will all affect a decision. Let us suppose, for example, that we are interested in studying the social structure of college fraternities. We might begin with the following descriptive hypothesis: Fraternities, appearances to the contrary, are fragmented noncohesive groups.

We are now faced with several options. Should we deal with only one fraternity? If so, how do we select that fraternity? Do we alternately deal with the several fraternities on one university campus? Or do we deal with some selected few fraternities on that campus? How is the university to be selected? And how might the selected few fraternities on that campus be selected? Should we attempt to deal with several fraternities selected from all the university campuses in a given country? And how might they be selected?

Note that only the first of these options really conforms to the option of a case study research format. If this first alternative were opted for, the researcher would presumably realize an intensive knowledge of this one fraternity. As we shall discuss in a subsequent chapter, there is a relationship between the type of format one selects and one's data-collection strategy, with a case study format typically being realized by utilizing some mode of observation, and a survey format typically employing the tools of questionnaire or interview.

Opting for the first strategy, the researcher would literally live within the fraternity, becoming a part of the group for several months; attending meetings, eating lunch, playing cards, and so on. The whole spectrum of interaction is available, providing a richness of data that is quite conspicuous when compared to the information obtained from relatively brief questionnaires or interviews. Indeed, there are those who feel that watching people in their ongoing social lives or in some way collecting data while in no way interfering with their lives is the only way to understand group behavior (Webb, Campbell, Schwartz, and Sechrest, 1966).

Of course the researcher could not generalize from one such experience, while he could generalize his results from a survey to a larger set of groups, assuming that proper sampling has been employed. That is, given a survey he would be able to make statements about all the fraternities on campus, whereas the case study method would not allow this. One of the criticisms often leveled at Freud was that although his case approach yielded a wealth of data, he should not have attempted to generalize his results to all human beings, particularly those of cultures other than the one he studied. Generally, short of an extensive cumulation of case studies, in obtaining such a richness of data, the right of generalization must be given up. If you wish to generalize you must sacrifice some of the potential richness of your data. This is the basic dilemma the choice poses.

Utilizing a case study approach provides a richness of depth of information, but also we are then faced with the possibility of idiosyncratic information. That is, when we deal with a single unit of study—what Galtung calls the "degenerate case" (Galtung, 1968)—then we may be dealing with a unit unique in some respects, and these unique characteristics may not be identified as such, while conversely, differences from other units may not be distinguished.

On the other hand, if we opt to maximize the units of study or adopt a survey format, then invariably we will have reduced the number of variables or dimensions associated with the given unit about which we will collect information. To the extent of the researchers' ability, the reduction might be minimized: Galtung argues, for example, that the contemporary trend in research is to maximize both the units of analysis and the variable attributes of the units (Galtung, 1967). But nonetheless, it is a fact that for any given unit the number of variable attributes studied will be fewer than in a case study investigation of a single unit; moreover, the given variable dimensions studied will probably be less intensively studied for the given unit. Thus the survey format sacrifices "in depth" study for a range of information along given variable dimensions such that the similarities and differences among the units can be identified—so that we might generalize from the research findings of the survey.

Some sociologists have resolved this rather frustrating dilemma by viewing the case approach as the exploratory phase of a larger study. The researcher carries out a case study in order to obtain some insights into the issues and relevant variables involved in the group in which he is interested. In our case, he may live in a fraternity for a couple of months. He then may use these insights to formulate a questionnaire which he administers to an appropriately drawn sample. The case study is thus perceived as a means of contributing to and polishing an instrument that will carry the brunt of the research.

CONCLUSIONS

Ultimately the choice of case study or survey is dependent on the sociologist's particular orientation to social research. The choice cannot be portrayed as that between a right and a wrong selection. As long as the researcher is aware of the limitations of the format he selects and does not attempt to exceed them, he can justify his decision and realize useful research.

The case study offers in-depth data which often permit a researcher to follow up with more intelligent explanatory research. In our view, lacking any accumulated findings that might guide explanatory survey research, the case study is often a wise exploratory measure.

A survey may, of course, also be exploratory. But by its nature, such an exploratory survey is apt to provide a more superficial view of the phenomena in question despite the greater number of units investigated. It would therefore serve as a less useful guide to follow-up research of an explanatory intent than would a case study.

REFERENCES

BLAU, PETER, "A Formal Theory of Differentiation in Organizations," *American Sociological Review*, Vol. 35 (1970), 201–18.

BREUER, J. AND S. FREUD, *Studies on Hysteria*. New York: Basic Books, 1957.

DURKHEIM, EMILE, *Suicide*. New York: Free Press, 1951.

GALTUNG, JOHAN, *Theory and Methods of Social Research*, chap. one. New York: Columbia University Press, 1967.

HORNEY, KAREN, *The Neurotic Personality of Our Time*. New York: Norton, 1937.

LAZARSFELD, P., B. BERELSON, AND N. GAUDET, *The People's Choice*. New York: Columbia University Press, 1948.

LIPSET, S., M. TROW, AND J. COLEMAN, *Union Democracy: The Internal Politics of the International Typographical Union*. New York: Free Press, 1956.

LYND R. AND H. LYND, *Middletown: A Study in Modern American Culture*. New York: Harcourt Brace Jovanovich, 1929.

THOMAS, W. AND F. ZNANIECKI, *The Polish Peasant in Europe and America* (5 vols.). Chicago: University of Chicago Press, 1918–1920.

WEBB, E. et al., *Unobtrusive Measures: Nonreactive Research in the Social Sciences*. Chicago: Rand McNally, 1966.

WHYTE, WILLIAM F., *Street Corner Society: The Social Structure of an Italian Slum*. Chicago: University of Chicago Press, 1943.

SELECTED ADDITIONAL READINGS (ANNOTATED)

EPSTEIN, A. L., ed., *The Craft of Social Anthropology*. London: Social Science Paperbacks and Tavistock Publications, 1967. This volume contains several papers which explicitly discuss case studies, and offers examples.

YOUNG, PAULINE, *Scientific Social Surveys and Research*, 4th ed. Englewood Cliffs, N.J.: Prentice-Hall, 1966. A thorough volume which pays considerable attention to exploratory, as well as explanatory social surveys, and also considers the role of the case study.

The Research Format II: Explanatory

As a science, sociology ultimately seeks more than a mere compilation of descriptive facts. Rather, the explanation of behavior is attempted; as such, many research projects are characterized by an explanatory rather than a descriptive format. The object of an explanatory study is to test specifically hypothesized relationships among variables.

As with descriptive studies, we might usefully view differences in the units of analysis subject to explanatory research. The units of investigation will at times be individuals, groups, or collectivities.

Figure 7–1 summarizes the options in explanatory research, indicating units of study and the research-format options of the experiment and the survey.

Explanatory Studies

Unit of Study

Format		Individual	Group
	Experiment	E 1	E 2
	Survey	E 3	E 4

Fig. 7-1

THE EXPERIMENTAL APPROACH

The chief characteristic of the experimental format relates to the control the experimenter has over salient variables. The experimental format permits designs such that, ideally, a researcher can limit the number of variables, and control or manipulate them as well. A researcher may design his experiment such that the variation in his independent or causal variable might, through experimental manipulation, be maximized so as to render its impact upon the dependent variable or effect more visible. Similarly, the experimenter might manipulate related variables that interfere with the central hypotheses to minimize or eliminate their effect on the dependent variable being investigated. In this last instance, we speak of the researcher controlling for *extraneous* variables.

Another advantage of experimental research is ease of replication. Typically the experiment is limited to only a few individuals as units of investigation. This in itself is a simplicity that facilitates full observation. And it facilitates replication; that is, the hypotheses can be readily reexamined in virtually identical conditions, for these conditions are created by the researcher.

Consider, as an example, the hypothesis: Students in situations where the teacher is confined to being a resource person will perform better than students in situations where the teacher's role is of the conventional, lecture type. The unit of study is thus the individual student, so we may classify the study in Cell E1

(Figure 7–1). Let us say that a "resource person" is someone who is available whenever a student wishes to consult with him; otherwise he does not intervene in the learning situation. On the other hand, let us consider the "conventional teacher" as one who presents material in a lecture context rather than allowing a student to proceed independently using a bibliography of salient works. Finally, let us assume that we have devised a satisfactory measure of student knowledge reflecting both familiarity with and comprehension of the course. We bring our students into a laboratory setting and set up the experimental strategy outlined in Figure 7–2.

The object of experimental research is to secure two groups virtually identical in all things conceivably related to the dependent variable (school performance)—for example, social class, IQ, and age. In our situation, the experimental group, after an initial test of knowledge at Time 1, is exposed to the *"treatment"* or "independent variable" of interest (the resource person). After a given length of time a second test of knowledge is administered (Time 2). The control group undergoes exactly the same process except that it is exposed to a conventional teacher rather than a resource type. The comparison of the After versus the Before differences is the relevant one in this case. How much of a gain from their initial state did the resource students make as com-

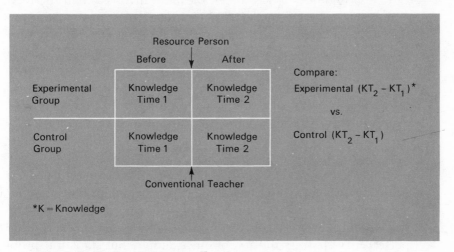

FIG. 7–2 AN EXPERIMENTAL FORMAT

pared to the conventionally led students? If the former gained significantly more, we have some basis to claim the superiority, at least in our study, of resource as opposed to conventional teaching.

There are at least three questions raised by this outline of the experimental procedure: First, why do the groups have to be identical? Second, how are they made so? And, third, why the control group?

The first we can answer rather briefly. If the groups are not identical in characteristics related to performance one does not know whether it was the treatment that caused the effect or whether it was this initial dissimilarity in the two groups. Suppose, for example, that the experimental group contained proportionately many more middle- and upper-class students. Suppose also that we find that the experimental group displays significantly higher gain scores than the control group. What then can we conclude? Is this result due to the resource technique or simply to the greater proportion of middle-class students in the experimental group? The point is we really do not know. This is an example of an extraneous variable that is confounded with our "independent variable." To ensure a relatively undistorted interpretation, the groups have to be as similar as possible.

The second question is somewhat more involved than the first, mainly because it requires the questioner to accept a basic assumption of statistics. In attempting to make the two groups similar, a common strategy is to assign students randomly to each of the two groups. If we have sixty students in all, the researcher may take a student, flip a coin, and assign him to the experimental group if it is heads, or to the control group if it is tails. He continues until all students have been assigned. The assumption is that the two groups will be the same on all variables, since they have been assigned completely at random. If twenty of the sixty are middle-class students, the assumption is that ten will end up in the control group and ten in the experimental group. If twenty are generally very successful students academically, the same result would be expected. We would never actually expect the perfect fifty-fifty distribution of our example, but statistical probability would predict a close approximation. In short, we put our confidence in the technique of *random allocation* rather than taking the time to make sure the groups are similar.

This is a relatively simple technique and is certainly efficient, especially when we are dealing with a relatively large group. Further, unlike the other two techniques to be discussed, it implicitly takes into account those variables that are related to performance but that we do not know about. Suppose, for example, that students with an excess of a particular hormone are more likely to do well than those with less of this characteristic. Further, past research has not yet discovered this relationship. By random allocation, we assume that this variable and all the other relevant ones we are not aware of are distributed approximately equally in the two groups. If we have carried out a rigid random technique this will be approximately true.

There are two other techniques for equating groups, both of which involve an explicit attempt to assure equality. The first, *pair matching*, involves finding a replica of each person in the experimental group and placing him in the control group. If one of our students is thirteen years old, has a physician father, and has an IQ of 140, we would attempt to find a student with exactly these characteristics and assign one to the experimental group and the other to the control group. We thus assure ourselves that the variables we know to be highly related to performance (age, social class, and IQ) have been cancelled out by equating the two groups with respect to them. The problem is, of course, that the relevant variables we do *not* know about have not been left free to distribute themselves equally in the two groups, as well as variables of which we might be aware but which we deem unimportant. We cannot state that variables like the hormone factor are roughly equated, since we have not allocated our students in such a way that we can defend this assumption, nor can we say that religion has been equated, for we have not matched on the religion variable.

The other obvious drawback of this technique is that it is very difficult to find in a limited population people who can be paired up in this way. To get around this problem, some researchers use a compromise strategy termed *frequency matching*. Here the researcher makes sure the percentage of various kinds of individuals are the same in both groups. The experimental and control groups might thus both have 20 percent middle-class students, 30 percent high IQ students, and 15 percent aged thirteen and over. Although less precise, frequency matching makes it much more likely than pair matching that a sufficient number of subjects in each group will be realized.

The third question raised above concerns the reason for the control group. Why not just have an experimental group and look at the effects on it of the resource person? (Figure 7–3).

Obviously, in our case, we desire a control group to serve as some kind of standard against which we gauge our resource person hypothesis. The standard is the conventional classroom situation, since we seek to find out whether the resource person technique is a better one in terms of magnitude of learning. But what if our purpose were different and for some reason we just wanted to see if some learning could take place in a resource. person setting; that there would be some gain from Time 1 to Time 2, quite apart from its size in relation to a conventional learning situation? In this case, one might well argue that we do not need a control group at all; we have only to measure the difference in knowledge between Time 1 and 2 and this will indicate the effect of our treatment.

In point of fact, though, we cannot with confidence reach such a conclusion. The reason is that many things have probably happened to our students between Time 1 and 2 in addition to exposure to the resource person. Two possibilities are: (1) they have matured and acquired experience, and hence are possibly more adept at tests of performance, and (2) they are so excited about

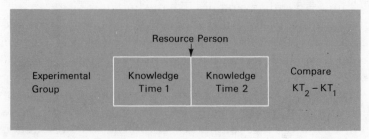

Fig. 7–3 Experimental Group Only

being involved in the experiment that they do unusually careful work to please all the observers and experimenters. The increase in performance may thus have occurred no matter what particular treatment was attempted. This latter possibility is often termed the "Hawthorne effect," after the industrial experiments of the early years of small group research (Roethlisberger and Dickson, 1939). As is perhaps clear, there is no way to separate out the relative effects of age, Hawthorne effect, and resource person on the performance of our students. Which is really the cause of any change is unanswerable in the 2-cell experimental design (Figure 7–3).

If we have an identically composed control group, though, we solve many of our problems. If we test a control group at Times 1 and 2 and allow it in the interim to be *observed* at work (thus duplicating the excitement generated in the experimental group) we are more likely to ferret out any effects of our teaching scheme. To do this we compare the gains in the experimental group with those in the control group. In effect, we are comparing the gains by virtue of age + Hawthorne + resource person with the gains due to age + Hawthorne. If the former gains are significantly larger we attribute them to the only factor that differs between the two groups—the resource person—and infer that some learning can indeed occur in such a situation. As a final note, it should be pointed out that the design outlined in Figure 7–2 is not perfect. Although we have handled most factors that might affect examination of the hypothesis, some difficulties remain. An obvious point is that the two teachers might be quite different in terms of personality. Separating out the teacher effect from the teaching *technique* effect might be problematic. To solve this, we would try to match the teachers carefully, perhaps getting the same person to act both as conventional and resource teacher, although here the difficulty might be that the same teacher would not be equally skilled using each technique.

A more subtle issue concerns the possible effects of *premeasurement*. Thus, although we have attempted to render the experimental and the control groups comparable by randomly assigning subjects, we have also introduced the possibility of premeasurement or practice effect. That is, we have measured such groups on the variable in question—performance level—prior to initiating the experiment. We required T1 in order to estimate whether T2 represents a significant change. But because of this premeasurement or testing, the contact with this testing procedure may affect either or both the control and the experimental group, and that effect may be confounded with the experimental treatment. It is possible that an interaction between conventional teaching and the premeasurement produces a change in performance level which would not otherwise have been apparent if the group was exposed to conventional teaching alone. Or, alternately, it is possible that the interaction between resource teaching and the premeasurement produces a higher performance level, which the experimenter could then mistakenly attribute to the independent variable alone —that is, resource teaching.

There are designs that attempt to deal with this difficulty of interaction effect, such as the Solomon 4 Group design (Campbell, 1957), which includes, in addition to the conventional control and experimental groups, two unpretested groups. Here, there is an unpretested experimental group and an unpretested control group. The effects of the independent variable, therefore, can be measured against four groups, two of which have been exposed to the experimental treatment, but only one of the two possibly affected by premeasurement effect.

Experimental Artificiality

In describing the potential of experiments to permit control of extraneous variables, and to manipulate the experimental variable, we have in effect described ideal or classical experimental designs. If a researcher confines his experiment to a laboratory setting, he will likely be able to maximize the control potential of the experimental design. He may also, however, create a contrived environment of such artificiality that he conceivably would be unable to generalize from the responses of the experimental subjects to nonlaboratory behavior. The laboratory setting, by virtue of its artificiality, may itself affect subject responses and thereby confound the effect of the experimental variable. One response is to reduce the artificiality of the laboratory; simulations to some extent achieve this effect, as will be discussed in the next chapter. To the extent that the environment can be made believable such that subjects lose awareness of being in an unusual setting, then the difficulty of artificiality is being at least partially corrected. In the teacher study referred to above, it might have been preferable to conduct the experiment in the classroom setting rather than by bringing the students into a laboratory. Needless to say, however, such interference with the functioning of our public schools is not always feasible.

Related to artificiality, there is also the effect of the experimenter's role in the research. In contriving his laboratory situation, the experimenter interacts with the subjects, either directly or indirectly. He defines the boundaries of behavior, and generally acts as a control agent. As Mills puts it:

. . . The experimental group is almost wholly dependent upon him for its substance, form and direction. Now, it is *he* who admits and excludes, *he* who assembles and dismisses, *he* who announces the purpose, sets the agenda, prescribes the rules, shifts direction, shields against outside influence, and so on—all in order properly to achieve comparable groups, standard procedures and a reduction in experimental error. The point of the comparison is that while earlier he encountered a group that performed its own executive functions, now it is *he* who performs those functions for the group. The group literally does not know what it is until he assembles the members; nor do they know what to do until he tells them (Mills, 1967).

Again, this difficulty is moderated to the extent that the experimenter remain unobtrusive, and to the extent that the laboratory environment is convincing or natural to the experimental subjects.

Field Experiment

Sometimes, of course, it is impossible to achieve the required degree of naturalness in an artificial setting. And sometimes the phenomena of interest are of such complexity that they cannot be easily reduced to a laboratory setting. Again, simulation is one recent mode of experimental examination of complex phenomena. But another has been the so-called *field experiment,* where the unit of study has often been the social group (Cell E2, Figure 7–1).

The field experiment lacks the advantages of control that characterize the ideal of classical experimental design. It consists literally of an attempt to explain the "real world" or actual environment. As such, it does not realize the closure of the laboratory setting, nor does it have the advantage of replicability or the advantage of a control group in many cases.

Typically, a field experiment consists of a researcher in some way intervening in a group and then, if there is some change in group interaction, attributing the change to the intervention. Thus, for example, one might introduce a new item of technology, such as metal, to a primitive and isolated people, and examine the changes in the social system subsequent to the introduction of the new item. In this example, we might have every reason to believe that there were no extraneous factors because of the isolation of the society in question. But in other less dramatic examples we can be less certain, as when an innovation is introduced among North American farmers who are exposed to a plethora of stimuli from the larger social system.

Thus in field experiments, we have T1 and T2, but we do not always have a basis for conviction that our experimental variable has been isolated. Extraneous factors have not been controlled. Thus, as illustrated in Figure 7–4, the field experiment lacks the *closure* of the classical experimental design.

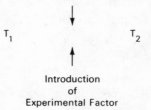

Environmental or Extraneous Effects (Uncontrolled)

T₁   T₂

Introduction
of
Experimental Factor

Fɪɢ. 7–4 Fɪᴇʟᴅ Exᴘᴇʀɪᴍᴇɴᴛ

THE CROSS-SECTIONAL SURVEY APPROACH

Let us now see what happens when we do what many sociologists do—attempt to test explanatory hypotheses *via* a cross-sectional survey, using what Campbell refers to as the "static group comparison" (Campbell, 1957); (also see Cell E3, Figure 7–1). We shall again use the example of conventional versus resource teacher in discussing the problems involved.

The cross-sectional survey is so named because we generally study *a cross-section of the population of interest at one time only*. Figure 7–5 compares this with the experimental design outlined earlier.

The dashed lines indicate what we do not have when we do a cross-sectional survey—some control over the nature of our two comparison groups before they got into the two different situations. That is, when we investigate the problem via cross-sectional survey, we might sample a number of schools, some of which

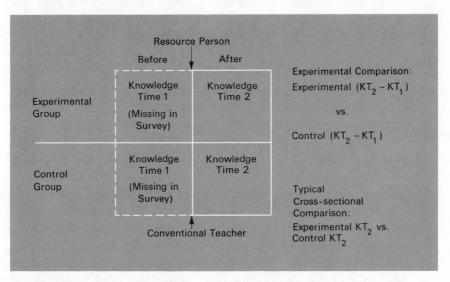

Fig. 7–5 An Experimental vs. Cross-sectional Format

utilize resource teaching, some of which are conventional institutions. We then compare the two groups of students on the performance level and attempt to attribute any difference to the
difference in instructional techniques. The difficulty arises because
the two groups have not been randomly assigned to the schools
they are attending. We cannot, therefore, assume they were equal
on all dimensions related to performance before their school experience. One might argue, then, that the resource person factor
is not the "real" reason for any difference in performance, but that
students entering a school that has this orientation are different
to begin with from those in the second school.

Suppose, for example, that parents who have had a college
education believe that independent study with a resource individual is philosophically superior to conventional instruction. Non-
college graduates, on the other hand, might prefer conventional
teaching for their children. The result would be that the resource
school would have a much higher percentage of middle- and
upper-class students, a factor which through past research we know
is strongly related to school performance. That is, at Time 1, before
they even entered the school, the experimental students were
higher on "knowledge." What has caused the difference, then, the
resource technique or the middle-class orientation of the student
body?

To compensate for the lack of initial equality of groups, cross-
sectional survey researchers are forced to match afterward instead
of before as with experiments. That is, data are gathered on
various characteristics of our students which we know or suspect
are related to performance (for example, social class). This enables
us to approximate the experimental design by matching, albeit
after the treatment rather than before. In this case we would
compare only middle-class students in both schools to see if the
resource effect was maintained. If so, we have ruled out the possibility that the middle-class orientation of the school was the
reason for our difference. The problem is, of course, that we can
only match on those variables we have reason to believe are related to performance. Because we were unable to assign students
randomly to the two school types, there are many variables we
undoubtedly have not taken into account. Cross-sectional survey

research is thus a much less precise technique than experimentation for establishing causality.

This issue is a specific brand of the chicken and the egg problem. Has the resource person affected "knowledge," or have students high on knowledge been attracted to and selected schools employing resource teaching? The direction of the relationship is often not at all clear in survey research, since we have no control over the time sequence of the two variables. Compare this with the experimental format, where we *know* the resource person has preceded our knowledge measurements in time. We ensure this by being able ourselves to manipulate the situation, thereby clarifying the direction and nature of causation.

All this would seem to imply that a carefully done experiment is generally superior to a cross-sectional survey. If one uses ability to control relevant variables as the yardstick, there is little doubt about this. However we would be remiss if we did not point to two advantages cross-sectional research has over experimental studies. There is, first, the greater likelihood of obtaining and actually reaching a representative sample when one is doing a cross-sectional survey. Carrying out a good experiment means persuading a group of people to appear at designated places usually several times over a long period. A survey, on the other hand, is typically a "one-shot" affair which can be conducted in the respondents' homes. One would expect, then, a better sample in the latter situation.

A second point, previously made, is that experiments are artificial situations. That is, they typically remove the individual from his natural environment and place him in one contrived by the experimenter. Mills has expressed well the nagging feeling of unreality experienced by the experimenter (Mills, 1967). The question is, how valid are the results of such studies; how close are they to actually capturing "real" behavior? In short, can we generalize from laboratory behavior to a population of behaviors, in natural settings? Since a survey is closer to an individual's ongoing everyday existence, it might be argued that it portrays a more realistic picture of behavior.

We will have more to say about problems of analysis with survey data in Part Three.

A Note on Longitudinal Survey Formats

A strategy that makes establishing causality somewhat less tenuous in survey work is the longitudinal format. Here one can gather data at two or more points in time on the same sample (see Figure 7–6).

The argument is that if one can compare the *change* in performance of the same individuals as exposure to the school increases, this change (as measured by the difference [Experimental KT_3 − Experimental KT_2] − [Control KT_3 − Control KT_2]) will reflect a "true" resource person effect. In other words, we are saying that, since gains in performance have been measured while the individual is in the school, any change will be assumed to be due to the school and not to any initial differences between the groups.

This is not necessarily the case, however. If an individual entering a school with resource teachers is there because of some prior commitment to learning, this in itself may cause a greater positive change in his performance, although its effect is likely to decrease

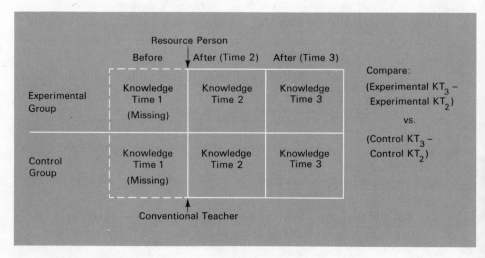

FIG. 7–6 A LONGITUDINAL DESIGN

in time. The longitudinal panel study does not completely take care of this possible inequality in motivation or commitment. Again, we will have somewhat more to say on problems of causal analysis in the last few chapters.

Cross-societal Research

Another means of gaining causal insight is cross-societal research. By cross-societal research we mean research involving a comparison between at least two societies. Such research is explanatory in nature, since explicitly or implicitly it involves the relationship between a minimum of two variables, usually conceived of in causal terms. The typical approach in comparative work is *via* surveys, hence we may classify the type as Cell E4 (Figure 7–1).

There are two major types of relationships with which such research is typically concerned—relationships in which the presumed causal factor is a characteristic of the societies being compared, and established relationships that one wishes to either replicate or generalize to other societies.

An example of the former type of research is the work of Rosen and his associates on achievement motivation. The strategy in this kind of analysis is to compare samples of individuals from various societies; in this case on the extent to which they possess motivation to achieve. The causal factors are generally taken to be differences in societal culture or structure (Rosen, 1962).

This kind of research can be diagrammed as follows:

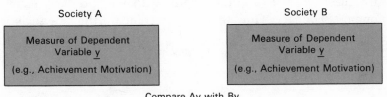

Society A

| Measure of Dependent Variable y (e.g., Achievement Motivation) |

Society B

| Measure of Dependent Variable y (e.g., Achievement Motivation) |

Compare Ay with By

FIG. 7–7 CROSS-SOCIETAL RESEARCH

Rosen's work illustrates a type of cross-societal work in which the data from both societies may be collected by the researcher himself. This implies relatively high reliability and validity of data, since the data collection instruments can be identical, as can the kinds of samples drawn and the time of the administration of the study. The researcher's confidence that any difference obtained is indeed a reflection of intersocietal variation, as opposed to defects in measurement and administration, is thus enhanced, although he is still faced with a language difficulty in establishing equivalences in meaning (Marsh, 1967).

Consider the situation, however, when we lack such control over the data. More typically in this type of research the data sources are censuses and other surveys already conducted within each society. Such studies exemplify the second major type of cross-societal research referred to above. Here we take a relationship already established in one society and attempt to document its tenability in other societies.

Robert Marsh has argued that two major functions of cross-societal analysis are replication and generalization. The first involves seeing if a relationship holding in one society obtains in other *similar* societies. The second involves seeing if a relationship verified in one type of society holds true in *other types* of societies (Marsh, 1964). In either type of study the problems are legion, and obtain mainly from lack of data comparability. Census administrators from various societies are often inconsistent in the kind of information they ask; and even when the variables are the same, the categories used may be quite different. One country may collect education data for its inhabitants by asking how many years of schooling have been completed. A second may ask for the level of education obtained; that is, primary, secondary, or postsecondary. How then do we compare the two societies in

Society A   Society B

$x -------\blacktriangleright y$ $x ------\blacktriangleright y$

Compare strength A ($x--\blacktriangleright y$) with strength of B ($x--\blacktriangleright y$)

FIG. 7–8 CROSS-SOCIETAL CONFIRMATION

educational attainment? When we use two noncensus surveys, these problems are multiplied. While there have been attempts to standardize census information, no such uniformity is guaranteed when two independent surveys are conducted.

One way of attaining a relatively viable replication is to collect *new* data in one society, using a study conducted in another society as a model. This ensures identical questions, sample, and mode of administration. Needless to say, however, we are typically unable to carry out such a study by virtue of limited resources. The tapping of secondary data is thus often the sole available mode of inquiry.[1]

The Matching Problem

The above difficulties in cross-societal research can be viewed as a further variation of the matching problem. In order to even begin arguing in a causal fashion, one must attempt to show that the units being compared are similar in all respects except for the variable of interest. As was pointed out earlier, this is difficult enough in a cross-societal survey that one conducts oneself. In a cross-societal study based on secondary data the difficulties assume immense proportions.

Let us suppose, for example, that you are concerned with aspirations for upward mobility in two societies. Specifically, you hypothesize that high-school-age individuals in Society A will be more likely to aspire to a university education than high-school-age individuals in Society B. You present as a reason for this the fact that the dominant religion in Society A reinforces such striving, while that of Society B assumes an indifferent attitude toward upward mobility. This kind of relationship thus exemplifies the

---

[1]To somewhat allay the pessimistic picture we present, we should point out that there has been much work done in organizing and systematizing cross-national data. While such work is far from complete, progress is being made. One massive comparative data storage project is the Human Relations Area Files, Inc. Working with a sample of 400 societies, data are gathered and classified into over 700 subject categories. For more detailed information, see R. Marsh, *Comparative Sociology* (Marsh, 1967, 261–67).

first type of cross-societal research referred to earlier—research in which the independent variable is a characteristic of the societies involved.

Before we even begin our analysis we must contend with the following questions:

1. Are the two samples equivalent in the degree of representation of the population they are drawn from?
2. Are the two questions on aspirations asked in the same way? If a language translation is involved, what attempts were made to determine equivalence of meaning?
3. How close in time were the two studies done? Could any differences found be due to the time discrepancy rather than the hypothesized causal variables?
4. Are the procedures of administering the surveys sufficiently similar in both cases?

Even if we assure ourselves that these difficulties are controlled, there are other matching problems in the analysis itself. A first step in the analysis would be to match the respondents on factors known to differ between the two societies, and which also relate to aspirations. One such possible factor might be social class. A smaller middle class in Society B might in itself be a cause of the lower aspirations of its members. To equate the groups here it would be necessary to compare students of equal SES in the two societies. But what does "equal" mean? Would comparing students from professional families in the two societies satisfy this condition? Not necessarily, since the relative position of professional people *within* each society might be quite different. Professionals might be quite common in the more economically developed Society A, but quite rare in Society B, where their status is likely to be extremely high. One possibility here is to use income as a measure and compare students whose families have the same relative position within each society. For example, one would compare those in the top 10 percent of income in each country, those in the next 10 percent, and so forth (Marsh, 1967).

This brief illustration, then, highlights the complexities of the matching problem in this kind of research.

The Survey vs. the Case Study Revisited

As a final note on cross-societal research, the reader might note that cross-national studies form the arena for much of the debate between those advocating case studies and those supporting survey approaches. The former, typically anthropologists, argue that the detailed and extensive study of a society *via* participant observation is likely to produce data of high *validity*. Surveys, it is argued, are often superficial and, perhaps more important, do not typically allow their administrators to become sufficiently known to the respondents to allay feelings of distrust and suspicion. Williams, for example, offers the general proposition that status distance between interviewer and respondent is positively associated with bias in the data obtained (Williams, 1964, 1968). In comparative research, in which status distance between Western sociologists and their respondents in other societies is likely to be maximal, confidence in the data is justifiably at issue.

Those on the survey side counter these arguments by pointing to the limitations of case studies in producing results that can be generalized for the entire society. Can the researcher indeed immerse himself in a total society? When these are anything but small, so-called "primitive" societies, the task is an enormous one. Further, the length of time necessary to produce a total picture via participant observation perhaps negates any gains accruing from the method.

This issue is in a sense a false one, however. Surely the choice of case study or survey depends not on any sense of the absolute merit of each, but on the purpose of the study. Intersocietal comparisons on specific variables such as educational attainment, political involvement, and crime rates demand some kind of survey approach. Comparisons on more complex variables such as familial relationships and normative prescriptions imply something akin to a case study approach.

In any event, there is no reason why both of these orientations cannot appear in the same study. Indeed, as will be argued later, such a combination can provide a richness of data not feasible with one approach alone.

CONCLUSIONS

In outlining experimental and survey formats we have pointed up the advantages and disadvantages of each. In point of fact, sociologists, interested in complex social behavior, have tended to resort to survey research far more than to experimental research. But the latter is represented in the discipline, particularly in social psychology. The experiment has the advantage of control and ready replicability. It often suffers from the disadvantage of unrepresentativeness. On the other hand, survey research, given proper sampling, may realize a representative cross-section of subjects. But in survey research, the variable behavior in which we are interested may not be satisfactorily measured because the behavior is simply not as visible as that in the laboratory setting of the experiment. Moreover, surveys are costly and replications accordingly few; generalizations are too often based upon a single survey lacking temporal perspective. The potential difficulty of "unnatural experimental setting" is somewhat corrected in simulations, the subject of our next chapter. The difficulties of representative cross-sectional surveys and data collection are considered in subsequent chapters, which discuss sampling and the research instruments, such as interviews and questionnaires, used by sociologists.

REFERENCES

CAMPBELL, DONALD, "Factors Relevant to the Validity of Experiments in Social Settings," *Psychological Bulletin*, Vol. 54 (1957), 297–311; reprinted in D. Forcese and S. Richer, *Stages of Social Research: Contemporary Perspectives*, pp. 116–32. Englewood Cliffs, N.J.: Prentice-Hall, 1970.

KISH, LESLIE, "Some Statistical Problems in Research Design," *American Sociological Review*, Vol. 24 (1959), 328–38; reprinted in Forcese and Richer, *Stages of Social Research*, pp. 103–16.

MARSH, ROBERT, *Comparative Sociology*. New York: Harcourt Brace Jovanovich, 1967.

MARSH, ROBERT, "The Bearing of Comparative Analysis on Sociological Theory," *Social Forces*, Vol. 43 (1964), 188–96; reprinted in Forcese and Richer, *Stages of Social Research*, pp. 154–66.

MILLS, THEODORE, "The Observer, the Experimenter, and the Group," *Social Problems*, Vol. 14 (1967), 373–81, reprinted in Forcese and Richer, *Stages of Social Research*, pp. 132–41.

ROETHLISBERGER, FRITZ J. AND WILLIAM J. DICKSON, *Management and the Worker*. Cambridge, Mass.: Harvard University Press, 1939.

ROSEN, BERNARD, "Socialization and Achievement Motivation in Brazil," *American Sociological Review*, Vol. 27 (1962), 621–24.

WILLIAMS, J. ALLEN, JR., "Interviewer-Respondent Interaction: A Study of Bias in the Information Interview," *Sociometry*, Vol. 27 (1964), 327–52.

WILLIAMS, J. A., JR., "Interviewer Role Performance: A Further Note on Bias in the Information Interview," *Public Opinion Quarterly*, Vol. 32 (1968), 287–94, reprinted in Forcese and Richer, *Stages of Social Research*, pp. 224–31.

SELECTED ADDITIONAL READINGS (ANNOTATED)

BURGESS, R. AND D. BUSHELL, JR., *Behavioral Sociology: The Experimental Analysis of Social Process*. New York: Columbia University Press, 1969. This recent volume describes many examples of experimental design applied to social research.

ETZIONI, A. AND F. DUBOW, eds., *Comparative Perspectives: Theories and Methods*. Boston: Little, Brown, 1970. A collection of papers which illustrate both the methods and the outputs of comparative research, with papers from sociology, anthropology, and political science.

CAMPBELL, D. AND J. STANLEY, *Experimental and Quasi-experimental Designs for Research*. Chicago: Rand McNally & Co., 1963. A superb monograph discussing design and analysis for experiments in social research, presenting practical elaborations of classical experimental design.

GREENWOOD, ERNEST, *Experimental Sociology.* New York: King's Crown Press, 1945. Despite its date of publication, still the most lucid presentation of the logic and difficulties of conventional experimental designs in social research.

MERRITT, R. AND S. ROKKAN, eds., *Comparing Nations: The Use of Quantitative Data in Cross-National Research.* New Haven and London: Yale University Press, 1966. The book presents the output of a conference on cross-societal comparison. The papers are uniformly excellent, keying the reader to many data sources for cross-societal or comparative research.

PORTER, JOHN, "Some Observations on Comparative Studies," *International Labor Studies: Bulletin,* No. 3 (November 1967), pp. 82–104, reprinted in Forcese and Richer, *Stages of Social Research,* pp. 141–54. A brief, well-written introductory overview of the logic, procedures, and difficulties of comparative research.

ROKKAN, STEIN, ed., *Data Archives for the Social Sciences.* Paris: Mouton Press, 1966.

ROKKAN, S., ed., *Comparative Research Across Cultures and Nations.* Paris: Mouton Press, 1969.

ROKKAN, S. AND J. VIET, eds., *Comparative Survey Analysis.* Paris: Mouton Press, 1969. Each of these three works by Rokkan, and Rokkan and Viet are particularly valuable in keying the reader to data sources for comparative research. The last of the three contains an extensive annotated bibliography.

Simulation

Simulation is a technique that has come to be used quite extensively in the social sciences. Simulations can be viewed as models, permitting both descriptive/exploratory research and explanatory research. In the latter instance, simulations can be viewed as variants of experimental design. In a sense, simulations are hybrids insofar as they may be viewed as teaching/heuristic devices, useful in exploratory research but also, rather more a potential than a realization, usable in explanatory research, and offering a richer environment for experimental design.

Simulation models are attempts to specify the parameters or boundary characteristics of some social system. This involves modeling the system and specifying the variables which constitute the model of the phenomena, suggesting links among these variables. Then a researcher might observe the interaction of the variable components of the system in order, literally, to see what happens: the heuristic function. Or a researcher, in varying the value of variable x, might observe the effect upon value y. Moreover, in doing so, he might hold constant the values of variables a, b, and c: the explanatory function.

This last is the ideal research function of a simulation: to determine what would happen to y, if x obtained. Thus, in constructing a simulation model, we may have specified values for x and y, and may have indicated that the relationship between x and y is such that variation in the value of x results in variation in the value of variable y. But we may not know what precisely occurs; that is, the full range of variation may never have been realized empirically, and the simulation offers the opportunity to explore the range of variation and the values assumed by the dependent variable y. Moreover, we might further employ the simulation to observe a more elaborate web of relationships: if x, then what happens to a, b, c, d, and y, all of which interact?

Simulation models can be thought of as three types: all-computer, all-people, and mixed people-computer (Meier, 1965). In *all-computer simulations* the variables are mathematically represented and are varied as represented by their programmed values. The variable components and the values and relationships they assume are dependent upon the programmed inputs—the instructions which the computer follows.

In *all-people simulations*, we have a situation similar to a game, in which people interact within the confines of some prescribed rules or boundaries. These boundary definitions serve to define the environment—the kinds of behavior required, the decisions required, and so on. Thus, for example, we might simulate the decision of persons who are acting as leaders of armies by asking persons to play the roles of generals making policy regarding troop movements, commitment to battle, and so on.

In *mixed people-computer simulations*, we have a simulated system in which some variables are programmed as in the symbolic or all-computer simulation. But also, some are unprogrammed and represented by human participants. These participants assume roles and interact with one another; their behaviors affect one another as well as the total system of interaction. They receive "feedback" on the consequences of this interaction from the computer. The feedback represents the way the researcher wishes to vary some of the variables in the model. The effect of this on the participant is then measured. Thus, in effect, the participants interact with one another and with the computer. For example, in simulating international behavior, if a participant allocates a certain number of resources to military equipment, the computer will calculate how the allocation affects the participant's nation and the other nations in the simulation. In other words, predetermined inputs or formulae govern the computer calculations. The calculations are initiated, however, by the behavior of a simulation participant. And in turn the calculated reaction or results of the decision maker's acts are fed back to him, thereby eliciting new responses. Thus, in man-computer simulation, people make the decisions and the computer represents the boundaries` and outcomes of decisions—in a sense, the computer acts as environment.

PURPOSE OF SIMULATION

Simulations, like any models, serve to simplify phenomena by reducing the number of variables considered, and their scale. Because of the scale of behavior, simulation research can be less costly than research in the real environment. In a sense, the variables relating to some phenomena are operationalized in a situation which is meant to represent the phenomena. Thus, for example, the internation simulation system represents the real world of international relations; it is a parallel environment. Within the internation simulation environment there are financial units, military units, consumers, wars, and so on. But this scale is such that the impact of these factors upon one another can be fully observed and recorded in a manner not possible in the real world. Simulation, therefore, has the advantage of *visibility*. Moreover, as we have previously suggested, a researcher could deliberately alter the values of one variable to produce a situation that he might never have an opportunity to observe in the real world. Simulations, therefore, have the advantages of *experimental control* and of *replicability*. In the real environment, where at best we approximate comparable situations when we attempt replication, often the occasion studied is a one-and-only thing, with no opportunity for replication. Using simulations, a researcher can with relative ease approximate a comparable environment at the point at which action is initiated, and thereby, like the laboratory researcher, is able to replicate his research.

The use of systems models is a sound engineering practice and a sound scientific practice. Miniature systems are more amenable to full observation, as well as manipulation, at low cost levels. Similarly, in the social sciences, models of the systems one wishes to investigate can be a boon to scientific studies—working models of organizations, national economies, or international systems, complete in every relevant detail, acting in the same manner as the real system, but on a reduced scale and over a much shorter period of time—and are proving ever more valuable. Using people, computers, or some combination of both, insight into system structure and behavior in a systems context is proving possible to an extent that we have been unable to achieve when dealing with the complete "real" world.

The Example of Internation Simulation

In order to convey some feeling for the way simulations work, we will describe one of the better-developed models in this area—the Internation Simulation. This is a computer-people simulation currently being employed by many social scientists interested in international relations. War gaming, one form of simulation, is by no means a recent innovation, probably having existed in at least prototypical form for as long as military conflicts themselves. In the nineteenth century, war games became very much the vogue, and they have been continuously refined and elaborated to the present time. Yet, although the Internation Simulation model is similar to war-gaming, it is also profoundly different.

Most basically, whereas the emphasis in war gaming is upon role playing and strategy projections with a view to a given conflict situation, the Internation Simulation model is an attempt to reproduce an entire international system. It enjoys the advantage, then, of a rich environment which produces in the participant a sense of genuine decision making.

It is true that sociologists always work with models; that is, they always abstract from reality. However the extent to which the model is made explicit will vary from the tacit and haphazard to the specific and systematic. Internation Simulation is an explicit and systematic abstraction. Moreover, it is a dynamic abstraction. It is a model or miniature reproduction of an international system involving actors and international interaction. Just as with any model, the researchers who have contributed to the development of the Internation Simulation model have made decisions as to which are the important concepts in international relations. These are the concepts we wish to examine and which therefore must be included in the model, while other less important concepts must be excluded. Thereby our research object is reduced to manageable proportions. Whether or not the researcher has done a good job in selecting the concepts and thus whether or not the model will have to be revised must be evaluated in terms of the research results derived from operationalization of the model.

The Internation Simulation model was developed by Harold Guetzkow and his associates at Northwestern University in the late 1950s (Guetzkow, 1963). The model is a composite of structured or programmed variables and "free variables." That is to say, the parameters of the system are established on the basis of specified values and relationships between key variables, these relationships expressed in mathematical equations. Yet a number of variables—the experimental variables, if you will—are free to vary subject to greater or less control depending upon the interests and needs of the given researcher.

The Internation Simulation model consists, at the operating level, of a number of decision makers who represent the nations of the simulated world. Each nation has at least two decision makers; a Central Decision Maker (CDM) and an External Decision Maker (EDM). There is some flexibility in the mode; some researchers have used a second External Decision Maker, and sometimes there is an alternative government. The division of labor between the decision makers is not structured; that is, it is a "free variable," the division of duties arrived at by the simulation participants.

There is also some flexibility in the number of nations comprising the Internation Simulation model. Generally there are at least seven nations, often nine, and as many as twelve. Each nation is represented by two or three decision makers. Tension, or potential conflict, is built into the model, and the nations form two opposing power blocs from the beginning of the simulation runs, as established by the histories or scenarios provided the participants. These bloc alignments may change in the course of the simulation. Often there is also a third bloc of nations consisting of "neutrals." There also exists an international body, the International Organization (I.O.). These, then, are the actors in the Internation Simulation world.

The decision makers represent their nations in the simulated international system, performing duties in relation to five basic variables: Basic Consumption units (BCs), Consumer Satisfaction units (CSs), Force Capability units (FCs), Validator Satisfaction (VS), and Decision Latitude (DL).

Basic Consumption units, or BCs, are precisely what their title implies—the fundamental resource of the simulate world. BCs are capital; they will produce more BCs, consumer items (CSs), or military materials (FCs). A critical duty for the simulate nation's decision makers is the adroit allocation of BCs. At the beginning of each simulation a nation has a specified number of BCs; as the researcher structures the system some nations will, of course, be more wealthy than others. The BCs a nation possesses must be distributed in such a manner as to satisfy the needs of the nation, including the production of consumer items and military defense.

Consumer Satisfaction units comprise the consumer items. During each simulation period a nation must allocate a minimum number of BCs to the production CSs. That is to say, there is a basic subsistence level, known as CS-min, which must be met by the decision makers of a given nation if they are to avoid loss of office or attempts to dislodge them from office. Allocation of BCs to the production of CSs over and above the minimum will depend upon the policies of the decision makers.

In addition to allocating BCs to the further production of BCs or CSs, a decision maker must concern himself with defense, both internal and external. Therefore there will generally be an allocation of BCs to the production and maintenance of Force Capability units. For most nations the force units will represent convention weapons (FCc), but at least two or three nations in the system will possess nuclear capabilities (FCn). A decision maker must file a defense plan with the simulation directors, allocating FCs to national defense and to internal police duties if he so chooses.

Finally, a decision maker may allocate BCs to research and development (R&D). Each simulate nation has three generation rates; that is, rates at which BCs will produce additional BC, CS, and FC units. Nuclear nations also possess a generation rate for the production of additional nuclear weapons. These rates will vary from nation to nation and it is this variation in generation rates that provides the rationale for international trade, since different nations find it to their advantage to apply their resources to different units on the basis of more favorable generation rates. An allocation of BCs to research and development represents an attempt to increase one's generation rates. Whether or not a nation will be successful in such an attempt will depend upon the extent of the allocation and is calculated by a preestablished formula.

All these budget allocations are carried out by the decision makers in a feedback situation. Since the simulation system is dynamic, there are necessarily, repercussions to decision. The decision makers enter their decisions on a decision form and the results of the decision are calculated, using a computer program, to provide feedback. Here Validator Satisfaction (VS) is basic. Validator Satisfaction, computed according to a preestablished set of equations, is a response to the relative allocations of BCs to consumer products (VScs) and to national security or military units (VSns), resulting in a mean score (VSm). Variation in Validator Satisfaction represents, to the decision makers, an indication of the extent to which the nation is satisfied with the performance of its decision makers. A decision maker's tenure of office will depend upon Validator Satisfaction; a low level of Validator Satisfaction will generally mean removal from office—violently or nonviolently, depending upon the military resources allocated to internal policing—and also depending upon Decision Latitude (DL).

Like Validator Satisfaction, Decision Latitude is computed by means of a predetermined formula. It reflects the extent to which a decision maker need be responsive to Validator Satisfaction. Decision Latitude represents a measure of the extent to which the decision maker can ignore the validators. The greater the Decision Latitude, however, the more likely a power change, if and when it occurs, will be violent. Decision Latitude varies from nation to nation.

Communications in the simulate world are, for the most part, written on standardized message forms. There are also opportunities for conferences and direct negotiations. And the simulate world newspaper, *The World Times*, is also a means of communication and an information source for the decision makers.

Thus the simulate world decision makers must allocate resources in order to produce additional capital, in order to satisfy the consumer needs of their nations, and in order to attend to the military requirements of their national positions. To these ends, as in the nonsimulate world or referent system, decision makers enter into negotiations, seek and secure trade and aid agreements, and establish treaties and alliances, and they may become involved in conflict.

Simulation Validity

Simulation models are useful as research tools only if they have reasonable parallel environments. Put more technically, if a simulation such as the INS is not *isomorphic* with the real world of international relations, then the findings of research conducted in simulation environments will not be able to be generalized to real international affairs. *Isomorphism* refers to an identity or congruence of structure and relationships. Thus, if the simulation model distorts that which is modeled, then the relationships observed to be occurring in the simulation will also be distorted and of no significant value to the social scientist.

The validity or isomorphism of simulations have been examined in essentially two ways. If a simulation model responds to appropriate inputs in such a manner as to produce events comparable to real-world events, we would have an indication of validity. For example, if researchers introduce conditions in the INS that are the simulate operational counterpart of factors and conditions preceding World War I, as the Hermanns did, and the simulate counterpart of World War I occurs a significant number of times through several simulation attempts or runs, then the coincidence of events or outcomes argues for the isomorphism of the INS to reality (Hermann and Hermann, 1967; Hermann, 1967).

Similarly, if we examine specific hypotheses relating "free" simulate variables, and the relationships identified are similar to those established between the "real" variables, then again we have an indication of simulate validity. In either of the above two validity checks, the isomorphism of the model will not have been invariably proven, but a validity claim will have been credited. Thereby a researcher might continue to utilize simulate environments in order to explore possible relationships for subsequent research in the real environment—simulation as exploratory research. Or the researcher can utilize the simulation environment to explore relationships for which there are no accessible data in the "real" world.

CONCLUSIONS

Simulation models—of nations, of schools, of business organizations, and so forth—are means of representing real phenomena in a simple, observable manner. Thereby, such simulations might serve to teach researchers and participants about the structure and functioning of the system that is being modeled. And given a sufficiently accurate simulation, the simulation environment may serve as a rich and detailed experimental environment, permitting the many variants of experimental design and research.

REFERENCES

GUETZKOW, HAROLD, et al., *Simulation in International Relations.* Englewood Cliffs, N.J.: Prentice-Hall, 1963.

HERMANN, C. AND M. HERMANN, "An Attempt to Simulate the Outbreak of World War I," *American Political Science Review*, 61 (1967), 400–416.

HERMANN, CHARLES, "Validation Problems in Games and Simulations with Special Reference to Models of International Politics," *Behavioral Science*, 12 (1967), 216–31.

MEIER, DOROTHY, "Simulation Techniques in a Realistic Policy Context," *Journal of Human Relations*, Vol. 13 (1965), 356–71.

SELECTED ADDITIONAL READINGS (ANNOTATED)

BOGUSLAW, ROBERT, *The New Utopians.* Englewood Cliffs, N.J.: Prentice-Hall, 1965. A discussion of contemporary system design, with consideration of the role of various forms of simulation models.

BOOCOCK, S. S. AND J. COLEMAN, "Games and Simulated Environments in Learning," *Sociology of Education*, Vol. 139 (1966), 215–36. This paper discusses simulations developed in the field of education.

COPLIN, WILLIAM, ed., *Simulation in the Study of Politics.* Chicago: Markham, 1968. This contains a wide range of papers, discussing simulation as a study tool for international relations, urban affairs, organizations, voting behavior, and modernization. It includes an extensive bibliography.

GAMSON, WILLIAM, *Simsoc: Simulated Society.* New York: Free Press, 1969. An instructor's and a participant's manual designed to simulate aspects of social behavior for use in instruction in introductory sociology courses.

RASER, JOHN, *Simulation in Society.* Boston: Allyn & Bacon, 1969. A brief but very good introduction to the various simulation approaches, including descriptions of several examples of simulation models and research.

Sampling: Estimating Population Characteristics

chapter nine

In order to engage in social research, it is necessary that there be some practical and scientifically acceptable means of selecting subjects for the research. The selection of such subjects is achieved through some form of sampling. If the researcher has previously decided to implement a case study research format, the basic principles of probabilistic sampling, which will be discussed in this chapter, are not relevant. Normally the prior decision for a case study will have precluded any sampling procedure, although it is conceivable that a researcher might select his case(s) for intensive study on the basis of some probabilistic sampling procedure. In most instances, if a researcher is determined on a case study, he will pragmatically select his "case" (e.g., preindustrial society, youth gang, etc.) considering such factors as researcher access. This principle also applies to individuals *within* the society or group selected. Access to potential informants is the dominant criterion for selection. This is quite unlike survey research, in which sampling is integral to the research process. The essence of sampling is the selection of a part (*sample*) from the whole (*population*) in order to make inferences about the whole.

The main purpose of sampling is to reduce the time and money that would be spent if the total population were studied and yet still realize data that are accurate representations of the entire population. Typically, sufficient time and money are lacking for a study of an entire population. For example, interviewing all ten thousand students at Northeast Tenuga University is much more costly than interviewing only one hundred. If we can achieve an accurate portrayal of the ten thousand by studying only one hundred, we will surely do the latter. Grebenik and Moser make the following point: "Normally, we are interested in large populations, and the additional expense and trouble of a full inquiry are rarely repaid in terms of increased accuracy; indeed the reverse may be the case, for the study of a selected sample may be easier to control, and more money may be available to obtain and process the information for each unit studied, whilst yielding considerable economies in total expenditure" (Grebenik and Moser, 1962; 189).

The success of any sample lies in its accuracy in reflecting the state of affairs in the population. This accuracy in turn is inextricably related to the concept of *sampling error*, as Fig. 9–1 indicates.

Because we do not study the entire population of Tenuga University, there will inevitably be some error in inferring from our sample to population. If 30 percent of our sample subjects say they have plagiarized on term assignments and cheated on examinations, we want to be able to say that roughly 30 percent of

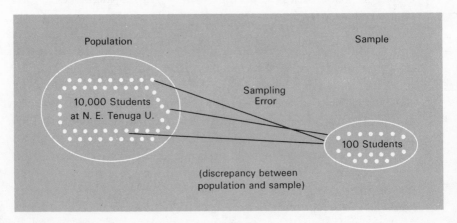

FIG. 9–1 POPULATION, SAMPLE, AND ERROR

Northeast Tenuga University students have plagiarized and cheated. The sample has no interest for us except as a representation of the population.

How can we make the step from statements about the sample to statements about the population? In order to do this we must have some way of calculating the amount of sampling error. This would allow us to say how wrong we are likely to be in our estimate of the population, providing some indication of the confidence we may have in our estimate. *Probability sampling* permits the measurement of sampling error and hence is the most desirable kind of sampling. We may define a probability sample as one in which *every person in the population must have a known probability of being selected for the sample.* Once the probability of each individual entering the sample is known, the extent of error is measurable.

The two probability samples most frequently used by sociologists are simple random and stratified samples. We shall talk about these two sampling strategies, then briefly consider cluster sampling, a more complicated technique, and conclude with a note on nonprobability sampling.

THE SIMPLE RANDOM SAMPLE

In a simple random sample, each individual in the population must have an *equal* chance of being included in the sample, a chance less than one (certainty) and more than zero (impossibility). This equality of chance is peculiar to simple random samples. In other types of sampling, some individuals have better or worse chances than others of appearing in the final sample. As suggested, this is fine as long as these chances or probabilities are known. If they are, we can compensate for the initial inequalities.

In simple random samples, though, all individuals in the population have an equal chance. Suppose we desire a simple random sample of Northeast Tenuga students representing the whole student body. On the surface this seems a simple matter, but there are two basic obstacles to overcome: (1) a precise definition of the population and (2) a complete list of the population as defined.

First, since we want our sample to be as close as possible to a replica in miniature of our population, it is vital to know exactly what the population is—what do we mean by "the Northeast Tenuga University student body"? Are evening as well as full-time day students included? Are graduates as well as undergraduates included? These questions must be answered not with reference to any statistical operations, but with reference to the aims and concerns of the study. Which group do we want to make statements about? If this question is not easily answered, the study's objectives are not sufficiently worked out. Suppose, then, we decide to define the population as *all full-time day students presently enrolled at Northeast Tenuga University.*

The second problem concerns the list. In order to acquire a satisfactory sample, we must have a complete list of all members of the population—in this case, all full-time day students at old Tenuga U. If luck is with us, exactly such a list will be available at the registrar's office. What is more likely, however, is that any list obtained will be a partial coverage of the population.

Let us suppose that the registrar has not yet listed all the foreign students on campus. Here there are two alternatives—either we attempt to complete the list ourselves from his files or other sources, or we redefine the population as all full-time, *nonforeign* day students at Northeast Tenuga U. Again, the decision should be made in terms of the study's objectives. If attitudes toward cheating and plagiarism are being studied and we have in mind the typical American student, we may be justified in excluding foreign students from the population. In any event, we should be able to defend in a reasonable fashion all such decisions.

It should be realized that no list can be taken at face value. It is necessary to check for units appearing more than once, or for units that might be systematically excluded. Generally, the sample list should be examined for any systematic bias. If a telephone directory is used as a sample list, for example, it is possible that houses in new suburban developments are excluded—that is, the directory is simply not up-to-date. Thereby any sample drawn on the basis of such a list may significantly misrepresent the larger population; the sample may not be representative because some suburban homes have zero probability of inclusion. Similarly, a telephone directory may underrepresent the extremes of lower-class and upper-class individuals in a population, for the impoverished may not have telephones, while the very rich may have unlisted numbers. The possibility of such biases and their implications must therefore be considered prior to the utilization of a sampling list.

Once we have assured ourselves that we possess a satisfactory list, the problem then becomes the actual selection of the sample. Here there are two issues: how many elements should we select, and how should we select them?

First, how many individuals can confidently be taken to be representative of our population—fifty? one hundred? one thousand? There are, of course, rules of thumb. Some researchers suggest 10 percent of the total population as a crude estimate which, if conformed to, should be representative of the population. When researching large populations, however, a smaller percentage would suffice. There are precise statistical calculations that can be employed to give appropriate sample sizes for varying degrees of error a researcher might judge as tolerable. Alternately, there are statistical tables prepared and readily available that summarize the relationship between sample size and population size (M. Arkin and R. Cult, 1963, 145–52).

Roughly speaking, the larger the sample, the more representative it will be. This would suggest, perhaps, that since sampling is intended as a means of reducing temporal and financial cost, we pragmatically opt for a maximal sample size consistent with these constraints of time and money. In addition, however, the sample must provide enough individuals to enable us to examine our hypotheses. There is a useful guide to sample size related to this issue suggested by Galtung. He suggests that research hypotheses be carefully examined, and the number of variables to be examined for relationships in any given cross-tabulations be estimated. Then the researcher must incorporate the number of values these variables might assume, knowing that a minimally acceptable average number of cases in any cell of a cross-tabulation should be ten, and ideally twenty. Thus if the hypotheses suggest the need to examine the relationship between student age and attitudes toward plagiarism and cheating, controlling for student socio-economic standing, we are dealing with three variables. If, in addition, the measurements permit three values for the variable "attitude toward cheating and plagiarism" and three values of socioeconomic status and age, we would estimate required sample size as:

$$r^n \times 20 = 3^3 \times 20 = 540$$
$$\text{where } n = \text{number of variables}$$
$$\text{and } r = \text{number of values on each variable}$$

Five hundred and forty individuals would thus provide us with a reasonable sample size (Galtung, 1967, 60).

The issue of mode of selection is of next concern. As suggested, this must be done in such a way as to conform to the principle of equal probability of inclusion. There are various devices to ensure this, the two most common being a table of random numbers and systematic sampling.

Random Numbers Tables

These are simply collections of numbers selected in a completely random fashion and put in table form. Continuous drawing of the numbers 0–9 from a hat is one way to construct such a table; the numbers organized in row and column form as in the following:

A Hypothetical Collection of Random Numbers

A	B	C	D	E	F	G
1	0	3	4	6	9	5
2	1	8	7	1	0	8
9	0	1	1	8	2	7
6	0	4	0	7	2	3
1	9	0	7	0	1	1
6	4	5	8	4	0	2
4	3	9	1	1	4	1

Tables of random numbers can be found in most standard statistics texts or in any volume of tables for statisticians. To use such a table, we must first number the population. If there are five thousand nonforeign full-time day students, they must each be assigned a number from 1 to 5000. Since the largest possible number is four digits long (5000) we can choose any four columns (let us say D, E, F, and G). Starting in the first row (although any row will do) we have the number 4695. Student number 4695 thus becomes a member of our sample. The next is 7108. Since we have no such person in our population, we go on to the next, 1827, who is included. Numbers 0723 and 1141 also become sample members. This process is continued until we reach the desired sample size, in our case, let us say, one hundred students.

Systematic Sampling

Another technique for obtaining a simple random sample involves sampling directly from the list. Again, assume we want one hundred students out of five thousand. To carry out a systematic sample, we would take every fiftieth person on our list, starting with a randomly selected person among the first fifty on the list. If number 24 is selected to start with, the first four people in the sample would be numbers 24, 74, 124, and 174.

Although this technique is certainly less time-consuming than utilizing a random numbers table, it is necessary to be wary of sampling biases which could arise because of the way the list has been compiled. To take an extreme case, suppose students were listed according to their grade averages so that those most successful academically were at the beginning of the list and those with the least success at the end. This means that the person selected to start with will have a large bearing on the sample with which we end up. If number 24 is selected, as before, there will be a much less successful group of students academically than if number 5 were selected. If academic success is positively related to cheating/plagiarism attitudes, the extent of pro-cheating/plagiarism attitudes at Tenuga University may well be underestimated. A good sampling technique should not permit such built-in departures from sample representativeness. The population list should be checked carefully before the method of systematic sampling is chosen. As a rule, lists arranged alphabetically are safe bets for the employment of this technique. They will generally provide samples which are virtual replicas of the population.

This is not to say that all sub-groups in the population must necessarily be represented in the sample. For example, even if there were a perfectly unbiased list, there might still not be any straight A students in the sample, since these are likely to be a very small proportion of the student body. They might simply be missed. Nevertheless, the sample would still be a good one because the straight A student had the same chance as anyone else of appearing in the sample. As Cochran, Mosteller, and Tukey, put it, "Representation is not, and should not be, by groups. It is, and should be, by individuals, as *members* of the sampled population. Representation is not, and should not be, in any particular sample. It is, and should be, in the sampling *plan*" (Cochran, Mosteller and Tukey, 1954, 172).

The Measurement of Error

If the above sampling principles have been followed, the extent to which the sample characteristics are also characteristic of the population can be readily indicated. Mathematicians have discovered that when samples are relatively large, population characteristics (for example, a percentage) will fall most of the time into a given interval, termed a *confidence interval*. What they have done in arriving at this conclusion was to experimentally draw simple random samples of the same size (for example, one hundred) from a population in which the characteristic in question was known. One could have a thousand balls in a bowl, half of which are white and half black. The percentage of white balls in the population is thus 50 percent. A large number of random samples of one hundred balls will produce a distribution approximating a normal distribution. That is, most of the samples will have close to 50 percent white balls, some will have percentages deviating somewhat from this (for example, 45, 55, 43, 56, and so forth), while a very small number will represent extreme deviations from the expected 50.0 percent (for example, samples with 30 or 70 percent white balls). The statistic called the *standard error* is a measure of this sample to sample fluctuation. Combined with a normal curve attribute reflecting the number of standard errors we wish our interval to contain, we have a simple formula for computing the probability of the sample characteristic reflecting the true population characteristic.

To illustrate, suppose we find that 50 percent of our sample of one hundred students advocate cheating and plagiarism as a legitimate response to the demands of the university educational system. The formula for the standard error (likely fluctuation from sample to sample) is

$$\sqrt{\frac{P\,(1\,-\,P)}{N}}$$

where P = the sample percentage and N = the number in the sample. Notice that the larger the sample size the lower the standard error will be, a pleasing phenomenon, since we intuitively have more confidence in our estimate when it is based on a large rather than small segment of our population. In our case

$$\text{standard error } = \sqrt{\frac{.50\,(.50)}{100}} = \sqrt{\frac{.25}{100}} = .05.$$

We know from statisticians' experiments that we will be right 95 percent of the time if we predict that the population characteristic lies within 1.96 standard errors of our sample characteristic. In our case the probability is roughly .95 that the population percentage approving of plagiarism and cheating is in the interval $50.0 \pm 1.96\,(.05)$ or between 40.2 and 59.8 percent.

This means that if many samples of one hundred students are drawn and they are questioned on cheating/plagiarism, 95 percent of the intervals computed for the sample percentage would contain the true population characteristic. To repeat, we know this to be true because of the work of statisticians, who have carried out exactly this kind of repetitive sampling and recorded what actually occurred.

It should be emphasized here that it is because we drew our sample in accordance with the principle of equal probability of inclusion (as did the statisticians mentioned above) that we are permitted to use the statisticians' models for measuring error. Without employing such techniques we would have little or no idea of the accuracy of our estimate.

Sampling error, though, while it is a major source of error in most studies, is not the only source. We should also be aware of errors due to imperfections in the data collection techniques themselves. People who refuse to be questioned in the sample or who neglect to answer specific questions can be problematic if we wish to make inferences to the population. This kind of error can be partly dealt with by repeated follow-up questionnaires which attempt to impress upon the respondent the importance of his participation. Also, there are techniques of testing for sample representativeness which compare sample attributes with known characteristics of the population. These are briefly discussed in a later chapter. As a general rule of thumb, if responses are not obtained from at least 80 percent of the sample, we will have a hard time convincing readers that the data are realistic portrayals of the population.

STRATIFIED SAMPLING

Stratified sampling involves breaking up the population into various subgroups or strata and taking a separate sample within each subgroup. Instead of one composite list, then, the population may be broken down into any number of smaller lists and then samples may be taken from each one. There are three common reasons that would prompt a researcher to use a stratified sample.

First, a researcher might want to make an estimate of the population more reliable than would be the case if he were simply to draw one large sample. To take an extravagantly fictitious example, suppose that out of the five thousand nonforeign full-time day students, one thousand view themselves as anarchists. Since being an anarchist may be strongly associated with pro-cheating/plagiarism attitudes, it is quite important that the sample contain virtually the same percentage of anarchists as does the population so that a reliable estimate of cheating/plagiarism attitudes can be attained. If we simply drew a random sample of one hundred from the list of five thousand, we would hope for 1000/5000 (100) or twenty anarchists, and eighty nonanarchists—4000/5000 (100); a perfect reflection of the population. But there is no guarantee of this happening. We might end up with twenty-five anarchists and seventy-five nonanarchists, or perhaps no anarchists and one hundred nonanarchists. In any event, the overall estimate of cheating/ plagiarism for the population could be distorted. To increase the reliability of the estimate, we simply *make sure* we have a sample representative of the variables which we know to be strongly related to the variable we are estimating. We would, therefore, have two lists—one composed of the four thousand nonanarchists, the other of the one thousand anarchists. From the first we draw 1/50 of the population (eighty students) using a simple random technique. From the second we draw twenty (1/50 of 1000). We have thus increased our confidence in the cheating/plagiarism estimate, since now the proportion of anarchists in our sample is the same as that in the population.

This kind of stratified sampling is often termed *proportional* stratified sampling, since the proportion of each subgroup or stratum appearing in the sample is the same (1/50 of the anarchists and 1/50 of the nonanarchists were selected).

A second type of stratified sample is termed *disproportional* stratified sampling, for the obvious reason that the strata or subgroups vary with regard to the proportion of their members appearing in the sample. To illustrate, we may decide to select 1/80 of the nonanarchists and 1/20 of the anarchists, thus giving us fifty nonanarchists (1/80 × 4000) and fifty anarchists (1/20 × 1000). The rationale for carrying out such a procedure is related to a second common reason for stratified sampling—one allowing us to compare in a reliable fashion the characteristics of various subgroups. Suppose, for example, we wanted to compare anarchists and nonanarchists in their attitudes toward cheating/plagiarism. This requires enough anarchists in the sample to enable us to compute a fairly reliable estimate of characteristics of the anarchist population. Even a proportional stratified sample would yield only twenty anarchists—a number insufficiently large to have much confidence in. As pointed out earlier, the more people in a particular subgroup, the less the sampling error. In order to increase our confidence in the percentage of anarchists advocating cheating/plagiarism, we draw a disproportional stratified sample of fifty anarchists and fifty nonanarchists. We can then make statistically meaningful statements about the difference between the two groups as well as making statements about each group separately.

We can also, of course, make estimates for the *total* population of Tenuga University by simply adjusting for the fact that our sample contains an incorrect percentage of anarchists and nonanarchists. As mentioned earlier, as long as the probabilities of inclusion in the sample are known, we can compensate for any inequalities. To illustrate, suppose we find that 40/50 anarchists and 10/50 nonanarchists are in favor of cheating/plagiarism. We can reliably say, then, that roughly 80 percent of the anarchists at Northeast Tenuga U. (with an appropriate confidence interval) are in favor of cheating/plagiarism as opposed to roughly 20 percent of the nonanarchists. What we cannot say is that

$$\frac{40 + 10}{50 + 50}$$

or 50 percent of the full-time nonforeign students at Tenuga are in favor of cheating/plagiarism. This is because our sample was not drawn so that it reflected the population. We have proportionately many more anarchists and fewer nonanarchists than exist in the population. While 20 percent of the population are anarchists, there are 50 percent anarchists in the sample; while 80 percent of the population are nonanarchists, our sample contains only 50 percent nonanarchists. In order to make accurate statements about Northeast Tenuga students we must adjust our findings using the correct population breakdowns. This procedure is quite simple:

40/50 or 80 percent anarchists for cheating/plagiarism
multiplied by 1000 (anarchists in population)   = 800
10/50 or 20 percent nonanarchists for cheating/plagiarism
multiplied by 4000 (nonanarchists in population)   = 800
                                                         ——————
                                                           1600

So 1600/5000 is our estimate of the percentage of Northeast Tenuga students in favor of cheating/plagiarism (32 percent).

To establish confidence intervals for this statistic is not as straightforward, however. The standard error for each stratum must be computed and a procedure carried out for combining these into one error estimate.

Without elaborating this technique, it should be pointed out that such a standard error is likely to be somewhat smaller than one based on simple random sampling alone. This constitutes the third common reason for stratifying—to allow for smaller standard errors and hence more precise estimates of population characteristics.

CLUSTER SAMPLING

In cluster sampling, another mode of probabilistic sampling, individuals are sampled in groups rather than singly. For example, it might be the case that the five thousand Tenuga nonforeign, full-time students are all living in cottages of ten students each, giving us five hundred cottages. Rather than sampling by student, we may decide to sample the residences instead, and then interview all the students in the cottages we select. We may, for example, draw a random sample of ten cottages and interview all ten students in each one, producing a sample of one hundred students.

There are many possible reasons for doing this, some of them involving sophisticated statistics. On a time and cost basis, however, it is obvious that cluster sampling could be more efficient than either simple random or stratified sampling. One advantage concerns the list. Compiling and using a list of five hundred elements is simpler than working with one of five thousand.

A second advantage is that if a simple random or stratified sample were selected, we might have to visit as many as one hundred cottages to collect our data. This could be a tedious and time-consuming chore. With just ten cottages, however, the data collecting job is made much easier. Expenditures of time and money, if a concern, can thereby be significantly reduced with cluster techniques.

The main disadvantage of cluster sampling, a factor probably outweighing the advantages, concerns the difficulty of measuring sampling error. A sense of this problem is ably transmitted by Cochran, Mosteller, and Tukey:

We realize that if someone just "grabs a handful," the individuals in the handful almost always resemble one another (on the average) more than do the members of a simple random sample. Even if the "grabs" are randomly spread around so that every individual has an equal chance of entering the sample, there are difficulties. Since the individuals of grab samples resemble one another *more* than do individuals of random samples, it follows (by a simple mathematical argument) that the means of grab samples resemble one another *less* than the means of random samples of the same size. From a grab sample, therefore, we tend to *under*estimate the variability in the population, although we should have to *over*estimate it in order to obtain valid estimates of variability of grab sample means by substituting such an estimate into the formula for the variability of means of simple random samples (Cochran, Mosteller and Tukey, 1954, 168).

The statistical operations necessary for computing error are quite complicated and have not been thoroughly explored by mathematicians. This implies that cluster sampling techniques should not be used without either a thorough familiarity with the difficulties or access to a specialist in the area.

NONPROBABILITY SAMPLING

Nonprobability samples are those in which the probability of population members being included is not known. Although in the previous strategies we knew definitely that each person had a chance of 1 in 50, 1 in 80, or 1 in 20 of being in the sample, here we do not know. As suggested earlier, this means that we have no reliable way of calculating the amount of error inherent in our estimate.

One type of nonprobability sample commonly used in public opinion polls is termed *quota* sampling. Here the objective is to fill a quota reflecting the population. For example, in the student study we may make sure we get twenty anarchists and eighty non-anarchists in our sample—an accurate portrayal of the population. However, this is not done in a random fashion. Rather, the interviewer is simply told to go out and make sure he gets the required number of both types of students. Chances are, then, that the first twenty anarchists and eighty nonanarchists he meets on campus will comprise the sample. These are quite likely not representative of the total student body, however. If the interviewer is an arts student, he is most likely to meet arts students; he would therefore overinclude arts students and underrepresent those in other areas. There may be similar biases with respect to year in school, sex of student, and so forth. In short, the errors are likely to be considerable; but more important, they are unmeasurable—we have little basis for discerning them.

Despite these drawbacks, quota sampling can sometimes be justified. First, given a limited budget, quota sampling is undoubtedly more economical than probability sampling. Second, if the aim is not to obtain a picture of the population but only to explore certain hypotheses in a preliminary fashion, there is no reason the quota tactic should not be used. It is quicker and less complicated than a more precise technique. In no way, however, can the results be validly generalized to the population. This step must await a more carefully constructed sampling design.

CONCLUSIONS

To fully appreciate the import of sampling, contemplate the necessity for social researchers to somehow reduce a population to manageable size—that is, researchable size. The probability theory developed by mathematicians and underlying sampling procedures has permitted researchers to deal with moderate numbers of subjects and still accurately represent some larger population. The degree of accuracy—or conversely, the degree of error—is calculable. Similarly, the characteristics of the population are calculable, such that a researcher can estimate, on the basis of a sample, the constituent features of the population—factors such as the age, religion, or income distributions of some given population. Measures of central tendency, such as the mean or the average, can be calculated, as can measures of dispersion, such as the range or the standard deviation. Thus, on the basis of a sample, we can estimate, summarize, and relate the numerical values that represent the parameters of a population.

REFERENCES

ARKIN, M. AND R. CULT, *Tables for Statisticians* (2nd ed.). New York: Barnes and Noble, 1963.

COCHRAN, W. G., E. MOSTELLAR, AND J. W. TUKEY, "Principles of Sampling," *Journal of American Statistical Association*, Vol. 49 (1954), 13–15; reprinted in Forcese and Richer, *Stages of Social Research*, pp. 168–85.

GALTUNG, J., *Theory and Methods of Social Research*. New York: Columbia University Press, 1967.

GREBENIK, E. AND C. A. MOSER, "Statistical Surveys," in A. T. Welford et al., eds., *Society: Problems and Methods of Study*. London: Routledge and Kegan Paul, 1962; reprinted in D. Forcese and S. Richer, *Stages of Social Research: Contemporary Perspectives*, pp. 186–202. Englewood Cliffs, N.J.: Prentice-Hall, 1970.

SELECTED ADDITIONAL READINGS (ANNOTATED)

BLALOCK, HUBERT M., *Social Statistics*, chap. 22. New York: McGraw Hill, 1960. A good, thorough introductory examination of the statistical underpinnings and consequences of various types of sampling.

KISH, LESLIE, *Survey Sampling.* New York: John Wiley, 1965. A comprehensive look at the practical as well as theoretical aspects of sampling. Especially enhancing understanding are the many illustrations of particular techniques using social science data.

SUDMAN, SEYMOUR, *Reducing the Cost of Surveys.* Chicago: Aldine Atherton, 1968. A practical discussion of some of the strategies available to stretch one's survey budget.

PART THREE

Observation

Having decided what and whom to study, the problem of data collection confronts the researcher. Data-collection decisions, of course, are not made independently of prior decisions. As previously pointed out, the type of research format chosen delimits alternatives in other areas of the research process. Figure 10–1 presents the ideal-*typical* combinations in sociological research.

This figure is not intended to describe an inevitable relationship between format and technique of data collection. We have presented the modal patterns which have typically occurred in sociological research. There is considerable flexibility, with departures from the ideal type configurations represented in Figure 10–1. There will usually be some data-collection mix—for example, an experimenter usually supplements his observations with pre- and postexperimental interviews and/or questionnaires, as might a participant observer. Or similarly, observational data might profitably supplement survey research conducted primarily with the questionnaire.

Typical Format – Data Collection
Combinations in Social Research

		Case Study	Experiment	Survey
Data	Observation	X	X	
Collection	Interview	X		X
Techniques	Questionnaire			X

FIG. 10–1 TYPICAL FORMAT—DATA-COLLECTION COMBINATIONS IN SOCIAL RESEARCH

Nevertheless we may safely assert that when sociologists carry out case studies or experimental research they tend to use observational techniques; when a survey is undertaken, the questionnaire or interview is generally used.

There is no single answer to the question as to why these particular combinations have evolved. There is no doubt that the different objectives of the three types of study, as well as the differential cost in time, have been important factors. In case study research we aim for an in-depth description of the workings of a particular social unit. This implies a data-collection technique that would reflect this holistic perspective and preserve the "oneness" of the social entity. Questionnaires or interviews with individuals tend to present a fragmented view of the group. They are not perfectly compatible with the objective of gauging the interaction networks, friendship patterns, and so forth, which characterize it. Observing the group as it really is from day to day has generally been thought to be the most relevant technique. In a similar manner, the objective of surveys has tended to be generalization from a sample to a population. Further, the individual and not the social group has generally been the unit of investigation. Here the holistic perspective is conspicuously absent, and preserving the unity of a particular group is not salient. The time factor is salient. A study of several hundred or thousand individuals is impossible without a relatively rapid data-collection instrument. The questionnaire seems perfectly tailored to this end.

The above considerations have unfortunately led to a host of "one methodology" studies (Whyte, 1965) in which a combination of several types of data-gathering procedures would have been preferable. That is, although there are distinct advantages associated with each of the data-collection procedures, each also involves weaknesses that are eventually reflected in data deficiencies. The utilization of combinations of data-collection procedures is a means of correcting for such deficiencies.

THE CASE STUDY AND OBSERVATION

There are several distinct kinds of observation which sociologists have used in studying group behavior. These can be rank-ordered according to the degree to which the investigator preserves the "natural" character of the group he is studying (Figure 10–2).

As the term implies, in *participant observation* the researcher becomes a member of the group he is studying. The rationale is to gain insight into the group's character that could not be attained from the outside. Here the group is unaware of the researcher's true identity. *Nonparticipant observation* essentially involves observation without hiding one's identity. The group is told of the researcher's observational interest and access is sought on this basis. Many instances of observational research are in reality somewhere between these two alternatives of participant versus nonparticipant observation.

The first two types of study in Figure 10–1 thus involve observation (either participant or nonparticipant) in the group's natural environment. That is, the researcher decides to study the ongoing functioning of a group as it really is—a gang in the streets of New York, a work group in a railway company, and so forth.

In contrast, *nonparticipant observation in an experimental set-*

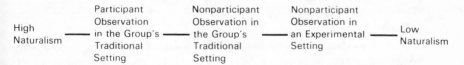

Fig. 10–2

ting involves a study in relatively artificial surroundings. A group of children may be brought into a laboratory and their play patterns observed through a one-way mirror. Or a group of complete strangers might be brought into a laboratory for the purpose of observing the development of group structure and function. In both cases, the situation is a contrived one, because the lab provides the context for interaction. Discussion of this latter type of observation is postponed until the section on experiment and observation.

PARTICIPANT VS. NONPARTICIPANT OBSERVATION

Let us assume we are studying fraternities as we did in Chapter 6. The descriptive hypothesis we began then with was that fraternities are fragmented, noncohesive groups. To study this, we might do one of two things: (1) enter the fraternity as a member, or perhaps as a janitor or cook, and observe the group under this role cover, or (2) inform the group members of our research interest and ask for permission to carry out the observation.

The first, participant observation, is argued to have a major advantage over the second strategy (nonparticipant observation), assuming that if the group members do not know they are being observed their behavior will be natural, and relatively unaffected by the researcher's presence. Since our ultimate goal as sociologists is to understand the uncontaminated everyday behavior of social groups, the argument continues, then the more the researcher blends into the group the more natural the group's behavior will be. On the other hand, if they knew he was an observer, the investigator's data could be inaccurate, a reflection of the possible self-consciousness of the group members.

Perhaps outweighing this considerably are a series of disadvantages of participant observation, many of them rectified by assuming a nonparticipant role: (1) we may not be able to see the forest for the trees—that is, when we are too close to a group the holistic perspective we are aiming for may be rendered impossible. As a member of the group the researcher will get to know some members better than others. His perception of group structure may thus be biased by his membership in a particular subgroup. Even if he enters as a peripheral member (cook, custodian) he is likely to be cut off from certain types of group behavior (fraternity meetings, parties, and so forth). (2) There may be a lack of data reliability. This is related to the preceding point. As defined in the chapter on measurement, reliability refers to the extent to which research can be duplicated by other research. The more likely this is, the more acceptable the work is scientifically, since we are always able to question and verify a colleague's results. When participant observation is used, it is extremely difficult for a second researcher to duplicate the work. The researcher's experiences as a group member are likely to be peculiar to him alone, simply because the relationship between him and other group members is dependent on the interaction between the group and his unique personality. The particular level he arrives at in the group—who his friends become—are factors mediating against duplication of results. (3) There is also a probability of "bad acting." When a researcher assumes a role in the group there is always the chance of being found out. The indignation of a group being observed without its knowledge might lead to a premature termination of the study. The possibility of failing because of bad acting must therefore be considered. Related to this, of course, is the ethical problem of doing research without informing the people being studied. Some sociologists feel that this is inherently wrong and that the real reason for interest in the group should be revealed. Others, however, take the stand that the end justifies the means, especially insofar as, presumably, no damage is being done to those under observation. If the researcher believes he can obtain the best data *via* participant observation, some argue, then he should do it. Ultimately, of course, every social scientist must make the decision himself; there are no clear-cut rules governing such issues.

Because of these problems, then, many researchers prefer nonparticipant observation. In this case, an executive committee member (for example, the fraternity president) could be contacted and told briefly what the purpose of the study is. It is probably a good idea not to reveal too specifically what the aims are, however; the researcher might express an interest in "fraternity life" and this would be appropriate. The less specific one is the less likely one is to affect the behavior of the group. If the president were told that "noncohesion and fragmentation" were being studied, he might urge his members to act quite the contrary in order to present a more positive picture of fraternity life. If the fraternity agreed to the study, the researcher would then enter explicitly as a sociologist. In this way the probability of maintaining a holistic perspective and collecting reliable data is increased.

The problem still remaining, however, is that the group knows it is being observed. As suggested, one way to cut down on this effect is to describe the study in terms as general as possible. In this way, the fraternity is unsure of the researcher's interest and cannot react to it. A second strategy is to be as inconspicuous as possible in recording the relevant data. This would imply a strategy of writing what is happening periodically rather than constantly. Training oneself to remember certain incidents for later recording is one way to decrease the group's feeling of constantly being watched.

Further, there are a range of opportunities for research which permit *unobtrusive or nonreactive observation*. There are instances in which the researcher, ideally with some specific notion of his interests, is able to record useful data by observing interaction but neither participating in it or affecting it by his presence. His presence is thus unobtrusive.

For example, he might be interested in the interaction of fraternity members at the local pub. The researcher need only frequent the establishment himself and observe their behavior, while neither participating as a fraternity member nor identifying himself.

Generally, there are occasions in which data can be collected without influencing whatever the behavior of the persons being studied. Observing motorists at a stop sign, people in a barber shop, ladies at a dress sale—these are all occasions for unobtrusive observation (Webb et al., 1966).

ETHNOGRAPHIC RESEARCH

The characteristic research format of anthropologists has been the case study—the intensive investigation of some given society. These case studies have accumulated to the degree that there are now data available for the derivation of cross-cultural generalizations.

Observational techniques have been integral to this anthropological research, or what anthropologists speak of as ethnographic research. Indeed, the reader might find that he shares the not uncommon stereotype of the anthropologists as the rather eccentric individual who "goes native." Anthropologists have relied to a considerable extent upon immersion in the society they are attempting to study. Since they usually come from North American or European complex/industrialized societies and inevitably share many of the values and outlooks of their own societies, the recording and interpretation of non-Western social behaviors by anthropologists have been subject to ethnocentrism. But the cultural acclimatization associated with some form of participant or quasi-participant observation has moderated such biases. Living with people and constantly sharing their style of life for an extended period of time have an obvious advantage over some form of external observation, for this supplies the opportunity to appreciate the nuances and meanings of the behaviors that are noted.

This is not to exclude the possibility of nonparticipant study. Nonparticipant observation may be of value, for the external characteristics of behavior can and must be noted. Animal ethnologists, for example, observe and record the behavior of monkeys, apes, birds, and so on, without attempting to emulate their subjects. And, on the basis of these observations of the characteristic behaviors of a species, the adaptive functions of these behaviors may be inferred. In a manner similar to that of ethnologists, then, an anthropologist or a sociologist may observe and record the behavior of a people and make inferences from a systematic record that is realized without participation in the social interaction of a given people.

However, quite realistically, anthropologists have been of the view that the greater the extent to which they remain external to the interaction they are studying, the more limited is their access to the full complexity of a society. More behavior will be hidden from them, and the meaning of such behavior will be obscured or deliberately hidden. They have therefore sought to maximize participation in whatever society is being studied.

Clearly, it may be impossible for the Western anthropologist, typically Caucasian, to become a full participant in a given preindustrial social system under study. The anthropologist will be conspicuously different in appearance, speech, and custom. He will not have a predefined role in the society. But, as participant observers have generally found, the visibility of the anthropologist can be gradually diminished. People become used to the presence of the observer. At the same time, the observer himself gradually learns to modify his behavior so that it comes to be less alien. Possibly the observer may come to assume some conventional role in the society. But in most instances, the very role of observer is gradually accepted, particularly if the observer is attempting to share the life style of those being studied. In this sense, a quasi-participant observation is realized.

Of course ethnographic research need not be exclusively dependent upon simple observation. Often the observational data collected by anthropologists or sociologists are supplemented by other sources of information. For example, where there is some recorded history, the analysis of this material is a vital data source, whether it consists of written records, songs or oral traditions, or the physical artifacts of a people. Similarly, interviews, usually informal, with members of the society are invaluable supplements, particularly in the case of key informants, such as the very aged, in a preindustrial society. Ethnographic research is, therefore, a mixed data-collection process, but its base is in observation.

Generally, ethnographies are illustrative of the intensive study of total societies or social systems that may be realized through the systematic observation and recording of behavior. They represent the most broadly based and perhaps most valuable data available in social science today.

RECORDING OBSERVATION

Thus far, we have described observation in very general terms. The practical question of actually recording observations must now be raised. How to do this is mainly related to the nature of the originating hypothesis. In case study research the hypotheses are often quite general. Indeed, some case studies start with as vague a purpose as "observing how group x works." Such studies are sometimes very exploratory in nature because the researcher isn't quite sure what he is looking for. In such a case he will probably record everything that goes on for a period of several weeks or months. The usual device for doing this is a diary with times, dates, and descriptions of events and people involved in them. As is quite obvious, this is an extremely difficult task to perform if the researcher is a participant observer. The sight of a supposed fraternity member writing constantly about his colleagues is sure to arouse suspicion. Even the nonparticipant observer has a difficult time. He must write down virtually everything that transpires, since he has not formulated his research problem in a sufficiently precise manner. This speaks for a more clearly spelled-out study objective.

The hypothesis we began with was that fraternities are "noncohesive, fragmented groups." This implies observing and recording friendship patterns, participation in meetings, and so forth. We may in fact decide to focus only on these two areas—friendship patterns and participation in meetings—taking these as indicators of cohesiveness and fragmentation. Refining our initial expectation somewhat, we might hypothesize that (1) the fraternity is composed of many little cliques with very little cross-membership, and (2) relatively few members attend meetings, and these are dominated by a very small and constant group. To test the first of these hypotheses, we decide to eat lunch regularly at the fraternity, watching carefully who sits with whom, the assumption being that lunch is the time when friendship patterns are most conspicuous. In this case, we can record our observations only at particular times, thus considerably reducing the tediousness and necessity for the constant observation that is characteristic of a more general hypothesis. Further, we can record the observations under general categories thought out in advance. The following is a partial example of a typical lunch session.

Monday, October 21—Lunch (12–1 p.m.)

Preliminary Interaction

John and Harry come in first. They get their trays and go through the lunch line together. They sit down and start eating, talking in low voices. Jerry comes in alone and sits at another table. No greeting is exchanged between Jerry and the other two. Joe and Marty come in and sit in the corner opposite Jerry. They shout a greeting to Jerry but have nothing to say to John and Harry. The president and vice-president (Bill and Curt) come in and shout a general greeting, "Hi guys, what's the word?" Joe and Marty wave curtly, Harry and John go on talking, while Jerry looks up but does not reply.

Interaction Over Lunch

John and Harry are talking about girls. Their discussion is occasionally disrupted by short bursts of laughter and knowing shoves. They are recounting exploits of the previous weekend. Jerry does not talk at all. Joe and Marty are talking about football and the upsets of the weekend's action. They are arguing mostly about the role of luck in the Colts' victory. The president and vice-president are talking about fraternity regulations. Occasionally they change to a more general philosophical discussion of moral versus social rules.

The second hypothesis—participation in meetings—might be tested by attending meetings in which the observer records information such as who sits with whom, the extent of one-way interaction in the meeting, and methods of decision making.

In short, recording observation in a natural setting tends to take a journalistic form wherein one records as accurately as possible the ongoing social interaction. The precision of one's hypothesis dictates the nature of the recording. If the hypothesis is general, the researcher will attempt to record virtually everything; if it is relatively precise, specific aspects can be looked for to the exclusion of others.

Hypothesis and observation are not only related by the effect of the former on the nature of observation, however. Observation may in turn feed back to hypotheses, changing them and providing the impetus for different phenomena to be the focus of observation. Indeed Becker argues that observation in a natural setting involves a constant interplay between hypothesis formulation, analysis, and formal observation itself (Becker, 1958). One may observe a phenomenon which changes a part of the conceptual framework, and this in turn may considerably change the shape and direction of further observation. Unlike other types of study, then, there is no easy way of separating the various stages of research.

SUPPLEMENTING OBSERVATION WITH OTHER TECHNIQUES

A problem with natural observation is that the data usually reflect the perception of one individual. Since it is practically impossible to record all relevant facets of the group's behavior, some things will be missed. Further, certain aspects of the situation deemed as important by one observer might be perceived as trivial by another. How accurate is the observer's picture of the group, then? This is a nagging question, as Becker indicates: "Faced with such a quantity of 'rich' but varied data, the researcher faces the problem of how to analyze it systematically and then to present his conclusions so as to convince other scientists of their validity. Participant observation (indeed, qualitative analysis generally) has not done well with this problem, and the full weight of evidence for conclusions and the processes by which they were reached are usually not presented, so that the reader finds it difficult to make his own assessment of them and must rely on his faith in the researcher" (Becker, 1958, 206).

To increase reliability, the usual suggestion is to increase the number of observers. With just one observer the probability of getting emotionally involved—of producing a biased description by virtue of selective perception—is quite high. Where there are at least two observers there are several separate sets of observations which can be compared. Any serious discrepancies can be discussed and, hopefully, resolved. Another alternative is to use objective recording devices such as tape recorders and films. While these are probably the ultimate tools for assuring reliability of observation, they are often not available or feasible. For example, while our fraternity members might permit informal observation via note taking, they might take serious objection to the use of tape or film. This leads us to a third mode of enhancing reliability—the use of more than one data-gathering technique.

As mentioned earlier, many works in sociology are "one methodology studies." That is, they utilize a single data-gathering device to the exclusion of others. The argument here is that a relatively inexpensive way of increasing accuracy is to collect the same information in several different ways. The basic principle is that the more independent confirmations of a hypothesis we can obtain, the more confidence we may have in its viability. Let us assume, for example, that we have pages of diary notes that tend to support the notion that fraternities are indeed "noncohesive, fragmented groups." At this point we might want to administer a very brief questionnaire to all the members aiming at further verification of the hypothesis. For example, the following data could be sought—frequency of attending meetings, number of "real" friends the respondent perceives he has inside the fraternity, extent to which he feels a part of the larger group, and his knowledge of names and interests of other members. If these data are found to support our observational data, we have built a strong case for the acceptance of our hypothesis. If they do not, we must take another look at our diary and try to reconcile it with our questionnaire results. In any event, both the reliability and the validity of our research is strengthened.

THE EXPERIMENT AND OBSERVATION

We have previously discussed the experimental format as one way of testing causal hypotheses. At that time the data-collection strategy alluded to was a test of knowledge, basically in questionnaire form. There is a group of sociologists and social psychologists, however, for whom experimental work consists largely of observation of small groups in a laboratory setting. Further, this is nonparticipant observation and is carried out with very carefully defined categories of observation in mind.

The archetypal work in this area is that of Robert F. Bales and his associates at Harvard University (Bales, 1950). The Bales strategy is to bring a group of people together in a laboratory for the purpose of observing the development of group structure. The individuals are given a problem to solve as a group and are observed at this activity through a one-way mirror. Further, they are aware of being observed.

This situation is thus antithetical to the observation previously discussed. The groups are artificial rather than "real" units, the setting is contrived rather than "natural," and the categories under which interaction is recorded are very clearly spelled out.

The Bales Categories and How to Use Them

After observing many groups over a long period of time, Bales was able to induce a set of categories which he believes cover all the possible kinds of interaction that could take place in a group context. These categories are twelve in number and are listed below (Bales, 1950):

–Shows solidarity: Raises other's status, gives help, reward
–Shows tension release: Jokes, laughs, shows satisfaction
–Agrees: Shows passive acceptance, understands, concurs, complies

–Gives suggestions or direction, implying autonomy for other
–Gives opinion, evaluation, analysis; expresses feeling, wish
–Gives orientation, information; repeats, clarifies, confirms
–Asks for orientation, information, repetition, confirmation
–Asks for opinion, evaluation, analysis, expression of feeling
–Asks for suggestion, direction, possible ways of action
–Disagrees: Shows passive rejection, formality; withholds help
–Shows tension: Asks for help, withdraws from field
–Shows antagonism: Deflates other's status, defends or asserts self

What the observer does is to code each bit of verbal and/or non-verbal behavior (the decision is the researcher's) into one of the twelve categories. According to Bales, each "bit" is ". . . the smallest discriminable segment of verbal or non-verbal behavior to which the observer, using the present set of categories after appropriate training, can assign a classification under conditions of continuous serial scoring. This unit may be called an act, or more properly, a single interaction, since all acts in the present scheme are regarded as interactions. The unit as defined here has also been called the single item of thought or the single item of behavior." (Bales, 1950, 37).

There is some flexibility here, however. Rather than defining the unit to be recorded as "the smallest discriminable segment" of behavior, one might prefer a more precise definition—the sentence could become the unit, or the amount of verbalizing an individual produces in one breath. Apart from which category the behavior is in we might also want to record who exhibits the behavior and also to whom it is addressed on each occasion. A typical interaction record sheet might look like Figure 10–3.

The entries enable us to see who talks to whom and under what categories. For example, person 1 said something to persons 4 and 2 (twice) in the category "shows solidarity." The original sentence might have been, "Nice going, John—that's what I call thinking." Person 2 talked to 3 in the area of "gives opinion"—for example, "I think this idea is an interesting one, Bill." Person 4 talked to 3 and 1 as well as the whole group, (symbolized by 0) in the area of "gives suggestion"—for example, "What do you think of trying John's idea?"

Person Exhibiting Behavior
(by number)

Categories	1	2	3	4
Shows solidarity	2, 4, 2	1, 3, 3, 1	2, 1	0, 1, 3, 1, 0
Shows tension	3	1, 0, 0	4, 1, 2, 4	2, 1, 0
Agrees	1, 2	4, 1, 3	2, 1, 2, 2	1, 2, 2
Gives suggestions	2	1	0, 1, 3, 1	0, 1, 3, 3, 3, 3
Gives opinion	4, 3	3	3, 2, 3	1, 3, 2, 2, 2
Etc.				

FIG. 10–3 DATA FOR A 15-MINUTE SESSION
(Only verbal behavior recorded)

These data do not give us the *sequence* of interaction, however, which is an additional piece of information we might want. There are various ways to build this time dimension into the observation. We might have a number of sheets like the above, each one corresponding to a minute of interaction; whenever a minute elapses the observer changes sheets. A second and more common device is to use an interaction recorder, which is a moving paper on a reel, allowing each individual piece of interaction to be recorded in sequence.

Needless to say, becoming an accurate recorder of observation à la Bales is extremely difficult. Much practice is needed before the technique can be mastered. Parts of the dialogue are often missed and hence lost forever. One way to enhance accuracy is to utilize a tape recorder to capture the entire session; the dialogue can then be coded directly from the tape, with replay of the sections that are ambiguous.

This formalization of observation is a far cry from the natural setting techniques discussed earlier. Its practitioners have alluded to the following two distinct advantages:

1. There are many relatively easy ways of increasing reliability. For

example, more than one person can observe the same session, and later they can compare the two or more data sheets and note any discrepancies. These can then be resolved by replaying tapes and discussing the nature of the differences. Further, the use of tapes is much more feasible in a laboratory than in a natural setting. This alone lends an additional measure of confidence to the observation procedure.

2. Since there is an exhaustive and standardized set of categories, the possibility of selective perception has been virtually eliminated. The problem becomes simply one of allocating the units of behavior to the proper categories. "Proper" allocation is in turn defined in terms of the inter-observer reliability of recording.

There are counter-arguments to these assertions, however. First, some researchers argue that the fact the group is aware of being observed is a distinct disadvantage. The behavior of the subjects is frequently argued to be distorted and artificial. In both participant and nonparticipant observation in a natural setting, this distortion is considerably less. In the first type, the subjects are unaware of being observed, and in the second, although they are aware of this, their natural setting serves to offset this effect, since they soon forget the observer is there and go about their regular business. In the laboratory situation, not only are the subjects aware of being observed, but they are also deprived of the props and setting of their own environment.

A second and related criticism is that, since we isolate groups in artificial laboratory settings, it is difficult to generalize the results obtained there to "real" groups outside the laboratory. No matter how representative a sample we may have, the fact that we have observed in a contrived situation might in itself prohibit generalization. And, since we are ultimately interested in understanding everyday group behavior, how can we justify a laboratory approach?

These issues are still being debated in the discipline, although the intensity of the discussion seems to have abated somewhat. In the final analysis, though, the researcher must select the data-collection technique most appropriate and feasible, given his particular problem. Again, as long as he is aware of the limitations of his approach he is in little danger of becoming dogmatic about one particular technique and the data generated through its use.

CONCLUSIONS

Observation is a time-consuming data-collection technique requiring much skill. Its effectiveness, particularly in the nonlaboratory setting of an ongoing social system, is largely dependent upon the patience and skill of the observer or team of observers. Thereby replications are rendered difficult, and the reliability and validity the data generates are often challengeable. Yet observation has the potential for insight and a richness of data that other data-collection techniques, such as the questionnaire, preclude. The researcher has the advantage of recording what people do, not just what they say. And he notes this behavior from the vantage point of knowledge of the social context of the behavior, while the researcher dependent upon the attitude survey often lacks such information about the social environment.

REFERENCES

BALES, ROBERT, "A Set of Categories for the Analysis of Small Group Interaction," *American Sociological Review*, Vol. 15 (1950), 257–63; reprinted in D. Forcese and S. Richer, *Stages of Social Research: Contemporary Perspectives*, pp. 216–24. Englewood Cliffs, N.J.: Prentice-Hall, 1970.

BALES, ROBERT, *Interaction Process Analysis: A Method for the Study of Small Groups*. Reading, Mass.: Addison-Wesley, 1950.

BECKER, HOWARD, "Problems of Inference and Proof in Participant Observation," ASR, Vol. 23 (1958), 652–60; reprinted in Forcese and Richer, *Stages of Social Research*, pp. 205–215.

WEBB, EUGENE, D. CAMPBELL, R. SCHWARTZ, AND L. SECHREST, *Unob-*

trusive Measures: Non-reactive Research in the Social Sciences. Chicago: Rand McNally, 1966.

WHYTE, WILLIAM F., *Toward an Integrated Approach for Research on Organizational Behavior,* Ithaca, N. Y., Industrial and Labor Relations Reprint Series No. 155, Cornell University, 1965.

SELECTED ADDITIONAL READINGS (ANNOTATED)

JUNKER, BUFORD H., *Field Work: An Introduction to the Social Science.* Chicago: University of Chicago Press, 1960. Problems of observation, recording, and reporting case study data are clearly discussed. Personal accounts of difficulties add a dimension of interest and reality.

POWDERMAKER, HORTENSE, *Stranger and Friend.* New York: Norton, 1966. Participant observation, a major technique in anthropological work, sensitively examined by a leading anthropologist. Four major research experiences are discussed—a study in Melanesia, one done in rural Mississippi, a third in Hollywood, and a fourth in Rhodesia.

WHYTE, WILLIAM F., *Street Corner Society: The Social Structure of an Italian Slum.* Chicago: University of Chicago Press, 1943. Whyte's classic work is perhaps the best observational case study of a social group ever completed in sociology.

The Questionnaire and the Interview

The observational modes of data collection we have just considered are ideally suited for in-depth descriptive investigations of units, whether individuals or groups. They often permit a degree of insight that would otherwise be lacking were it not for the sheer intensity of the observational investigation. However, observations are apt to be limited to a single unit of analysis, which may be unique. Moreover, there are problems of investigator reliability and validity peculiar to the observational techniques of data collection.

Accordingly, with an interest in generalization, social scientists frequently attempt to collect data which are not limited to the observations of a single unit of analysis. Survey research formats, rather than case study formats, characterize such research designs, and data tend to be collected by means other than observation. Of those data-collection tools associated with the survey format, *questionnaires* are frequently employed.

THE QUESTIONNAIRE

Questionnaires may be defined simply as forms for securing answers to questions. Further, they are forms which the respondent fills in himself. Instead of observing a person's behavior, then, we ask him in writing about himself, his behavior, or his attitudes, and he responds in writing.

The use of this technique is extremely widespread among sociologists. Indeed, of the four major data-gathering procedures employed by sociologists, questionnaires are perhaps the most frequently used. Given this, we would expect that the questionnaire has proved the most viable in sociological research, with the other techniques following in order of successful returns. There is no evidence to support this conclusion, however. Indeed, the proliferation of questionnaires in sociological research is less a function of their documented superiority in eliciting good data than their efficiency in terms of time and ability to reach a large number of respondents. That is, a large number of studies in sociology are large-scale sample surveys. This almost invariably implies a questionnaire format, since the other techniques tend generally to require more time per individual respondent than would be desirable.

Questionnaire Construction

There are two general types of question which appear on questionnaires—*structured* or *closed questions* and *unstructured* or *open-ended questions.* In structured questions the possible responses are all provided in advance for the respondent. For example:

What is your religion?

___ Protestant
___ Catholic
___ Jewish
___ Other

The respondent thus has no choice but to select one of these categories. In unstructured questions the respondent is allowed to put down anything he wishes as an answer. For example:

What is the most important quality you look for in a potential friend? _____

As is perhaps obvious, structured questions are used when we have a very good idea of all the possible responses to a particular question. For example, there is little doubt that the responses provided for the religion question will be adequate for all respondents. On the other hand, if we were to try a priori to construct a structured question on the friend's quality item, it probably would be incomplete:

What is the most important quality you look for in a potential friend?

___ Intelligence
___ Good personality
___ Good looks
___ Other

It might be expected that the presence of "other" as a category would ensure that each respondent would find his particular answer. The problem is, though, that in our case a relatively high percentage of respondents would probably check "other," giving us little information, simply because we've constructed the categories with little or no prior knowledge of our population. We have made a guess, not even an educated one, as to the possibly relevant items.

Given this situation, then, would it not be more accurate to leave the question unstructured, allowing the respondents freedom to express their own particular thoughts? The answer depends to a certain extent on one's purpose, but in general the following holds: in a sample survey, particularly a large one, we should aim for as many *structured* questions as possible. Structured questions are less time-consuming for the respondent. And, in effect, they constitute *precoding*.

In survey research, the researcher eventually wants to transfer the data to punch cards or magnetic tape in order to carry out the various tabulations. It is virtually impossible to analyze large quantities of data without such technical aids. The structured question is compatible with these procedures, while the unstructured question is not. In order to transfer unstructured question responses to card or tape, it is necessary first to go through each unstructured response and recode it into a set of induced categories. As might be obvious, this can be extremely time consuming, especially when a large sample is involved. The general conclusion, then, is that the more structured questions on the questionnaire the better. The following question then arises: How are we to construct accurate structured questions in advance of the administration of the questionnaire?

There are two ways to do this—using previous research, and conducting a pilot study. First, as much as possible should be learned about the research topic from the work of previous writers. This will give some idea of what factors are relevant in constructing the questions. Often structured questions have already been formulated in these works—questions which have been used with a similar sample and with regard to a similar topic.

A second strategy is to carry out a *pilot study*, which is really a "prestudy study." Here we select a very small sample (let us say fifty), and ask several unstructured questions, from which we will ultimately derive structured questions for the final questionnaire. For example, we may be interested in factors attracting people to one another and thus decide to ask the same question alluded to above: "What is the most important quality you look for in a potential friend?" We then look at all fifty responses, tabulating them in the following manner:

TABLE 11-1 ANALYSIS OF UNSTRUCTURED QUESTION ON
FRIEND'S QUALITIES

Item Mentioned	Frequency
Personality	13
Good looks	10
Intelligence	7
Car	3
Good dancer	2
Money	6
Compatibility	3
Strength	1
Emotional stability	2
College education	1
Unselfishness	2
	50

The strategy, then, is to look at the items most frequently mentioned, and to include them in the final version of the questionnaire. In this case, our final structured question might take the following form:

What is the most important quality you look for in a potential friend?

__ Personality
__ Good looks
__ Intelligence
__ Money
__ Car
__ Compatibility
__ Other

Since the other items are relatively infrequently mentioned, it is fairly safe to limit the items to those listed above. The "other" category remains, to allow for an exhaustive list. In short, we have taken a small sample from our population, questioned it about a particular issue, and incorporated this information into our final instrument. The result is a more accurate questionnaire.

As a further check on the clarity of questions, many researchers make use of a *pretest*, carried out just prior to the study itself. Here the questionnaire is again administered to a small sample. At this stage, though, it is pretty well in final form, with most or all of its questions in structured form. The focus here is on the percent of individuals not answering particular questions, either because they fail to understand what is meant or because they refuse for some reason to respond. The respondents should thus be asked to comment on each question and to indicate the particular defects they believe exist. With this information as a basis, the researcher then rewrites or eliminates completely the ambiguous or offensive questions.

A questionnaire, however, does not consist simply of an assortment of questions. The questionnaire must be assembled in some practical manner once the questions themselves have been perfected. The following are useful guidelines:

1. Give some information to the respondents at the beginning of the questionnaire as to the nature of the study. This should be a relatively short paragraph or two explaining the purpose of the study as well as stating who is carrying it out. A guarantee of anonymity should appear in this statement as well as an expression of appreciation for the respondent's time and effort. Should such information and assurances be lacking, the researcher risks failing to achieve the confidence and the cooperation of his potential respondent.
2. The various questions should fit together as a consistent, logical whole. This implies that questions dealing with the same or similar topics should be put together in the same section. Further, they should appear under a heading reflecting the substantive area to which the questions are related. For example, a questionnaire probing attitudes of high school students toward their future education and occupational plans might contain three sections: (a) respondent's background (containing general questions of a biographical nature), (b) respondent's future education, and (c) respondent's future occupation. This partitioning by subject matter reduces the likelihood that the respondent will have to perform mental gymnastics in going abruptly from one topic to another. It thus provides him with an indicator of what kinds of queries to expect in each section.
3. In general, the shorter the questionnaire the better. Data are likely

to be of higher quality when the researcher limits his questionnaire to a reasonable size. This means that we should be able to justify each question in terms of its relevance to the particular conceptual scheme we are interested in. If this cannot be done, the possibility of eliminating the question at issue should be seriously considered. As a general rule of thumb, a questionnaire demanding in excess of thirty minutes of a respondent's time is apt to discourage completion or return of the questionnaire.

Questionnaire Reliability

Much of what has been said could have been subsumed under a general title such as "Things to Do to Insure Reliability." As previously noted, reliability refers to the extent to which a study can be duplicated by another researcher. The easier it is for a second researcher to get the same results the more reliable the study is. When applied to questionnaires, reliability refers to the set of precautions taken in constructing and administering the questionnaire. These procedures must be carried out in such a way that a researcher wanting to duplicate the study would be able to do so with a minimum of effort. This implies that the sample is clearly defined, that all questionnaires in the study are administered in exactly the same way, and that the questions are as unambiguous as possible.

First, if a second researcher is going to repeat a particular study, he must know exactly the population the original sample reflects, as well as the procedure that was used in drawing that sample. This information should thus appear in the research report itself.

Second, there should be a uniform procedure in administering the questionnaires. The instructions to the respondents preceding the questionnaire should be identical for all respondents. This is particularly relevant when there are many people administering the questionnaires, a common situation in large sample surveys. The researcher should make sure that each administrator presents the study's aims and instructions for filling out the questionnaire in the same way.

Validity

Finally, the questions themselves should be as clear as possible, so that if another researcher administered the same questions to a similar sample he would get virtually the same results. The extent to which questions really measure what we think they do—is termed the *validity* of a question. If what a question is getting at is clear and hence recognized by both researcher and respondent, it is likely to produce the same results time after time.

As suggested, pilot studies and pretests are useful devices for detecting invalid and unreliable questions. A further device is one Schuman terms "the random probe." He makes the point that survey researchers are often in a dilemma as to the relative merits of closed- versus open-ended questions. The former are desirable in a large survey because of the ease with which they can be handled via computer technology. On the other hand, there is always the nagging doubt that perhaps the closed, structured questions are not really tapping the respondent's true feelings and that a more valid approach would be the open-ended device allowing the respondent to respond in his own fashion. Schuman argues that by using "the random probe," a researcher can have his cake and eat it too. The technique involves requiring the interviewer "to carry out follow-up probes for a set of closed items *randomly* selected from the interview schedule for each of his respondents. The probe does not replace the regular·closed question in any way, but follows immediately after the respondent's choice of an alternative. Using nondirective phrases, the interviewer simply asks the respondent to explain a little of what he had in mind in making his choice. The recorded comments (or occasionally, lack of comments) are used by the investigator to compare the intended purpose of the question and chosen alternative with its meaning as perceived and acted on by the respondent" (Schuman, 1966, 219). If a large percentage of the respondents display lack of understanding of a question—that is, see it as getting at something quite unintended by the researcher—the exclusion of this item from the analysis might be warranted. Although Schuman was explicitly discussing series of questions which are administered by an interviewer, some variation of his plan can no doubt be used with self-administered questionnaires.

A final validity check involves the use of *cross-check questions*. Here questions that can be checked against independent sources are included. The accuracy of a high school student's response to a question on his grade average can be checked against school records. An inmate's response to the question "How many years have you spent in prison?" can be validated against prison files. Such checks will provide a good barometer of the degree of confidence the researcher can place in his data. In addition, more than one question designed to elicit the same information might be included in the questionnaire. Two such questions, worded differently and located at different points in the questionnaire, would serve as cross-checks of a respondent's replies. For example, if the researcher were interested in identifying the decision makers in a small community as perceived by a sample of respondents, he could ask these two questions: (1) Who are the leaders in Dinkeyville? and (2) If there were a community problem here in Dinkeyville, what persons would be involved in correcting it?

Such an internal cross-check would be of aid when the means for external validation are lacking or impractical.

Administering the Questionnaire

There are two situations usually encountered in the administration of the questionnaire. The first might be called the "captive audience" situation, in which the instrument is administered to a group of individuals assembled in the same place. Research in schools, prisons, and other organizations are typically of this kind. In terms of maximizing response, this form of administration is the ideal situation. There is a good probability of a high response rate because the respondent lacks the ready option of refusal. In addition, there is always the opportunity to clarify ambiguous instructions, because the respondents are assembled in one group. For the same reason it is a relatively easy chore to retrieve the completed questionnaires.

The second type of situation concerns the mailed questionnaire. Here the respondents are mailed a copy of the questionnaire, asked to fill it out and return it using a stamped, self-addressed envelope.

Unfortunately, response rates to this kind of administration are typically low, for there are only limited means of encouraging the respondent to complete the questionnaire. Fundamentally, the respondent's cooperation is a function of his interest in the subject matter, which is itself a function of the respondent's education, intelligence, occupation and amount of leisure time. Similarly, a respondent's cooperation will depend upon how important he judges the research to be and how important his role in the research appears to be. Short of these, a researcher might resort to some form of payment or reward for respondent cooperation.

The following is a list of suggestions for maximizing the return of mailed instruments:

1. A stamped, self-addressed envelope is vital, for the researcher should attempt to minimize respondent inconvenience.
2. A *cover letter* spelling out the importance of the research and asking for cooperation may serve to generate respondent interest. If the research is shown to be affiliated with a university or research institute, any suspicion of the respondents may be allayed.
3. An intensive followup campaign should be planned for those not answering within ten days of the first mailing. Techniques such as followup letters, telephone calls, and actual visits are suggested. If a followup letter fails to elicit a response, a telephone call is advisable. If this fails, a visit by the researcher(s) is a possibility which should be considered. Although time-consuming, the gains in terms of sample representativeness are certainly worth the effort.

THE INTERVIEW

Two characteristics distinguish an interview from a questionnaire. First, the interview is recorded by the researcher rather than the respondent. This implies a dialogue situation—a give-and-take between researcher and respondent—a feature not possible in a self-administered questionnaire. Second, the interview contains many more unstructured questions than does the questionnaire. Indeed, it is precisely this feature that is best served by a dialogue situation.

An essential difference between the questionnaire and the interview is the detail obtainable in the latter; the respondent can be allowed to talk until he exhausts a particular topic rather than simply being presented with several structured questions containing a predetermined set of response choices. The interview form may look like a questionnaire except for its relative emphasis on unstructured questions. This means that in constructing the interview questions the researcher will leave a large space beneath each question so that extensive answers can be recorded. This is not to say that structured questions have no place in interview forms; in any study certain basic background data about the respondents will be needed—data that are compatible with structured items. Such data as age, sex, size of family, education, and marital status are always best sought by means of structured questions, whatever the main form of data collection employed.

Schedules and Guides

With reference to the degree of structure incorporated in an interview, we can distinguish an interview schedule from an interview guide. An *interview schedule* is virtually identical to a questionnaire in that it consists of precisely designated questions, worded in full, some precoded or closed, and others open-ended. Often, with such a schedule, an interviewer will have explicit instructions to ask the question in exactly the manner indicated on his interview schedule, in the order indicated, and, if asking a closed question, the interviewer will be instructed to require one of the indicated alternate responses.

An *interview guide* provides the interviewer more discretion. It is literally a guide outlining the kind of information required and perhaps suggesting means of wording the queries. But the interviewee is allowed greater scope of response, while similarly, the interviewer is allowed to govern the interview situation insofar as determining how he elicits the required information.

The rules for constructing interview questions and putting them together are essentially the same as those already discussed for questionnaires, with one addition: aside from the questions themselves, the researcher should also construct "probes." These are devices to be used when the initial question fails to elicit the desired information. For example, suppose, in a study of interfaith marriages the following question was asked of a Protestant respondent:

What would your reaction be, Mr. X, if your daughter wanted to marry a non-Protestant?

Answer: Well, I guess I'll have to wait and see what happens when the time comes.

Here the respondent avoided answering the question. If his answer is accepted, how he feels about interfaith marriage will remain unknown. The strategy is to anticipate this difficulty by constructing "probe questions" in advance as part of the interview form itself. Two examples are the following:

I'd really like your opinion on this, Mr. X. I'm extremely interested in your reaction to a situation like this.

Take all the time you want on this, Mr. X. I realize it's not an easy question to answer; but if you could give me even a vague idea of your feelings, it would be considerably helpful.

It is advisable to construct probes in advance of the interview rather than making them up as various situations arise. If we were to improvise in each interview, sometimes relying on one probe and sometimes on another, the probability that a second researcher could duplicate our study would be very low. The creation in advance of appropriate probes brings a measure of control to a potentially haphazard form of data collection.

Carrying Out the Interview: Access to Respondents

In early texts on social research the novice interviewer could take heart from the oft-repeated phrase that "people like to be interviewed." Access to respondents was not particularly problematical and the emphasis tended to be on styles and techniques of eliciting data once the interview was underway. Contemporary interviewers, however, are finding more often that the major problem is to convince the potential respondent that he should grant an interview. We are perhaps an overtested, oversurveyed, overpolled society. Further, with increasing social unrest, suspicion of strangers is yet another impediment to social research. The interviewer who knocks at the door of a randomly sampled household can therefore no longer be guaranteed instant and automatic cooperation. In fact, unless various preinterviewing steps are instituted, the response rate in such studies is likely to continue to decrease. The following steps are suggested as possible preinterviewing strategies:

1. If at all possible, and if the size of the sample warrants it, the media (TV, Radio, Newspapers) should be informed of the study so that appropriate publicity can be given. For example, in a recent study of attitudes toward the Canadian government's enactment of the War Measures Act, radio publicity was secured. The general purpose of the study and the names of those involved were broadcast a day before the administration of the study. This apparently had the effect of legitimizing the project, because many respondents referred to the broadcast while admitting interviewers to their homes (Forcese, Richer, deVries, McRoberts, 1971). Detailed information as to the nature of the questions to be asked, as well as any comment, should of course be avoided in order not to bias respondents.
2. With a relatively small sample the above technique would certainly be extreme. As a substitute, the use of preinterview letters or telephone calls is suggested. Letters or calls from representatives of the project will prepare the respondent for the interviewer's call and might have a positive effect on his reception.

3. All interviewers should carry a letter of introduction from those responsible for the project, as well as identification cards. If the interviewers are predominantly students, a student identification card can be a valuable legitimizing device.
4. If at all possible, the interviewing should be done in the daylight hours. Any suspicion and anxiety the respondent might have could conceivably be magnified in the evening.

Carrying out the Interview: The Notion of Social Exchange

Once confronting the respondent, what should the interviewer bear in mind? What every interviewer works for is the situation in which the person interviewed feels completely at ease and uninhibited. Achieving this end is a function of recognizing that the interview, like all social relationships, is a social exchange situation; that is, it involves the interaction of two people. In order for any social interaction to be enjoyable, both parties have to receive social rewards. Each party must receive from the other sufficient social rewards to allay the cost he is suffering in terms of time given up. The researcher or interviewer's rewards are obvious—he is getting data for his study. He is further enjoying a position of power, since he, during the interview, guides and initiates the respondent's behavior. But what of the respondent—what is he receiving?

From the outset, the respondent should be receiving a combination of subtle flattering and attention. The first contact should impress upon the respondent that here is a person, probably with a university affiliation, seeking *his* opinion on various issues. During the interview itself, this should be maintained as the interviewer does nothing more or less than simply *listen*. As suggested, people seem to enjoy expressing their opinion about an issue once they have accepted the study as legitimate. A sympathetic ear, eyes fixed attentively on the talker—these are social rewards which for most respondents are adequate compensation for spending an hour or so being interviewed.

The actual recording of the interview is generally a matter of writing down the exact words of the respondent, if possible. This is not easy; indeed, many interviewers compromise by recording only the main phrases and then reconstructing the rest of the conversation after the session is over. Capturing in writing the naturalness of free-flowing dialogue is not easy but is well worth the effort in view of the authenticity and richness such data can lend to a research report. The use of tape-recording devices, should be considered because if this type of recording device does not inhibit the particular set of respondents, it can be of considerable value.

When to Interview

There are distinct roles that sociologists have assigned to interviews in their studies—they have been used as the sole data-gathering instruments in studies, as pilot study instruments only, and as supplementary instruments to questionnaires. These are now discussed in turn.

First, some studies consist solely of reports of interviews. A sample is drawn and the researcher(s) arrange and carry out interviews with the selected individuals. Use of interviews, however, is contingent on the size of the sample. Interviews, being in-depth discussions, take much more time than do questionnaires. If a small sample is involved, the interview is a feasible alternative to the questionnaire. On the other hand, when there is a large survey, the most efficient procedure is a questionnaire. Aside from the time factor, the other advantage is that because of the self-administrative nature of the technique, questionnaires allow the respondents to proceed without direct one-to-one supervision. This cuts down the actual number of man-hours required to complete the project. A first consideration in deciding between the questionnaire and interview is thus the sample size.

A further factor is the kind of respondent being studied. There are certain explicit skills involved in filling out a questionnaire. The minimum, of course, is that the respondent be able to read and write in an intelligible manner. If this is not the case, the quality of the data is likely to be quite low. For example, when studying prison inmates or "culturally deprived" individuals, this fact must be considered. Verbal dialogue in an interview situation presents fewer problems for such groups than written questionnaires. It should also be pointed out, however, that although interviewing such respondents solves the problem of eliciting data, it may create new problems of data quality. For example, Williams and others have argued that when the interviewer is considerably different from the respondent in social background, biases may appear in the form of the respondent's attempts to answer in order to achieve what he perceives to be the interviewer's preference (Williams, 1968).

A related data quality problem has been argued to accrue when so-called "deviant" groups are being interviewed. There has been some evidence that deviant groups occasionally conceal or deny their deviant activities. In an effort to shed more light on this, John Ball has investigated both the reliability and validity of interview data obtained from fifty-nine narcotics addicts. The former was measured by comparing age data given by the subjects at two points in time—at hospital entrance and later—during Ball's interviews. Validity was gauged in part by comparing offenses reported by the subject during the interview with arrest records obtained from F.B.I. files.

In Ball's study, the interview data correlated well with the previously obtained data, indicating high reliability and validity. The author attributes this success to several factors peculiar to his study —factors which prospective interviewers of deviant groups should perhaps attempt to duplicate:

It seems likely that the completeness and validity of the interview data were related to a number of factors. The principal interviewer was extremely competent and familiar with interviewing procedures in Puerto Rican slums. The use of an interview schedule which focused upon specific topics (such as the group situation at time of first drug use) usually precluded vague or off-hand replies. Of considerable importance was the fact that our project staff was not associated with police authorities and that our study was exclusively a research undertaking. In this respect and others, the prior Lexington hospitalization of the subject seemed significant: We were outsiders from Lexington who had come to ask about his post-hospital adjustment. And it soon became known in the San Juan addict community that we were not reporting to any police authority. Further, we felt it was often efficacious to have knowledge of the local community in questioning a subject (Ball, 1967, 653).

A second major use of interviews has been in pilot studies. As pointed out earlier, one way to refine a questionnaire is to carry out a pilot study, essentially a series of unstructured questions which the respondent fills in and which later become the basis for a final set of structured items. Rather than having the respondent fill in these questions, however, some researchers have carried out interviews with pilot study respondents. The advantage of this, of course, is that the skillful interviewer using probes is able to completely exhaust the respondent's attitudes toward a particular issue. Any set of response choices ultimately appearing on the final questionnaire is thus likely to be much more accurate and comprehensive than that based on self-administered questions.

A final use of interviews, though one that has received relatively little attention, is that of *supplementing* data received from questionnaires. This use explicitly recognizes that questionnaires are fairly limited in their capacity to produce more than cursory explanations of human behavior.

The strategy advocated, then, is to combine both questionnaire and interview techniques in the same study. If we have an overall sample of a thousand individuals, we might take a subsample of fifty of these and interview them in depth about certain key items in the questionnaire. These data would be incorporated into the research report as illustrative material, providing a nice complement to the more quantitative data of the questionnaires.

CONCLUSIONS

As with any data-collection tool, there are various advantages and disadvantages of the use of the questionnaire and the interview in survey research. Questionnaires, as opposed to interviews, are appropriate when a large number of respondents is desired, when one has sufficient knowledge of the topic to include many structured questions, when one has limited personnel resources, and when one's potential respondents possess adequate literacy. However, pitting the questionnaire against the interview hides the potential complementarity of the two types of instrument. A study utilizing both devices would embody a richness of data not possible with one technique alone.

REFERENCES

BALL, JOHN, "The Reliability and Validity of Interview Data Obtained from 59 Narcotic Drug Addicts," *American Journal of Sociology*, 72 (1967), 650–54; reprinted in D. Forcese and S. Richer, *Stages of Social Research: Contemporary Perspectives*. Englewood Cliffs, N.J.: Prentice-Hall, 1970, pp. 231–36.

FORCESE, D., S. RICHER, J. DEVRIES, AND H. MCROBERTS, "The Methodology of A Crisis Survey," Paper presented to the Canadian Sociology and Anthropology Association, St. John's, Newfoundland, June 1971.

SCHUMAN, H., "The Random Probe: A Technique for Evaluating the Validity of Closed Questions," *American Sociological Review*, 31 (1966), 218–22; reprinted in Forcese and Richer, *Stages of Social Research*, pp. 240–46.

WILLIAMS, J. ALLEN, JR., "Interviewer Role Performance: A Further Note on Bias in the Information Interview," *Public Opinion Quarterly*, 32 (1968), 287–94; reprinted in Forcese and Richer, *Stages of Social Research*, pp. 224–31.

SELECTED ADDITIONAL READINGS (ANNOTATED)

GORDON, RAYMOND L., *Interviewing: Strategy, Techniques, and Tactics*. Homewood, Ill.: Dorsey, 1969. An exhaustive examination of various types of interviews and their appropriate applications, including some comparison with questionnaires.

HYMAN, H., *Survey Design and Analysis*. New York: Free Press, 1955. A classical treatment of the administrative and statistical aspects of large-scale surveys.

STEPHAN, F. F. AND P. J. McCARTHY, *Sampling Opinions*. New York: John Wiley, 1958. Although concerned predominantly with sampling strategies, the book also contains useful information on general problems of survey design and the practical problems of actually conducting surveys.

The Use
of
Secondary Sources

Secondary data may be defined as preexisting or prerecorded data which were not collected for the specific ends of a given social researcher. This includes three major types of data: expressive documents, mass media reports, and official records. Each of these can be placed on a continuum going from low to high reliability, and from low to high prequantification. In the first instance we are speaking of the extent to which the data are accurate and replicable representations of some phenomenon. In the second instance, in speaking of prequantification, we are concerned with the extent to which the data are amenable to tabulation and counting such that variables might be distinguished and measured.

Of the secondary data sources we have distinguished, expressive documents are those that most reflect the writer's own perception and interpretation of events. As such, they are extremely low in the extent to which a second observer would produce the same data. That is, their reliability is very questionable. Mass media reports avoid this somewhat in that the writer or reporter, even though he may have an interest in biasing his reports, is con-

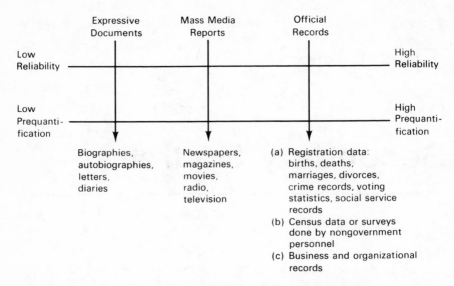

FIG. 12–1 TYPES OF SECONDARY DATA

strained by a network of editors, colleagues, and public sentiment. Further, the notion of objectivity is a fairly powerful journalistic norm. Nevertheless, he remains a selector and interpreter of what he considers relevant events, a fact one should bear in mind. Finally, official records are most free of selective recording and personal whim. As such, their reliability is relatively high, allowing reasonable confidence in their accuracy.

Sociologists have used secondary sources in three ways. First, they have been used as ends in themselves, as providing all the data for a complete study. Second, they have been used as partial data for a study; that is, as "fillers" for variables the researcher has decided not to collect himself. And third, they have been used to validate and check data gathered by the researcher.

SECONDARY DATA AS ENDS IN THEMSELVES

The first use of secondary sources is probably the most common. Here an analysis based exclusively on secondary data is done. A well-known example is Thomas and Znaniecki's *The Polish Peasant in Europe and America*, in which the use of diaries and letters was conspicuous (Thomas and Znaniecki, 1918). Similarly, any study that utilizes census data is making use of secondary data, for the census data were not collected for the explicit ends of the researcher.

In the study mentioned, the authors attempt to describe the relationship of family members who have been separated due to the emigration of certain members to America. The major data source was the letters written between separated members. Through these, Thomas and Znaniecki derive various insights into the problems and strains associated with separation and hence family fragmentation. Such data are equivalent in "naturalism" to those obtained through participant observation, since at the time the letters were written the correspondents were unaware that their writings would be analyzed. Further, the major disadvantage associated with participant observation is not present—the researcher is not a "group member," so his perspective is likely to be unbiased. The main disadvantage of such data is that they are often hard to obtain, and even so, it is probable that there will be deficiencies in certain respects. Some whole documents may be missing, or else they might not contain exactly the information the researcher had hoped for. This latter possibility is a problem with secondary data in general; that is, the data have not been gathered by the researcher and hence will not conform exactly to the specifications he desires.

Perhaps the most commonly used secondary data source is the census. This is a complete enumeration of the population taken every ten years in Canada and the United States (as well as in many other countries). In Canada, the data are gathered in years ending with the numeral 1—1941, 1951, 1961, 1971—while in the U.S. the years follow the decade—1940, 1950, 1960, 1970. The minimum data recorded by international agencies and hence available for most countries are the following: sex, age, marital status, place of birth, citizenship (or nationality), and language, educational characteristics (including literacy), fertility, urban and rural residence, size of household, economically active and inactive population, occupation and industry, industrial status (class of worker), population dependent on agriculture (Petersen, 1969, 35).

The use of census data thus permits the specification of individuals, communities, states, and finally entire societies in terms of these and other attributes.

The reliability of census data is theoretically superior to either mass media reports or expressive documents, since the data collectors have no vested interest in biasing the results. Census data are collected by people who proceed from door to door asking the same questions in virtually the same way. Or, as was done for the first time in the 1971 Canadian Census, the data are derived from brief questionnaires mailed to each adult Canadian. The questionnaires are returned subject to fines for those who fail to do so. In addition, a random representative sample of Canadians were asked to answer a longer, more elaborate questionnaire, again subject to legal penalty should they fail to respond.

There are various problems with census data, however. First, there is generally no direct supervision of the many census interviewers. For the 1960 U.S. census roughly 160,000 interviewers were used. These were mostly women who received nine hours of classroom training before they began their door-to-door enumeration. Using this tremendous number of people means that keeping track of the activities of individual workers is practically impossible. This, in turn, means that cheating is a possibility. Interviewers, who often receive piece rate payment, are occasionally known to make up answers and fill in questionnaires at their leisure. Further, although instructions are often given on how to handle respondents not at home and the lack of answers to particular questions, there is no guarantee that these are followed.

A second problem is that the census uses many residual categories. Categories like "other professionals" are quite common. This means that often we have no information on fairly large segments of the population.

Finally, the fact that the researcher has no control over the kind of data collected means there will again be items that are incomplete from the analyst's point of view. Categories that are too gross and questions not worded exactly the way one would like are inevitable characteristics of census data and of secondary data in general.

Treinen reports that such problems are often frustrating and work to greatly limit the amount of theoretical mileage that can be squeezed out of data that the analyst has not himself collected. In a postgraduate seminar, Treinen and his students reanalyzed the data from several well-known surveys (Lipset, Trow, and Coleman, *Union Democracy*; Lazarsfeld and Theilens, *The Academic Mind*). The major difficulty was the lack of sufficient and appropriate indicators to introduce new variables into the analysis. Often his students came up with new models which they felt could be fruitfully applied to the data. Unfortunately, however, many of the hypotheses could not be tested due to the lack of adequate measures: "The difficulty of operationalizing variables is even greater in secondary analysis, because indicators must be found within a small universe of given survey questions and their answer categories. Thus, attempts to deal with new hypotheses resulted in endless discussions about validity. . . . Such a dilemma could only be avoided when hypotheses, not encompassed in the research design of the authors, but bearing on already operationalized variables, were chosen" (Treinen, 1970, 128).

The challenge of comparative research may be more fully appreciated in the light of Treinen's remarks. As suggested earlier, much comparative research relies on secondary data. We need only add the difficulties already inherent in comparative research to those accruing from analyses with secondary data to appreciate the problems involved.

SECONDARY DATA AS PARTIAL DATA

The second use occasionally made of secondary data is as partial data—data that complement what is gathered by the researcher himself. For example, suppose a researcher is doing a study of high school students. Apart from the variables of particular interest to the researcher, there are a host of variables which he is interested in collecting as a matter of routine, regardless of the study's purpose. These are factors like sex of student, age, parents' education, and so forth, standard components of most questionnaires. Rather than gather these himself, the researcher might take advantage of the fact that most school boards usually collect such information on all their students. To illustrate the wide range of data often available, the following lists information routinely collected on all students attending collegiate board high schools in the city of Ottawa: sex, age, number of rooms in house, parents' education, parents' occupation, IQ scores, language spoken, number of brothers and sisters, birth order, marital state of parents, area of residence, number of people in house, high school program, and health history. Data of this nature are typically on record in any given community, although the willingness of a school board to permit access varies widely.

From the researcher's point of view, such data can be utilized to produce at least two positive results—greater efficiency and less data loss.

It seems senseless for a researcher to administer his own IQ test or a question on father's occupation when such information already exists in school records. By utilizing these data, the sociologist reduces considerably the length of his own questionnaire, thus reducing the amount of time he has to disrupt the class, as well as raising the quality of data he obtains from the questionnaire. Generally, the shorter the instrument the higher the quality of response.

The second advantage concerns the loss of data on certain key questions when questionnaires alone are employed. A prime example is the category of father's occupation. It is typically the case that this question produces an inordinately high proportion of nonresponses. Since this is an extremely relevant bit of information in most sociological research, the problem is a serious one. The use in our example of school records and files here is a possible solution. Because these are constantly updated and validated, the information is likely to be complete and accurate. The researcher's instrument can then be concentrated on eliciting information relevant to his own particular set of hypotheses.

SECONDARY DATA AS VALIDATION

A final advantage of secondary data lies in the possibility of enhancing the reliability and validity of data. This was already touched upon when the potential of shorter questionnaires and more accuracy on variables such as father's occupation was noted. We are speaking here of an opportunity to actually cross-check respondent data in order to increase our confidence in his overall accuracy. For example, comparing the student's answer regarding his father's occupation with the equivalent data in school records would provide such a test. If the two match, we have increased our confidence in the respondent's reporting; if they do not, we may want to check other questions and ultimately make a decision as to the advisability of using that particular student's questionnaire. We could do this, as well, with factors like failure history, grade average, and truancy, all of which are likely to be available in school records.

In short, secondary data allows us to check the accuracy of our data and hence leaves us in a better position to defend their quality.

CONTENT ANALYSIS

It may often be the case that secondary data such as letters, newspapers, and magazines may not be objective. But the nature and extent of bias may itself be the object of research. For example, we may wish to analyze newspapers with a view to political partisanship. Or we may wish to analyze textbooks with a view to racial prejudice. For these and like research problems, we are literally intent upon analyzing the content of the printed or vocal record in which we are interested. This analysis may be with a view to isolating and quantifying an attitude, such as prejudice, or, using the record as a chronology of fact, in isolating and counting the reports of some category of events, such as wars. *Content analysis* refers to techniques used to quantify secondary data. Basically, it consists of the systematic isolation and counting of units or indicators of the phenomena in which we are interested. The method consists of essentially three steps.

First, as in any research, the phenomena in which we are interested must be defined. Perhaps we are interested in three alternate political ideologies or attitude sets; fascism, conservatism, and liberalism. We would have to define, at the conceptual level, exactly what we mean by these concepts.

Second, again as in any research, we must define the units of investigation. This must be done with a view to both physical and temporal space. Thus, let us define our unit of analysis as the newspapers of city X, for the time period—temporal space—of six months of the current year.

Third, our definitions would lead us to a specification of the operational indicators of these conceptual categories. We must specify those items to be found in the newspapers which will serve to indicate fascism, conservatism, or liberalism. These unit indicators may be of varying size—that is, they may be news items, editorials, paragraphs, sentences, phrases, or words. They might also be the space utilized per topic, the type size, or the location in the newspapers.

The predesignation of such indicators is the vital step in content analysis. Once they have been clearly identified they can be counted. Moreover, given that they have been clearly and unambiguously identified, different individuals analyzing the same newspaper should produce essentially identical counts—that is, precisely designated indicators are the key to content analysis reliability.

Thus, in our example, we might take as our indicators certain key words: "punishment" as indicative of fascism; "order" as indicative of conservatism; and "reform" as indicative of liberalism. In point of fact, one would use several such indicators, but the idea is to isolate units—in this case, words—that one has reason to believe would disproportionately occur in the literature of the three political ideologies. These indicators would be isolated on the basis of some preresearch or exploratory research and/or on the basis of previous research reported in the literature.

Words as unit indicators are preferable to more complex units. Obviously the more simple the indicator the less subjective the counting. Thus, the researcher need only recognize and categorize —count—the words. But imagine the instance in which he is asked to categorize paragraphs, or entire news or editorial items; this is invariably attempted on the basis of ideological content as assessed by the researcher. Although it may be the case that often a researcher can identify one given editorial as more conservative than another, obviously this becomes a very subjective thing. Less precision is attained the more the analysis depends upon *judgement* as opposed to *recognition* of units as indicators.

A relatively recent innovation that enhances precision, hence reliability, consists of computer techniques for content analysis. The General Inquirer is a program that can be used in the content analysis of printed material. Thus, once a researcher has identified his categories and his indicators, he would then type in the text he wishes analyzed. The computer reads the text, isolates the cues or indicators, and counts them (Stone *et al.*, 1966).

But note that the key to the analysis remains the isolation and specification of indicators. Computer counting reduces error, for it eliminates subjective judgement. But the computer's identification of indicators is only as good—as valid—as the designation of indicators programmed by the researchers. If the researchers have not keyed upon the correct or adequate indicators, then the computer analysis may prove extremely reliable but quite invalid.

A NOTE ON DATA ARCHIVES*

A discussion of secondary data would be incomplete without a brief section bringing the reader's attention to the existence of data archives. These are organizations devoted to the collection

*We acknowledge the advice of John deVries regarding this section.

and maintenance of secondary data acting as repositories or "warehouses" for the storage of such data.

Data archives may be classified according to the range of people having access to them as well as on the scope of data they are concerned with. Bisco, for example, differentiates between two types of archives—those which provide data for the entire community of social scientists and those which limit access to social scientists affiliated with the particular university containing the archives. An example of the former is the Inter-university Consortium for Political Research, which is based in Ann Arbor, Michigan (Bisco, 1967). The more limited-access type of archives may be found in most major universities with great variation, however, in the scope of data maintained. Archives, for example, may be concerned primarily with data relating to census characteristics of a particular municipality; or they may be much broader in scope, collecting data speaking to state and perhaps national levels.

Bisco (1967) has summarized the several functions served by data archives. Following is an elaboration of some of his points:

1. *Acquiring secondary data*: First and foremost, archives provide the service of locating and securing secondary data. Governments are a major source, because they are custodians of vast arrays of census information, but often data from studies conducted by nongovernment personnel appear in archives (surveys done by sociologists, political scientists, market researchers).
2. *Processing the data*: The processing function consists of "cleaning" data files. Often computer cards or tapes are not usable in the form in which they arrive. Card columns may contain multiple punches, the data may be incomplete, or the way the researcher has coded his data may be incompatible with standard coding schemes used by the archives. For example, archives may be custodians of comparative data on educational development. Further, they may have devised a standard scheme for classifying levels of education attained in any given country. If data they secure manifest a different classification of levels, the intersocietal comparability of the information is seriously weakened. The data must therefore be worked through and if possible, transferred into codes comparable with those of other societies. Once data are cleaned, the archives will duplicate a particular study or set of studies so that they may be

diffused to other universities, research institutes, or interested researchers within the same university.

3. *Maintaining current data*: In the case of data that are being constantly updated (for example, census data), the archives will attempt to secure and process the most current data available.

4. *Providing resource staff for consultation*: Most archives have a full-time staff available to assist potential users of their data. Such assistance may be extremely valuable. Often coding schemes are quite complicated and demand explanation. Also, the careful researcher is always interested in how a particular study was conducted—what kind of sample was used? Are there any likely systematic sampling errors? Who administered the data collection instruments and exactly how was this phase organized? When was the study carried out? These are just some of the relevant pieces of information about a particular study an archivist would be prepared to provide. It is even possible in some archives to receive certain standard analysis runs, such as marginals for the data and basic "cross-tabulations."

Any researcher should consider exploring the potential data archives in his university or municipal area before embarking on a piece of research. If his interest is in attaining analysis skills, the researcher will find such data extremely convenient, since they obviate the need to collect one's own data. If he is interested in intersocietal research, data archives are often gold mines of secondary data gathered from several countries. The expense and effort of doing an original piece of cross-societal research are irrational when such data are readily available. Not least important, secondary data provide ideal opportunities for an all too rare activity in the social sciences: the systematic reanalysis and criticism of an existing study.

CONCLUSIONS

In some sense, the expression secondary data is a misnomer in that the data may, in given instances, prove more than sufficient for a total research project. Frequently data are gathered and analyzed by a researcher, the results published, and the data filed. Yet reanalysis, from a different point of view, may yield significant insights.

In the more general sense of reference to the printed artifacts of our culture, the analysis of secondary data will often serve to provide information of a longitudinal nature. For example, the material in a newspaper exists for a period of many years and thereby offers a researcher information with a significant advantage over the "one point-in-time" data generated in conventional case studies or in survey research.

REFERENCES

Bisco, R. "Social Science Data Archives: Progress and Prospects," *Social Science Information*, 6 (1967), 39–74.

Petersen, W., *Population*. New York: Macmillan, 1969.

Stone, Philip, et al., *The General Inquirer: A Computer Approach to Content Analysis*. Cambridge, Mass.: M.I.T. Press, 1966.

Thomas, W. I. and F. Znaniecki, *The Polish Peasant in Europe and America*. Chicago: University of Chicago Press, 1918.

Treinen, H., "Notes on an Experience with Secondary Analyses of Survey Data as a Teaching Device," *Social Science Information*, 9 (1970), 123–32.

SELECTED ADDITIONAL READINGS (ANNOTATED)

Berelson, B., *Content Analysis in Communication Research*. New York: Free Press, 1952. This early example of content analysis is still very useful for its series of examples of the actual process of content analysis.

Council of Social Science Data Archives, *Social Science Data Archives in the United States*, New York, 1967. A listing of all the major data archives in the U.S., as well as type of data held and to whom access is permitted.

DUVERGER, MAURICE, *An Introduction to the Social Sciences*, pp. 105–123. New York: Praeger, 1961. A good introduction to the techniques and problems of content analysis.

LIPSET, S. M. AND R. HOFSTADTER, eds., *Sociology and History: Methods*. New York: Basic Books, 1968. A collection of papers in the application of sociological techniques for the study of history illustrating the use of secondary data.

ROKKAN, S., ed., *Data Archives for the Social Sciences*. Paris: Mouton Press, 1966. An extremely useful collection of articles on data archives in various countries. Occasional discussion on how to use such sources.

PART FOUR

Descriptive
Analysis

It was pointed out in Chapter 6 that there are two fundamental types of hypotheses which occupy sociologists: descriptive and explanatory. The former posit the existence of some phenomenon, as for example, the statement: "Prison inmates form a very highly organized informal structure." A causal hypothesis, on the other hand, refers to a relationship between two or more variables, as for example, the statement: "The authoritarian character of prisons (x) produces a highly organized informal inmate structure (y)"—$(x \rightarrow y)$. As suggested in earlier chapters, data collection for each of these types has generally been handled in different ways. Descriptive hypotheses are typically tested in case study research and survey research, while the testing of causal hypotheses generally involves experimental and survey formats. This chapter deals with the analysis carried out when a researcher has obtained data from a descriptive case study or a descriptive survey.

ANALYSIS IN THE DESCRIPTIVE CASE STUDY

In Chapters 6 and 10 we used the following descriptive hypothesis: "College fraternities are fragmented, noncohesive groups." It was pointed out that this type of hypothesis can often be best served by a case study of one fraternity, utilizing a form of observation. It is possible to record in diary form the ongoing social interaction of the group members over a relatively long period of time, perhaps several months. The data that will form the basis for analysis thus consist of pages and pages of notes on group interaction. The following is an elaboration of the hypothetical diary notes presented in Chapter 10 on lunchtime interaction:

Monday, October 21—Lunch (12–1 p.m.)
Preliminary Interaction

John and Harry come in first. They get their trays and go through the lunch line together. They sit down and start eating, talking in low voices. Jerry comes in alone and sits at another table. No greeting is exchanged between Jerry and the other two. Joe and Marty come in and sit in the corner opposite Jerry. They shout a greeting to Jerry but have nothing to say to John and Harry. The president and the vice-president (Bill and Curt) come in and shout a general greeting, "Hi guys, what's the word?" Joe and Marty wave curtly, Harry and John go on talking, while Jerry looks up but does not reply. Two other groups come in at the same time. One consists of four people— Jack, Mike, Tom, and Steve; the other a group of five—Fred, Sam, Tim, John, and Terry. The first group joins Joe and Marty, who put two tables together to accommodate everyone. The group of five sits together at one table.

Interaction over Lunch

John and Harry are talking about girls. Their discussion is occasionally disrupted by short bursts of laughter and knowing shoves. They are recounting exploits of the previous weekend. Jerry does not talk at all. Joe and Marty's group is talking about football and the upsets of the weekend's action. They are arguing mostly about the role of luck in the Colts' last victory. The president and vice-president are talking about fraternity regulations. Occasionally they change to a more general philosophical discussion of moral versus social rules. The group of Fred, Sam, Tim, John, and Terry are talking mostly about cards, specifically bridge and poker. Occasionally the race track and horses are brought into the conversation. Fred dominates most of the conversation, giving an occasionally interrupted account of how he had done playing poker on the weekend. He frequently seeks Sam's confirmation of certain parts of the story. Sam nods or perhaps throws in a slight elaboration of Fred's description; the other members make periodic comments.

After Lunch

Jerry is the first to leave. He eats quickly and leaves right after his dessert. John and Harry leave next. On the way out John asks Bill, "How's it goin'?" Bill S. says "O.K. John—you?" John nods and leaves, followed by Harry. Joe and Marty's group continue talking sports, mainly football, until one o'clock. Two of the group, Mike and Steve, rush off to a class; the other four leave together, still talking sports. Bill and Curt (president and vice-president) also leave around one o'clock, talking in relatively low voices as they depart. Sam and Fred's group start playing five-handed nickel and dime poker around 12:30. Tim leaves at one o'clock for a class, at which point the game changes to bridge. The game goes on until 3:30 in the afternoon.

The above data represent the interaction for only one lunch session. If the observer is "in the field" for two months, then he will have sixty of these recordings. It is from these that his ultimate picture of the group's structure will emerge. The strategy of building such a picture consists of a constant reading of one's observations. The object is to see if a more or less stable pattern of group interaction emerges—a pattern which will reflect more than any other possible pattern the group's peculiar organization. For example, after sixty such lunchtime observations, as well as additional observations at social events and fraternity meetings, certain characteristics of the group hinted at in the above data might be confirmed. The major finding might take the following form: The fraternity in question is in reality composed of three distinct subgroups, or cliques, each organized around a different kind of activity. One group consists of those on the executive level of the fraternity—the president, the vice-president (Bill and Curt), the secretary (George), and the treasurer (Larry). The main impetus for their interaction is their common membership on the executive level. They sit with each other at lunch every day and organize their social activities primarily with each other. The leadership structure of this clique appears to follow the organizational chart of the fraternity. The president typically dominates the conversation and tends to initiate interaction for the other three more than the reverse. The vice-president appears to be the second man in the clique. Bill often seeks Curt's advice, as well as eating with him proportionately more than with the others. The other two seem roughly equal in terms of clique status.

The second subgroup consists of Joe, Marty, Jack, Mike, and Tom, the main bond linking them being a common love for sports. The five may be found together often discussing football, baseball, or hockey. Joe and Marty are both on the college football team, Joe a first-string guard and Marty a second-string halfback. The other three, though not on any varsity teams, play several intramural sports. The group also forms the nucleus of the fraternity football team which competes regularly in the inter-fraternity league. Joe and Marty are the leading members of the clique, due to their success in varsity football.

The third group may be termed the "gambling clique." It consists of Sam, Fred, Tim, John, and Terry. These five are to be found playing cards together at various times in the day. They also frequent the local race tracks and occasionally the pool halls. Fred is clearly the dominant member of this clique. This is hypothesized to be related to his incredible gambling successes—he loses very rarely, typically winning large sums. Of all the cliques, this appears the most cohesive and clearly defined. There is very little association with members outside the subgroup; indeed there appears to be an implicit hostility between the gambling group and other groups. To some extent the latter view the gambling clique as inferior.

Apart from these three basic and relatively constant cliques, there are members whose subgroup affiliation is either very unclear or nonexistent. John, Harry, and Jerry are examples. John and Harry are obviously close friends, but otherwise have no clear-cut affiliation with any other clique. Jerry is an isolate—he rarely talks to other group members and in fact is usually absent from fraternity meetings and social events.

The above analysis might be depicted in a sociometric matrix, as discussed in Chapter 5, or in a sociometric "picture" of the group's structure, know as a *sociogram*.

This graphic representation is one of the products of several

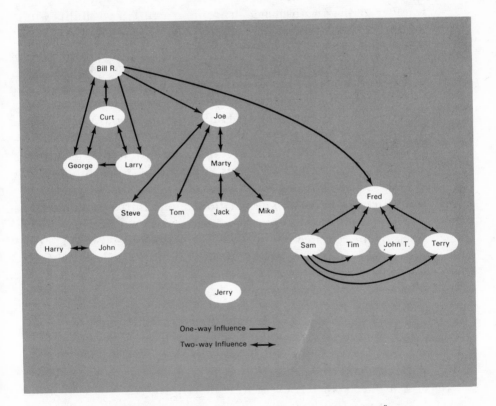

FIG. 13–1 SOCIOGRAM: FRATERNITY INFORMAL STRUCTURE*

*Position of the circles indicates relative status within the fraternity.

months of observation. Along with supplementary data from questionnaires and/or interviews, the group structure of the fraternity can be clearly documented. As part of the analysis a description of the group in terms of standard demographic factors like age composition, social class background, size, and length of existence, should be included. These data should always be sought as a matter of routine, no matter what group is being studied.

It should be realized that it is possible to have more than one chart of group organization. For example, a sociogram might be constructed after the first two months of observation and a second constructed two months later. Such a procedure allows the researcher to investigate change in group structure, a possibility with long-term case studies which should not be ignored. Change in clique membership and in relative status of members and cliques are fascinating dimensions of group structure which add immeasurably to the sociologist's understanding of behavior.

The sociogram has frequently been used to represent leadership structures. For example, Floyd Hunter in his famous work, *Community Power Structure*, graphically indicated the reputational interchange of selections among the identified leaders (Hunter, 1953). The volume of selection is indicative of leadership stature. To take a fictional example, the sociogram (Figure 13–2) indicates the pattern of leadership designation among thirteen influentials.

The sociogram thus summarizes patterns of interaction as identified by the repeated observations of the researcher, or perhaps as identified by the respondents themselves in interviews or questionnaires.

ANALYSIS IN THE DESCRIPTIVE SURVEY

The survey that is exclusively descriptive is a rarity in sociological research. What one usually finds is that surveys permit of both descriptive and causal analyses, with the former introducing the major variables which will appear later in the causal analytical section. The purpose of a descriptive survey (or the descriptive

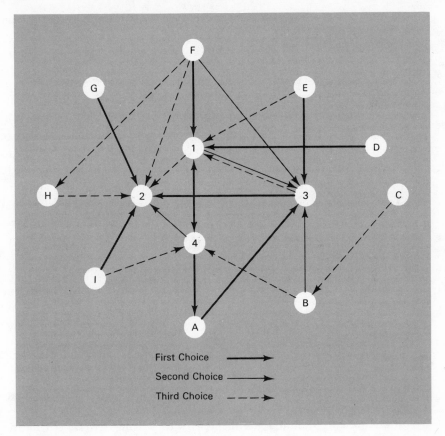

First Choice ——————▶
Second Choice ——————▶
Third Choice — — — —▶

Fig. 13–2.

part of a survey containing both types of analysis) is simply to describe the population represented by our sample. The raw data for this task usually consists of the questionnaire or interview responses of a sample of individuals. The objective is to organize these into tabular or graphic form so that we may describe in as clear as possible a way the salient features of the population. There are three phases characterizing such analyses: the preparation of the data for analysis, the conducting of tests for sample representativeness, and the description itself, the nature of which is determined to a large extent by the level of measurement characterizing our variables.

Preparing the Data

In a large survey (over one hundred respondents, as a rule of thumb) it becomes necessary to use computer facilities for tabulating data. Manually counting the number of respondents who said *x* or *y* is extremely tedious and time-consuming. In order to utilize the advantages of computer tabulation, however, it is necessary to transfer the questionnaire responses to punch cards or possibly magnetic tape, which form the basic input for machine analysis. To illustrate the principle of converting raw questionnaire data to punch card form, the following are an individual's possible responses to two questions on a questionnaire concerned with student activism:

1. Have you ever participated in a student protest demonstration?
   ___ Yes
   ___ No

2. How far do you feel students should go in expressing their grievances?
   ___ Students should not express their grievances
   ___ Students should limit themselves to writing letters and circulating petitions
   ___ Students should limit themselves to writing letters, circulating petitions, and boycotting classes
   ___ Students should limit themselves to writing letters, circulating petitions, boycotting and picketing classes
   ___ Students should limit themselves to letter-writing, circulating petitions, boycotting, picketing, and sitting-in.
   ___ Students should do all of the above plus be willing to use force

These data, along with the rest of this individual's responses, are to be assigned to a punch card which stands for that individual's questionnaire. Let us assume that we have the questionnaires of one hundred individuals, the questionnaires having fifty structured questions. This particular individual will be assigned a number from 1 to 100, let us say 010. The data for individual 010 appear on a punch card, the first three columns representing his assigned number. Figure 13–3 is a hypothetical punch card containing 010s data.

A punch card is traditionally eighty columns long, so that eighty pieces of data can be stored on one card. Since we are assuming a set of fifty structured questions, each card will have data up to column 53, the first three indicating the respondent's number. As we see, for our particular illustration, the first three columns contain punches 0, 1, and 0, indicating respondent 010. Each number entered on the card will in reality be indicated by punching a hole in the appropriate punch number. We have chosen to portray the data by penciling in the number in the appropriate place. Letters of the alphabet can also be punched on these cards. To do this one combines in a single column a 1–9 punch and either a 0, 11, or 12 punch. Punches 11 and 12 are not used for numerical data, a 12 indicating a plus sign, an 11 a minus sign.

We decide to let the data for questions 1 and 2 be punched in columns 4 and 5 respectively. A 2 in column 4 thus means that individual 010 answered "no" to question 1, which asked about his participation in protest demonstrations. The 3 in column 5 means he selected the third choice to question 2, indicating he

Punch Number	Respondent's Number			Question Number 1	2					Column Number					
	1	2	3	4	5	6	7	8	9	10	11	12	13	14	15_____53_____80
12															
11														0	
0	0		0												
1		1													
2				2		2									
3					3										
4								4	4						
5						5									
6												6			
7													7		
8											8				
9										9	9				

FIG. 13–3.

believes students should limit themselves to letter-writing, circulating petitions, and boycotting classes as expressions of discontent.

The remaining responses are transferred in the same way. The accuracy of the punching can be checked by a repunching operation which uses a machine termed a *verifier*. We end up with a numerical representation of the individual's entire questionnaire, one that can thus be manipulated statistically by machine in a straightforward, convenient manner. Needless to say, we should always keep track of which card columns contain the data for which questions. This information is usually kept in a "coding manual," which contains a list of card column numbers and their corresponding question numbers.

It should be pointed out that the task of allocating data to column numbers can be done either before the questionnaire is administered or afterward. The above illustration is an example of allocation done after the questionnaires were completed. That is, the coding manual would in this case be constructed after the survey was terminated. If a researcher wanted to, however, he could set up these equivalencies between card column number and question number beforehand. In fact, some researchers actually record these equivalencies on the questionnaire itself, so that the questionnaire is also a coding manual as well. To illustrate, the two questions alluded to above might have been set up on the questionnaire in the following way:

1. Have you ever participated in a student protest demonstration?

                 ___ 1. Yes   Col. 4
                 ___ 2. No

2. How far do you feel students should go in expressing their grievances?

                 ___ 1. Students should, etc. Col. 5
                 ___ 2. Students should, etc.
                 ___ 3. Students should, etc.
                 ___ 4. Students should
                 ___ 5. Students etc.
                 ___ 6. Students etc.

We can thus go directly from the questionnaire to the punch card, since the code has already been established. Such a questionnaire is often termed a "precoded questionnaire."

It should be mentioned that cards are punched using a machine called a "key punch," which closely resembles a typewriter. It is fairly easy to use and probably worth the effort of learning.

After the data preparation phase is ended, then, the researcher should have one hundred punch cards containing data in the first fifty-three columns. Further, he should have some kind of coding manual which tells him where on the punch card the responses for each question may be found. With very large samples (say over two thousand), it is much easier to work with magnetic tape than with cards. Although it is an oversimplified description, we can think of a tape as containing a series of card images, each card (or respondent) image separated from adjacent ones by a gap on the tape.

Testing for Sample Representativeness

The first thing that one should do when the data are on cards or tape is test for sample representativeness. This involves comparing known characteristics of the population with characteristics of the sample to see if it is indeed a replica in miniature of the population. For example, suppose we know from data obtained from the registrar that the percent of boys enrolled at Tenuga University (our population of interest) is 70.0 percent, while the figure for girls is 30.0 percent. We compare these data with those computed for our sample of Tenuga University students to see what differences, if any, exist. Two possible outcomes are portrayed in Table 13–1.

We can often carry out a simple visual inspection of the population and sample statistics to discern the existence of any departure from representativeness. A look at Outcome 1, for example, assures us that virtually the same sex distribution existing in the population can be found in our sample (70.0 vs. 68.0 and 30.0 vs. 32.0). With regard to the sex variable, then, our sample is a good

TABLE 13-1 COMPARISON OF SEX DISTRIBUTIONS FOR
POPULATION AND SAMPLE

	Sample Percent	Population Percent
Outcome 1		
Boys	68.0	70.0
Girls	32.0	30.0
Outcome 2		
Boys	60.0	70.0
Girls	40.0	30.0

one. If we then carried out similar comparisons for several other variables and found the distributions again virtually identical, we would be satisfied with our sample. It should be pointed out, though, that the variables we choose to compare should be, to the extent that such population data are available, those variables that are important in our analytical scheme. If we are studying the relationship between fraternity residence and political activism it does make sense to see if the sample is representative with respect to hair color. It does not make sense, however, to see if it is representative with respect to fraternity membership, for the proper distribution of this variable in our sample is of major concern. Obviously, though, we cannot compare on fraternity membership if there are no population data available on this aspect. In fact, it is usually the case that the variables we are most interested in have not been collected beforehand on a population basis. In this case, we should compare those factors for which we have population and sample information. A test on several factors, even those not directly relevant to the research, is better than no test at all.

Outcome 2 in the above table represents a possible discrepancy between sample and population. We say "possible" because there are two alternative explanations for the 10 percent difference between sample and population—sampling error and a truly biased sample. One possibility is that the difference reflects only sampling error. Because we only have a sample there will be some departure from the population value due to chance alone. The question we must ask is the following: Is the difference we observe (10 percent more girls and 10 percent fewer boys) due only to sampling error, or is there something really wrong with our sample? In order to investigate this there exist several statistical *tests of significance* which measure the following: On the assumption that there is no difference between population and sample (that any difference only reflects sample fluctuation), what is the probability of getting the difference we observe? If this probability is quite high, we conclude that our sample is satisfactory since by chance alone we could easily have obtained such a difference. If the probability is low, however, we must begin to question our sample, since it is unlikely that our difference was due to sampling fluctuation. It might therefore be due to a bias in our sample which produced an overrepresentation of girls and an underrepresentation of boys. If nonchance differences are found with variables other than sex, we must carefully review our sampling procedure in order to detect the source of the possible bias. While a deficiency cannot always be corrected, we are at least aware of it and can hence be cognizant of the limitations of our research.

As a final note in this connection, some researchers argue that testing for representativeness is only necessary when we have a low questionnaire return. In this view, if a high percentage of our questionnaires are returned (for example, 80.0 percent or more), then there is no reason to suspect gross departures from representativeness and we may proceed without population-sample comparisons. The position taken here, however, is that regardless of the return rate it is advisable to carry out the comparison procedure. It serves as an additional check, allowing us to detect possible deficiencies in our sampling procedure which we might have been totally unaware of.

Describing the Population

The next step is to describe the population. As suggested earlier, though, we cannot proceed without considering the level of measurement of one's variables. The kind of description we carry out is closely related to the type of variables with which we are working. If as in most sociological research, the variables are nominal in nature, the description will be in terms of proportions or percentages, with graphical diagrams as possible supplements. If interval data are available, however, we can use, in addition to these, measures of central tendency or dispersion. We shall begin, then, with the kind of description that is possible with nominal variables—one relying basically on percentages or proportions.

DESCRIPTION WITH NOMINAL VARIABLES. The major tools for doing a descriptive analysis with nominal variables are the "marginals" obtained for the data. Marginals are simply a tabulation of the responses to each question—the percent of respondents that gave each of the possible responses to each question. The marginals for the questions on student activism might thus look like the following:

TABLE 13–2

Responses to the question: Have you ever participated in a student protest demonstration?

		Percent
	Yes	15.0
	No	83.0
	No Answer	2.0
N(=Total Number Respondents)		100

TABLE 13–3

Responses to the question: How far do you feel students should go in expressing their grievances?

	Percent
Should not express their grievances	0.4
Should write letters or circulate petitions	30.5
Letters, petitions or boycotts	27.8
Letters, petitions, boycotts, or pickets	9.4
Letters, petitions, boycotts, pickets, sit-ins	28.2
All of these plus force	3.7
N(=Total Number Respondents)	100

Marginals are thus simple percentage distributions for each question. In order to acquire these the standard practice with relatively large surveys is to utilize a marginals "program" written for the computer. A computer program consists of a set of instructions telling the machine to perform certain operations on the data that is fed to it, the data being in card or tape form. The question on participation in protest demonstrations, for example, might have been assigned to column 4, as in the section on preparing the data. Further, a 1 punch in column 4 might mean "yes," a 2 "no," and a 0 that the respondent did not answer the question. The program tells the machine to read each card, counting the number of 1s, 2s, and 0s in column 4 and any other column tabulations desired. The computer then calculates the percentage distributions for each question. In our particular example it would output the following three percentages:

$$\frac{1s}{(1s \,+\, 2s \,+\, 0s)}; \quad \frac{2s}{(1s \,+\, 2s \,+\, 0s)}; \quad \frac{0s}{(1s \,+\, 2s \,+\, 0s)}$$

Tables 13–2 and 13–3 are the results of the calculations—marginals for the two questions. They are also common forms for presenting descriptive data. We might also decide to present for each percentage the appropriate confidence limits (see Chapter 9). With a relatively small number of respondents (say less than five hundred), the same operation can be performed with a machine termed a *counter-sorter*. This machine simply sorts punch cards into designated groups and counts the number in each group and the researcher then calculates percentages by hand (Janda, 1965, 53–62).

As a substitute or supplement to these tables it is often a good idea to present graphical pictures of the distributions. A long series of tables is rather tedious to read, so the incorporation of visual aids is frequently advisable. One common device is the bar graph, or histogram. Rather than presenting Table 13–3, for example, we might present the data as shown in Figure 13–4.

The height of the bar indicates the percent of students selecting each response. The reader can thus see at a glance that the ma-

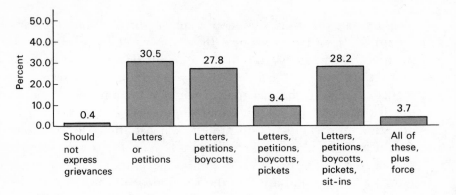

FIG. 13–4 HISTOGRAM FOR DATA IN TABLE 13–3

jority of students advocate a fairly moderate strategy in expressing grievances and that a very small percent advocate either no expression at all or actual violence.

It must be emphasized at this point that these graphs and the earlier tables form only the skeleton or framework for the actual description. They must be connected and filled out with the researcher's descriptive commentary. Further, it is not sufficient to simply point to the graphs or tables and repeat in commentary form the information contained in them. The analyst must dress up the data with a well-organized and well-written narrative. The tables and graphs should be organized in a coherent fashion; each should fit logically, on a substantive basis, with the one before and the one after. As the data are being discussed, their possible social or theoretical significance should be alluded to, with the views of other writers brought in as supportive or contrasting argument. In short, good description is an art, and the mere stringing together of data is not good description.

DESCRIPTION WITH INTERVAL-RATIO OR ORDINAL VARIABLES. Higher level variables are not as easy to organize for presentation as are nominal variables. In the former case there are usually relatively few response categories, and the task of displaying the percent in each category is quite straightforward. With ordinal or interval-ratio data, however, it is possible to have as many categories as there are respondents, which means that we must somehow reduce our data to manageable proportions before they can be summarized. To illustrate with ratio data, suppose we have the wages before taxes of a sample of fifty high school teachers from a metropolitan community:

TABLE 13–4 SALARIES FOR EACH OF FIFTY TEACHERS

$5500	$ 6500	$ 4500	$ 5000	$5500
6000	8500	9000	4500	8500
9000	5000	10,000	6000	6000
7000	10,500	6000	8500	8000
8000	6000	8500	8000	9000
8500	7000	8000	9500	5500
7500	8500	8500	11,000	8000
8000	6000	7500	10,000	6000
7500	4500	5500	6500	7500
4500	6500	6000	5000	8000

In order to describe our population in this case, we must organize the data so that the reader can make sense of them. A glance at the salaries reveals that grouping them into the following categories would be fairly reasonable—$4000–$4999, $5000–$5999, $6000–$6999, $7000–$7999, $8000–$8999, $9000–$9999, $10,000–$10,999, and $11,000–$11,999. The data might therefore be presented as follows:

TABLE 13–5 THE SALARIES REGROUPED

Income	Number in Each Category	Percent
$ 4000– 4999	4	8.0
5000– 5999	7	14.0
6000– 6999	11	22.0
7000– 7999	6	12.0
8000– 8999	14	28.0
9000– 9999	4	8.0
10,000–10,999	3	6.0
11,000–11,999	1	2.0
	50	100.0

The table indicates, then, that most of the teachers make under $10,000 (92 percent); the heavy concentration of salaries being in the range $6000–$8999. Further, the modal or most common interval is that of $8000–$8999, with 28 percent of the teachers falling there. The information can also be presented graphically, as in the previous example for nominal variables.

Two other items of information can also be derived from these data—more precise measures of central tendency and of dispersion. The arithmetic mean is a common and useful summary of the distribution.
In our case it is

$$\frac{\$5500 + 6000 + 9000}{50} \text{ etc. or } \frac{360,000}{50} = \$7200,$$

the average salary of our teachers.

We can also compute a measure of dispersion of the ratio scores. Such a measure indicates the extent to which the values (in our case, salaries) are similar or different from one another, an often useful bit of information. If all the teachers made between $5000 and $7000 this would mean that teachers are very similar in their salaries. On the other hand, incomes ranging from $4500 to $11,000, as in our distribution, imply considerable variation in our sample. A common summary measure of the extent of dispersion of a distribution is the standard deviation, which may be viewed as a kind of average of the difference of each value from the mean. That is, if you took each income score, subtracted the mean from it, summed these differeneces and took the average difference, you would have an intuitive notion of what the standard deviation is. You can see that the larger the differences from the mean the larger the overall standard deviation, which is one way to indicate how disperse a distribution is.

The formula for the standard deviation is

$$S = \sqrt{\frac{\Sigma (X_1 - X)^2}{n}}$$

x_1 in our case stands for each teacher's income; X for the mean of the distribution, and n the total number of teachers involved. The symbol before the bracket means we sum each mean $-x_1$

difference squared. That is, we square each difference between mean and salary value and then sum them—($5500-$7290)^2 + ($6000-$7200)^2 + ($9000-$7200)^2, and so forth. The standard deviation for our data is

$$\sqrt{\frac{141,000,000}{50}} = 1679.29$$

As suggested, the statistic 1679.29 may intuitively be seen as an average discrepancy from the mean of our teachers' incomes. It would be much smaller if our teachers were more alike in their salaries.

Again, we should emphasize that simply presenting means and standard deviations is not adequate description. The writer must build an interesting commentary around his data. Sophisticated speculation (perhaps in the form of hypotheses) on why teachers' incomes are so divergent or similar would be a welcome part of the narrative. In addition, contrasting the mean income of teachers with those known for other occupations would provide an interesting comparative perspective. Such commentary guides the reader to the significance of statistics presented, and broadens an otherwise mechanical, predominantly statistical, presentation.

CONCLUSION

Descriptive analysis consists fundamentally of precise summaries of the data that have been collected by a researcher. Summary statistics appropriate to his levels of measurement permit him to digest the frequency distributions representing the mass of data collected. Simple statistics, such as percentages, conveniently indicate the relative distribution of values, such as the categories of attitude response. Similarly, measures of central tendency such as the mode, median, or arithmetic mean serve to represent the "typical" value or mode of response for any given variable. In the same manner, measures of dispersion such as the range or standard deviation provide a readily comprehensible representation of the range or extremes of value or response for a given variable.

In general, good descriptive analysis consists of the careful use and presentation of statistics, and interesting and instructive commentary.

REFERENCES

HUNTER, FLOYD, *Community Power Structure*. Chapel Hill: University of North Carolina Press, 1953.

JANDA, K., *Data Processing*. Evanston, Ill.: Northwestern University Press, 1965.

SELECTED ADDITIONAL READINGS (ANNOTATED)

BLALOCK, HUBERT, *Social Statistics*. New York: McGraw-Hill, 1960. A lucid presentation of statistical applications, oriented specifically to sociological research.

COLEMAN, JAMES, *The Adolescent Society*. New York: Free Press, 1961. This study of high school students in several midwestern U.S. schools is a good example of what can be done with descriptive survey data.

COLMAN, H., C. SMALLWOOD, AND C. BROWN, *Computer Language: An Autoinstructional Introduction to FORTRAN*. New York: McGraw-Hill, 1962. Computer systems have changed considerably since 1962, but this volume is still a useful first-learning device. It is a self-contained set of instructions and exercises.

FRANZBLAU, ABRAHAM, *A Primer of Statistics for Non-Statisticians*. New York: Harcourt Brace Jovanovich, 1958. A very good first exposure to statistics for social science. This brief paperback is especially lucid in discussing descriptive statistics.

SIEGEL, SIDNEY, *Nonparametric Statistics for the Behavioral Sciences*. New York: McGraw-Hill, 1956. An excellent volume devoted to statistical tests utilizable for ordinal data for which the assumption of random selection from a given population cannot be made.

WHYTE, WILLIAM F., *Street Corner Society: The Social Structure of an Italian Slum*. Chicago: University of Chicago Press, 1943. This work, which we have had occasion to cite frequently, is a fine descriptive analysis of a social group.

ZEISEL, HANS, *Say It With Figures* (rev. 7th ed.). New York: Harper & Row, 1957. An excellent treatment of the manner in which one should analyze and present data, including consideration of use of percentages and the setting up of tables.

Explanatory
Analysis

chapter fourteen

THE EXPERIMENT

As pointed out in Chapter 7, the experimental method typically involves a comparison between at least two groups which have been randomly composed. One group is exposed to a "treatment," the other to a different treatment or to nothing at all. The two groups are compared on the particular variable the researcher thinks will be affected by the treatment. The treatment is usually referred to as the "independent" variable in the research, and the variable it will affect is termed the "dependent" variable, since, if our hypothesis is correct, its nature will "depend on" the treatment. The dependent variable comparison between the two or more groups can take many forms. We can compare the percentage of individuals in each group displaying a particular characteristic, compare the arithmetic means in the groups, or do more sophisticated kinds of analysis, such as analysis of variance. Which form we choose depends partially on the level of measurement of our dependent variable. If we have nominal data the percentage is the common statistic; if our data are ordinal, interval, or ratio, a simple comparison of means, medians, or a more complex analysis of variance is feasible. To illustrate the general strategy with a simple comparison of percentages, we shall refer to a possible experiment using the Bales interaction categories discussed in a preceding chapter. We choose this type of experiment as an illustration because when sociologists do experimental work (which is not too often), they often utilize the Bales categories.

Let us assume we are looking at the relationship between the sex composition of a group (the independent variable) and the kind of group interaction (the dependent variable). We have ten university students as subjects—five women and five men. We make certain by one of the techniques discussed in Chapter 7 that the groups are equivalent on all relevant dimensions. To the extent that this is successful, the only difference between them should be their sex composition. Each subject is given a report of a hypothetical problem which has supposedly arisen among employees in an organization. Each is made uncertain as to whether or not his report contains the same facts as the other members of his group, although he is assured that the facts are accurate. The subjects are given time to read the reports individually and are then observed for a given length of time as they attempt as a group to come up with a solution to the problem. Our general expectation is that the kind of interaction taking place in the men's group will be different from that in the women's group. Specifically, we might hypothesize that women will emit a greater frequency of socioemotional behavior than will men. After coding the interaction in each group (as outlined in Chapter 10) we tabulate the number of units of interaction in each category. The fictitious data in Tables 14–1 and 14–2 are illustrative.

The figure 900 means that during the men's session there were 900 units of interaction recorded. For the women the figure was 1000. In order to make it possible to compare the two groups we must eliminate the discrepancy in total number of units of interaction. Standardization is accomplished by converting the raw frequencies to percentages (Table 14–2).

TABLE 14–1 THE FREQUENCY OF KINDS OF INTERACTION IN THE
TWO GROUPS

	Men's Group	Women's Group
Shows solidarity	90	300
Shows tension release	40	200
Agrees	40	100
Gives suggestion	100	50
Gives opinion	200	50
Gives orientation	100	30
Asks for orientation	80	40
Asks for opinion	80	30
Asks for suggestion	45	50
Disagrees	40	100
Shows tension	40	25
Shows antagonism	45	25
	900	1000

TABLE 14–2 THE PERCENTAGE OF KINDS OF INTERACTION IN THE
TWO GROUPS

	Men's Group	Women's Group
Shows solidarity	10.0	30.0
Shows tension release	4.4	20.0
Agrees	4.4	10.0
Gives suggestion	11.1	5.0
Gives opinion	22.2	5.0
Gives orientation	11.1	3.0
Asks for orientation	8.8	4.0
Asks for opinion	8.8	3.0
Asks for suggestion	5.0	5.0
Disagrees	4.4	10.0
Shows tension	4.4	2.5
Shows antagonism	5.0	2.5
$N(=100\%)$	900	1000

Having made both total interaction units equivalent to 100
percent, it is now possible to compare the nature of the interaction in the two groups. The main observation is that the
women's discussion contained a much greater percent of positive
socioemotional reactions than the men's. The first three categories
are much more likely to appear in the women's than the men's

group (30.0 vs. 10.0, 20.0 vs. 4.4, and 10.0 vs. 4.4). The men, on the other hand, were much more task oriented—giving suggestion, opinion, and orientation are much more common in the men's than in the women's group. (11.1 vs. 5.0, 22.2 vs. 5.0, and 11.1 vs. 3.0). In short, the men's interaction appeared to revolve around the assigned task, the women's around the task of socializing with one another.

One experiment, however, is hardly sufficient. In order to verify the finding, we should carry out several more sessions with other groups. If all of them show the above pattern, then we would have some basis for confidence in the results.

Prior to initiating the research, the experimenter would have had some reasons or explanations in mind for the hypothesized relationship. Offering various possible explanations as to the reason for the relationship is part of the analyst's job. For example, he may suggest that when young women are in groups without men there is a leadership vacuum resulting from the learned expectation of women that men tend to make the decisions. As a consequence, attention is turned away from the task and fixed instead on nontask interaction—interaction reflecting a socioemotional emphasis. The analyst may consequently design a new set of experiments to test the explanation. For example, his reasoning implies that women would be more task-oriented in sexually mixed groups than in all women groups, since the presence of men would focus their energies on the task at hand. His next series might thus involve comparing sexually heterogeneous and homogeneous groups in their extent of socioemotional versus task interaction.

THE CAUSAL SURVEY

One of the common kinds of research used in sociology is the cross-sectional survey, which aims at establishing a causal relationship between two variables. Here the researcher might administer a questionnaire to a cross-section of the population at one point in time, utilizing these responses as variables to be related in the analysis. To illustrate, we may be interested in the relationship between a high school student's involvement in extracurricular activities and his desire to finish high school. We hypothesize that students involved in such activities will be more likely than those not involved to want to complete high school, since the former would presumably be more satisfied with their high school experience. We therefore administer a questionnaire to a sample of high school students, questioning them on both their dropout plans and their extracurricular involvement. As well, we include a host of questions tapping other possibly relevant variables, such as the student's social class, his grades in school, and his year in school. The high school plans question might read as follows:

Do you intend to finish high school?

___ Yes

___ No

The question on extracurricular participation might take this form:

Are you a member of any school clubs, teams or organizations?

___ Yes

___ No

Once the data are collected we may discern four distinct phases in survey causal analysis—sample testing and description; computation of a measure of association; testing for the significance of the association; and testing hypotheses alternative to the one stating the two variables are causally related. We shall discuss each of these in turn, move on to a section emphasizing the relationship of type of analysis to measurement level, and conclude with a discussion of mixed unit analysis. The discussion will assume that we begin a survey with one or more clearly spelled-out hypotheses, although this ideal is often not reached. Indeed, researchers are frequently guilty of relating a large number of variables after the data are in with the hope of discovering viable relationships (Selvin and Stuart, 1966).

Sample Testing and Description

This initial phase has already been discussed in the section on descriptive surveys. As in a descriptive survey, the causal survey should include tests for sample representativeness. Here we would take the key variables in our analysis (for example, participation in extracurricular activities, students' grades) and compare sample distributions to population distributions (to the extent, of course, that the latter are available). In our case, we probably would find that a record is kept of each student's grades but that data on membership in school clubs are not collected. We would have to be content, then, with the comparison between the grade distribution in our sample and that in the population of students. We might do the same for sex and year in school, both of which are likely to exist in school records.

The ensuing step is a description of the population in terms of the key variables in our analysis. Because we are carrying out a causal survey does not imply that we leap right into the causal analysis. Before this step, we must describe our population. Providing the reader with basic information about the population sets the stage for later, more complicated analysis. The percent of students planning to finish and drop out of high school, the percent participating in various kinds of extracurricular activities, the percent in each school or type of school in the area, the social class level of the students—all these serve to orient the reader with respect to the group being studied. Once he has digested this fundamental information he can more easily be led into the causal analysis itself.

Measures of Association

There are various statistical techniques for establishing that two variables are related to one another. These are termed measures of association in that they indicate how closely one variable is associated with another. By association we mean the extent to which one can know about one variable simply by knowing about another. For example, sex and hair length are fairly closely associated. If we know a person's hair length, we also usually know his sex. Although this association has weakened in the past decade or so, it still exists to some extent. In our case, we are investigating the hypothesis that extracurricular participation and high school plans are associated. We hypothesize that if we know a person's extracurricular involvement we will also tend to know his high school plans. Specifically, we expect that those involved will be likely to plan on finishing high school, and those not involved less likely to do so. Our immediate task, then, is to compute a measure of association between participation in extracurricular activities and high school plans.

We must first make the point that both our variables, as we have defined them, are nominal variables. The respondent either is a member of school clubs or organizations or he is not. Further, he either plans to finish high school or he does not. There is no degree of finishing or of extracurricular membership in our measure; there is no continuum along which individuals can be ranked. This situation in which both variables to be related are nominal variables is, except for demographic and ecological work, a most common situation in sociological research.

Because of this state of affairs in sociology, we shall illustrate the phases of causal analysis utilizing the two nominal factors referred to above. We shall talk in a later section on analysis with ordinal and interval data. The point to be emphasized, however, is that the logic of causal analysis is the same whatever the level of measurement of our variables. Once a researcher understands the basic strategy, he can apply it in all situations where causal inference is desired regardless of the measurement sophistication of the variables and the specific measures of association used.

This point made, we return to the computation of a measure of association between extracurricular involvement and high school plans. The basic operation is simply counting the number of individuals who fall into each category formed by combining the two variables. The following table represents the four possible combinations:

TABLE 14–3 THE TWO VARIABLES RELATED

		Extracurricular Involvement	
Finishing High		Yes	No
School	Yes	1	2
	No	3	4

We thus have four kinds of individuals—those involved in activities and planning to finish high school; those not involved and planning to finish; those involved and not planning to finish; and those not involved and not planning to finish. Counting the number in our sample in each category can be rather tedious by hand, so we again make use of the computer. Here the machine is simply programmed to count the number of cards in the appropriate categories. For example, let us assume participation in extracurricular activities appears in column 5 of an individual's punch card, with a 1 punch indicating involvement and a 2 punch noninvolvement. The variable of high school plans is found in column 18, with a 1 indicating that the individual plans to finish, a 2 that he does not, and a 3 that he is not sure. We decide to leave the 3s and no answers (represented by 0s) out of the analysis, concentrating on the four types alluded to above. The machine is programmed to count the number of individuals who have: (a) a 1 in column 5 and a 1 in column 18 (Cell 1 of Table 14–3); (b) a 2 in column 5 and a 1 in column 18 (Cell 2); (c) a 1 in column 5 and a 2 in column 18 (Cell 3); and (d) a 2 in both column 5 and 18 (Cell 4). The computer can also be programmed to output the data on printed sheets in the following form:

TABLE 14–4 THE FREQUENCIES IN EACH CATEGORY

		Col. 5 (Participation in Extracurricular Activities)		
		Yes (Punch 1)	No (Punch 2)	
Col. 18 (Finishing	Yes	40 (A)	25 (B)	65
High School)	(Punch 1)			
	No	10 (C)	25 (D)	35
	(Punch 2)			
		50	50	100

Tables such as this are termed cross-tabulation tables ("cross-tabs") since they involve the tabulations for the "crossing" or combining of two or more variables. Most computer centers have standard cross-tab programs which one can use to generate such tables. As can be seen, the data do not consist solely of the number of individuals in each category, but various totals are also given— the total number of individuals involved in extracurricular activities (50); the total number not involved (50); the total finishing high school (65); the total not finishing (35); and the total number of individuals in our sample (100).

This table will serve as the basis for our analysis. A cursory inspection reveals that we do seem to have a relationship between the two variables. If involvement in extracurricular activities is related to high school plans, we would expect the individuals to be concentrated in Cells A and D of the table. That is, most people should be involved and finishing high school or not involved and not finishing. Those that fall in Cells B and C are not compatible with our hypothesis. These are the people who are not involved and who nevertheless plan on finishing, and those who are involved but who do not plan on finishing.

There are a series of measures of association for nominal variables which explicitly make use of this cell distribution notion, among them the *Phi* coefficient and the *Q* coefficient. Both of these are applicable only for 2 × 2 tables such as ours, where there are two dichotomous variables involved. Others, such as the *C* coefficient, can be used with any number of categories of nominal variables (Ferguson, 1959, 194–96).

To illustrate how the appropriate cell distributions are the bases for these measures, the following is the formula for the *Q* coefficient:

$$Q = \frac{AD - BC}{AD + BC}$$

Cells A and D of Table 14–4 are those which, according to our hypothesis, should contain most of the individuals. Cells B and C are inconsistent with the hypothesis. The measure *Q* reflects this by subtracting the product of the undesirable frequencies (BC) from that of the desired ones (AD). The greater the difference, the closer the two variables are related. In our case,

$$Q = \frac{40 \;\; (25) \; - \; (25) \;\; 10}{(40) \;\; 25 \; + \; (25) \;\; (10)}$$

$$= \frac{1000 \; - \; 250}{1250}$$

$$= \qquad + \;.60$$

The coefficient Q, like many other measures of association, ranges from -1 to $+1$; the closer one gets to $+1$ the more closely are the variables positively related. By a positive relationship is meant one that has the following characteristic—as you increase one variable the other also increases. In our case, as you go from no extracurricular involvement to some you also go from not planning to finish high school to finishing. A negative relationship exists when as you increase one variable, the other decreases. If students involved in activities would be less likely to finish high school than those not involved, our relationship could be described as a negative one. As the $+.60$ indicates, we have a fairly high positive relationship. Students involved in activities tend also to plan on finishing high school.

The Q statistic represents a class of measures of association which work with cell frequencies to arrive at the final coefficient. Probably the most common measure of association in sociology, however, works not with frequencies but with percentages. The strategy is to compute the percentage of individuals wanting to finish high school for each extracurricular group, as reflected in Table 14–5.

The data from Table 14–4 have thus been converted to per-

TABLE 14–5 THE RELATIONSHIP IN PERCENTAGE FORM

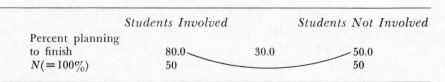

	Students Involved		Students Not Involved
Percent planning to finish	80.0	30.0	50.0
$N(=100\%)$	50		50

centages. There are several characteristics of the table which require emphasizing. First, it is not necessary to present the percentage of students *not* finishing high school for each of the two involvement groups. Obviously, if 80 percent of those involved in activities are planning to finish high school, 20 percent are not. The table is cleaner and less cumbersome to read when we eliminate unnecessary data. A second point is that the total number of individuals on which each percentage is based (the total "Ns," as they are termed) are always given (50 and 50). This allows the reader to see exactly how many respondents the researcher is basing his arguments on. Third, the percentages have been calculated vertically instead of horizontally; that is, we could have computed our percentages in two different ways—using the Ns for high school plans as the base, in which case our percentages would have been

$$\frac{40}{65} = 61.6 \text{ and } \frac{10}{35} = 28.6,$$

and doing it as we have done in Table 14–5 (producing 80.0 percent and 50.0 percent). The first (horizontal) calculation would have given us the percent of students involved in extra-curricular activities for two groups: those planning on finishing high school and those not planning to finish. But we are not interested in the extracurricular involvement, we are interested in the distribution of high school finishing plans, particularly as these are affected by participation in activities. In other words, for us the relevant calculation is the percentage planning on finishing high school for the two involvement groups. We have shown that this is greater for the group involved than it is for those not involved (80.0 percent vs. 50.0 percent). In short, involvement seems to some extent to have affected the distribution of high school finishing plans. The general rule for deciding on vertical vs. horizontal calculations is thus the following: percentages should be computed in the direction of the assumed causal factor—in our case vertically (Zeisel, 1957).

A final point is that our measure of association in the case of percentages is the percentage difference between the various groups pertaining to the variable one is interested in. In our case the percentage difference in high school finishing plans between the two groups is 30.0 (80.0 percent vs. 50 percent). The larger this difference, the closer the two variables are associated. At the extreme, if 100 percent of those involved in activities were planning to finish high school and 0 percent of those not involved were planning to finish, we would have a perfect association—our percentage difference would be 100 percent.

The Statistical Significance of the Association

Thus far we have only computed a measure of the strength of our relationship. The higher the Q or the greater the percentage difference the more strongly do our two variables appear to be related. We say "appear to be related" because we still must deal with our old nemesis—sampling error. What seems to be a relationship between two variables may only reflect sampling fluctuation. In survey research we work with a sample—in our case one hundred students out of a high school population of, let us say, one thousand. Our sample yielded a difference of 30 percent between those involved and those not involved in activities. Had we selected another sample, however, we may have obtained a difference of 20 percent, or perhaps 5 percent; simply because a sample is just that—a piece of the population. Suppose, for example, that in reality there is no difference in high school plans in the population between those involved and those not involved in activities. If the entire one thousand students were surveyed and Table 14–5 were then computed, there would be no percentage difference. The statistical fact is, though, that sometimes, even if there is no difference in the larger population, one will be found in the sample, *by chance alone*. As suggested in Chapter 9, statisticians have carried out experiments showing that even when there is no difference between, say, the number of black and white balls in a drum, any particular sample we draw might nevertheless contain a difference. If there are five hundred white and five hundred black balls in a drum and we select one hundred at random you would expect fifty black and fifty white. But samples are not always perfect—you may get a 55–45 split, a 60–40 split, and upon occasion even such an extreme departure from population reality as a 70–30 split. The question we must ask in our case is the following: Could we have gotten the difference we did (30 percent) if there is in reality no difference in the population? That is, we assume what is commonly termed the *null hypothesis*—that there is really no difference in the population (Grebenik and Moser, 1962).* We then ask the question: What is the probability of getting our sample difference (30 percent) if the null hypothesis is true? We can compute this probability using various statistical procedures to be briefly outlined below. If this probability is small, it means that the difference we found is highly unlikely under the assumption that there really is no difference. That is, the probability that our difference is due to sampling error is quite low. We therefore reject the null hypothesis and infer that we have a "real" difference. If, on the other hand, the probability is high that our difference could have been obtained even though there is no true difference in the population, we fail to reject the null hypothesis, attributing our sample difference to sample error.

To clarify the above discussion, we make use of the concept of standard error. In Chapter 9 we defined this term as a measure of the sample to sample fluctuation of a statistic. In that chapter we computed the standard error of a percentage. Here we shall compute the standard error of a percentage *difference* as a step to computing the probability that our percentage difference could have occurred under the null hypothesis. That is, just as we can conceive of percentages varying from sample to sample, we can conceive of percentage differences varying from sample to sample. The formula for the standard error of a percentage difference is

$$\sqrt{PQ\left(\frac{1}{N_1} + \frac{1}{N_2}\right)}$$

where P = the total percentage of the sample possessing the attribute of interest (in our case "planning to finish high school").

*The null hypothesis method of hypothesis testing is but one approach. One may discern two other schools—the Neyman Pearson approach and the Bayesian approach. These alternative strategies are held by some to be superior techniques (Heerman and Brackamp, 1970).

$Q = 1 - P$; $N_1 =$ the number of respondents on which the first percentage is based; $N_2 =$ the number of respondents on which the second percentage is based. In our case

$$P = \frac{40}{50} + \frac{25}{50} = \frac{65}{100} = 65\% \quad \text{(see Table 4)}$$
$$Q = 35.0$$
$$N_1 = 50$$
$$N_2 = 50$$

so the standard error of our 30 percent difference =

$$\sqrt{(65.0)(35.0)\ \frac{1}{50} + \frac{1}{50}}$$
$$= \sqrt{.46}$$
$$= 7.0 \text{ (approximately)}$$

The standard error is thus roughly 7.0 percent. Statisticians have shown that if there is really no percentage difference in the population, samples will nevertheless vary in their percentage differences. It has been shown that the percentage differences of 68.0 percent of a very large number of samples drawn will fall within ± 1 standard errors, and that slightly over 95 percent of the percentage differences will fall between -2 and $+2$ standard errors. In order to prove this, we would have to draw an extremely large number of samples. Statisticians talk about an "infinite" number of samples. Figure 14–1 illustrates this phenomenon.

That is, if there is no difference in the population (population difference $=0$) 68 percent of the samples drawn will nevertheless show differences ranging from -7 to $+7$ percent, or differences falling between -1 and $+1$ standard errors. Ninety-five percent will fall between -14 and $+14$ percent. Ninety-nine percent of the samples will have differences falling between -2.56 and $+2.56$ standard errors, or between -17.5 and $+17.5$ percent. Any difference outside these limits would be extremely rare if there was no difference in the population. In fact, the probability of getting a difference of 14 percent by chance alone (that is, when there is really no difference in the population) is approximately .05 (since roughly .95 fall between -2 and $+2$ standard errors).

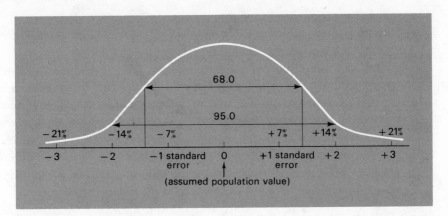

FIG. 14–1 THE PROBABILITY OF VARIOUS DIFFERENCES ASSUMING THE NULL HYPOTHESIS

Indeed, our difference of 30 percent is seen to be an occurrence so rare that it is not even portrayed on the curve. The figures .05 and .01, or their standard error equivalents of -2 and $+2$ and -2.56 and $+2.56$ are usually used to indicate that we have a "real" difference, and not simply one due to chance.

It should also be pointed out here that these standard errors of 2 and 2.56 will change somewhat depending on the specificity of our hypothesis. In our case we could have stated two hypotheses, one a general hypothesis that there is some relationship between activity involvement and high school plans (we do not specify a positive or negative relationship). The second alternative is the one we adopted, specifically predicting the kind of relationship— a positive one, that involvement would lead to a greater probability of wanting to finish high school. In the first situation we would investigate the null hypothesis that there is no relationship at all, either positive or negative, between the two variables. In this case we make use of the whole curve in Figure 14–1 and both positive and negative outcomes are taken into account in computing the significance. In the second instance, however, we would be interested in only the positive side of the curve, since a negative finding would obviously be inconsistent with our hypothesis right from the start. We would not even bother to test for significance if we found a negative relationship. This issue is discussed in most statistics texts under the heading "1 versus 2 tailed tests" (for example, see Blalock, 1960, 127–28).

Because our difference is thus so rare if we assume the null hypothesis, we reject the null hypothesis, arguing that there is a "real" difference in the population. We conclude, then, that those involved in extracurricular activities are truly different in their high school finishing plans from those not involved. We thus have a strong association between the two variables (30 percent difference) as well as a statistically significant one, whose probability of occurring by chance is extremely small.

As a final point, there are tests of significance other than the above, a commonly used alternative being the X^2 test which gives virtually the same results for a 2×2 table. The X^2 has a wider range of applicability, however, since it can be used in tables with more than two categories per variable.

Causality or Not—Alternative Hypotheses

At this point in our analysis we must seriously investigate the hypothesis that our two variables, which are strongly and significantly related, are also causally related. Thus far we have only an association. Moving from this to a causal statement is a fairly elaborate process. We can clarify the problems involved by comparing our position with that of the experimental researcher.

The ideal research format from the point of view of scientific perfection is the experimental design. Here we randomly assign subjects to experimental and control groups, being assured that any variables which could distort the results are pretty well equally distributed in the two groups. One group is then exposed to the independent variable, the other is not. Any difference between the two groups in the dependent variable can then be argued as being due to the independent variable, since the two groups are randomly equivalent in all respects except for the differential exposure to the treatment.

Often, however, it is not possible and/or practical to carry out such a research format. In our case, adopting such a strategy would have meant selecting a sample of one hundred students and randomly assigning fifty to extracurricular activities for a period of time and withholding such activities from the other fifty. Needless to say, such a manipulation of our schools is not typically feasible. The alternative is a survey of high school students which seeks information on extracurricular involvement, high school plans, and a host of other variables which must be collected to investigate the alternative hypotheses to be outlined below. There are two basic and related problems that arise because we did not have experimental control over our project: (1) It is difficult to establish the time order of our variables, and (2) it is difficult to sort out the effects of our independent variable from those of any number of other possible factors.

PROBLEMS OF TIME ORDER. In an experiment we introduce the independent variable at one point in time and then gather data on the dependent variable at a later point. In short, we know the independent variable has preceded the dependent variable in time. As is perhaps obvious, establishing this time sequence is a fundamental prerequisite for arguing causality. If you cannot show that x preceded y, x can hardly be considered a cause of y. In our case this time issue is an important one. Is it the case, as we would like to believe, that extracurricular involvement affects high school plans, or could it be that the nature of a person's high school plans determines whether or not he will become involved in extracurricular activities? A not unreasonable argument is that our relationship is due to the fact that people planning to leave high school are less likely to invest time and effort in school clubs and organizations simply because they have already decided to terminate connections with the school.

One way to begin sorting out these two hypotheses is to include in the questionnaire a few items probing the respondent's memory regarding the time certain decisions took place. What we ideally want to show is that the two groups—those involved and those not involved in activities—were similar in their high school plans at some point prior to the "experimental" group's exposure to extracurricular activities. Suppose we asked, for example, the following question:

When you first entered high school, what were your intentions about finishing?

_____I fully intended to finish high school
_____I wanted to finish but I had some doubts about it
_____I did not think I would finish
_____Don't remember

The following table would then be set up:

TABLE 14-6 ORIGINAL INTENTIONS BY EXTRACURRICULAR INVOLVEMENT

		Member	Nonmember
Percent fully intending to finish when entering high school	a	85.0	83.0
	b	83.0	51.0

Outcome (a) would give us somewhat more confidence in our causal argument. It would indicate that upon entering high school the two groups were similar in their intentions. Whatever happened to change this therefore happened after exposure to high school life. Needless to say, of course, other things could have happened to the experimental group other than exposure to school activities, but at least we can say that it appears that the difference between the two groups emerged within the high school context. A more valid test would be to present only first-year students in Table 14-6. This would cancel out some of the memory problems that would obtain for the upper years. It is assumed to be easier for a first-year student to remember his thoughts on entrance than it would be for a student who had entered three or four years before.

Outcome (b) would be quite threatening to our hypothesis. It would indicate that students who are members of clubs and organizations were different to begin with from those who ultimately did not join activities. This leads to the hypothesis that variables other than the extracurricular factor are involved.

A second and perhaps less tenuous strategy would be to compare the high school finishing plans of students who had been involved in activities for varying lengths of time. The argument would be that if extracurricular involvement did indeed affect high school plans, then the longer the individual has been involved the more likely he would be to want to finish. Table 14–7 supports this hypothesis:

TABLE 14–7 HIGH SCHOOL PLANS BY LENGTH OF EXTRACURRICULAR INVOLVEMENT

| | Those involved in Activities for: | | |
	Less than 3 months	Between 3 and 6 months	Over 6 months
Percent wanting to finish	60.0	75.0	90.0
$N(=100\%)$	15	15	20

The table reveals that wanting to finish high school increases with increasing exposure to activities; a finding which should emerge if indeed activity involvement causes high school plans. It must be recognized, though, that a student who has been much involved in activities is probably different in other respects as well from those not involved. For example, he may be in his later years of high school, a fact which alone could cause him to be more likely to state he will finish. In short, other factors must be taken into account in the analysis. We shall return to this point when we explicitly discuss the matching problem.

A third way of dealing with the time problem is to question the respondents at more than one point in time. We could, for example, measure the commitment to a high school education of a group of students before they entered high school. Some time later, perhaps six months, we might question them again. At this second questionnaire adminstration we would also secure data on extracurricular involvement. The question we would ask is the following: What effect does activity involvement have on the change in a person's attitudes toward high school? If we can show that a greater percentage of club members change from negative to positive attitudes, we have considerably strengthened our causal argument.

The conclusion in all the above strategies cannot be that we have "proven" our argument, however. Because we were not able to randomly equate our two groups prior to the experimental group's exposure to extracurricular activities, we can never be sure that our relationship is indeed a causal one. All we can do is present a good argument and build a plausible case through techniques like the ones we have discussed. As a final note here, the time order issue is not always the serious problem presented above. It is often quite obvious which variable preceded which in time. A hypothesis asserting that the social class position of one's family affects one's high school plans is not plagued with time problems. The hypothesis that one's high school plans have "caused" one's social class status does not make much sense. It is only when the two variables to be related are ambiguous with regard to sequence that we must be concerned with the hypothesis that y causes x rather than the reverse.

PROBLEMS OF MATCHING. As stated, our two groups of students were not equated before the study. They may be different in many respects aside from their difference in extracurricular participation. We must somehow match the two groups after the fact, as it were, to be able to attribute the difference in our dependent variable to the factor of activity involvement. In short, we must attempt in survey research to approximate as closely as possible the experimental situation of groups randomly equivalent on all factors except the "treatment" or independent variable. This means that in the questionnaire we include questions designed to gather data on those variables in which we think the two groups might differ and which are at the same time probably related to high school plans. For example, it may well be the case that social class is related to club membership. The higher the social class position of a student's family, the more likely he might be to engage in extracurricular pursuits (Hollingshead, 1949). The involvement and noninvolvement groups are therefore likely to differ in their social class composition. Further, we know from previous research that social class is related to educational plans. Generally, the higher the social class of an individual's family the higher he aims in the educational system (Boocock, 1966). It may well be, then, that the reason for our original relationship is not causal at all, but arises out of the relationship of social class to both our variables:

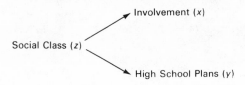

Fig. 14–2.

To use the common terminology, our relationship may be a *spurious* one. As Figure 14–2 indicates, *x* and *y* may only be associated because a third variable, *z*, has caused them both. To investigate this possibility we must seek information on the social class position of our respondents. This is typically done by several questions on father's occupation, education, or income. There may also be variables other than social class about which we must gather data. A person's academic average might also be relevant, as well as his year in school. Our questionnaire should thus be carefully constructed, containing questions relating to various alternative hypotheses such as that in the above diagram. With such data we are able to match our two groups on various factors that might be distorting our results.

To illustrate the process, let us "match" on social class. To do this, we simply repeat Table 14–5, except that we do it separately for each social class group we distinguish. (Cross-tabulation programs which do this are available in most research institutions.) Let us suppose we are working with two social class groups—those students whose fathers are nonmanual workers we consider as one class level, while those whose fathers are manual workers we consider as a second level. We then look at our involvement—high school plans relationship for each of the two groups (Table 14–8).

The table depicts, in extreme form, each of the possible outcomes of the matching procedure. What we have done by looking at our relationship for each social class group is equated the groups on social class. The left side of the table portrays the relationship for students with nonmanual fathers only. The right side

TABLE 14–8 HIGH SCHOOL PLANS BY ACTIVITY INVOLVEMENT, MATCHING
ON SOCIAL CLASS

		Nonmanual			Manual	
		Involved	Not Involved	Involved		Not Involved
Percent wanting to finish H.S.	a	80.0 — 0 —	80.0	50.0 — 0 —		50.0
	b	80.0 — 30.0 —	50.0	80.0 — 30.0 —		50.0
	c	80.0 — 0 —	80.0	75.0 — 30.0 —		45.0

does the same for students with manual fathers. The logic is the
following: if social class *is* the reason for our involvement/high
school plans relationship, then when we match on social class our
relationship will disappear, since there is no longer any difference
in social class for our involvement groups. In fact, outcome (a)
would indicate precisely this—when one matches on social class,
our involvement comparisons yield no difference at all. Eighty
percent of nonmanual students who are involved in activities wish
to finish high school, while 80 percent of the same nonmanual
group who are *not* involved wish to finish. The manual comparison is 50.0 percent versus 50.0 percent. In short, when we equate
on social class there is no longer any difference. This means that
the reason for our initial relationship was due solely to the fact
that individuals with nonmanual fathers are more likely to join
school clubs and also more likely to want to finish high school
than sons and daughters of manual workers. We must, therefore,
reject our initial causal hypothesis. It should be noted, however,
that in practice we never get a complete disappearance of a relationship, partially because of measurement error. In the above
table, for example, a manual-nonmanual measure of social class
would in all likelihood be too crude a measure of social class to
effect a complete disappearance. This point will be dealt with in
more detail later.

Outcome (b) however forces us to reject the alternative hypothesis. When we match the two groups on social class they still
show a large difference in high school finishing plan. For both
manual and nonmanual groups the association is 30.0 percent.

Here we conclude that social class is not the reason for our relationship. The next step is to match on various other relevant factors (for example, academic grades or year in school). If our relationship holds up under all such tests we increase our confidence in its viability.

Outcome (c) is an example of what has been termed *specification*, or an *interaction effect*. We find that our relationship still holds, but only for manual workers. That is, membership in clubs does affect high school plans, but only if the subject is from the lower socioeconomic stratum. If the father is a nonmanual worker, involvement in activities makes absolutely no difference to a student's high school plans. We have thus specified one of the conditions for our relationship to emerge.

Matching thus aids both in determining spurious relationships and in discovering conditions under which our relationship is more or less likely to hold. It must be reemphasized, though, that we can never conclude that our relationship is in fact a causal one or even a nonspurious one. We can only increase our confidence in this probability. Because we were not able to randomly equate the groups prior to the study, there is always the possibility that there are variables other than the ones in our questionnaire —variables which we did not know about and which could be distorting our results. We can, however, do our best to see that variables discerned as important by pervious researchers are included in our questionnaire, as well as any others which we personally feel are relevant to the problem.

Once we have carried out several tests of our original hypothesis and have assured ourselves as well as we can that we have a "real" relationship, the next step is to attempt, again by matching,. to "explain" our relationship. Here we seek to answer the following question: Why does x affect y? Why does involvement in extracurricular activities produce a greater likelihood of wanting to complete high school? What variable or variables come or intervene between our independent and dependent variables? Note that here our purpose is different from that of spuriousness testing. In spuriousness testing we were concerned that a third variable, z, which preceded or occurred at the same time as x, was producing a false picture of the relationship between x and y. Here we want to find out if a third variable, which occurs after or at the same time as x but before y, will explain our relationship. This is a major step in theory building. We are attempting to determine the process or processes linking our two original variables. The relevant diagram is the following:

$$x \longrightarrow z \longrightarrow y$$

This is a fourth major possibility, apart from the $x \longrightarrow y$ hypothesis, the $y \longrightarrow x$ hypothesis, and the $z \overset{\displaystyle x}{\underset{\displaystyle y}{\diagdown}}$ hypothesis. Suppose in our case, for example, we suspect that the variable intervening between x and y is satisfaction with the school experience. Further, we have included the following question on our questionnaire:

How satisfied would you say you are with your high school experience?

___ Extremely satisfied

___ Moderately satisfied

___ Moderately dissatisfied

___ Extremely dissatisfied

We match our two involvement groups on this variable, as the following table illustrates:

TABLE 14-9 HIGH SCHOOL PLANS BY ACTIVITY INVOLVEMENT, MATCHING ON SATISFACTION

		Satisfied		Dissatisfied	
		Involved	Not Involved	Involved	Not Involved
Percent wanting to	a	80.0 ____ 0 ____ 80.0		50.0 ____ 0 ____ 50.0	
finish	b	80.0 ____ 30.0 ____ 50.0		80.0 ____ 30.0 ____ 50.0	

Again, the two ideal type outcomes are presented. The first indicates that when one matches on satisfaction there is nothing left of our involvement–high school plans association. We have shown that the reason for our relationship is the presence of a third variable, which is related to both of our original variables. As will be recalled, this is exactly what we concluded when we considered the social class variable. Here, however, our stance is quite different. Whereas the social class factor obviously preceded both involvement and high school plans in time, the high school satisfaction variable can be argued to be a consequence of extracurricular involvement but an antecedent of high school plans. This decision to treat satisfaction as an intervening- rather than as spuriousness-producing variable is thus not only based on the time ordering of the variables. In our case this is a hazy situation and we are not sure of the exact order—for example, we cannot be certain that satisfaction came before or after the student's decision to stay in school. Nevertheless, we build a reasonable case for the $x \longrightarrow z \longrightarrow y$ interpretation based, we believe, on a plausible argument; it makes sense to see satisfaction as emerging out of extracurricular involvement and in turn affecting high school plans. We conclude, therefore, that we have explained our relationship—our key intervening variable is general satisfaction with one's high school experience.

Outcome (b) indicates that whatever the reason for our assumed causal relationship, it is not general satisfaction with high school. Matching our groups on this factor did nothing to our original association; it remains as strong as ever (30.0 percent). If we found this or something similar we would turn our attention to alternative possible intervening variables, the ultimate object being explanation as we have defined it.

To conclude this section, we must again emphasize that our attempts at matching must be regarded as at best compromises. Not only do we not have all the relevant variables at hand but we are also limited to a certain extent in that the variables we do have may be poorly measured. For example, measuring social class by two categories of father's occupation (manual and nonmanual) may be too crude to allow us to match with confidence. Within each of these social class groups there may be considerable variation in father's occupation. The nonmanual worker could be a lower-level clerical worker or a physician. Are we really matching, then, when we look at our two involvement groups within the manual and nonmanual categories? This has serious consequences for our analysis. One of the main bases of inference is observing what occurs when we introduce a third variable into the analysis. Whether the original relationship changes or not is crucial for the analytical scheme we impose on our data. The fact is that virtually never does a relationship disappear after matching on another factor. First, this would mean that the variable was the sole cause of the relationship—an extremely unlikely situation in sociology, where multiple causality has been the most prevalent conclusion in research. Further, even if the third factor truly is causing the initial association it will not cancel completely the relationship, since we never have perfect measurement. Our illustrations are thus "ideal" types, occurrences which would take place if our variables were perfectly measured. One solution, of course, is to have more refined categories for our major variables. Instead of two social class categories one might have three or four, thus improving our measure of this variable. If we do this, however, we create more problems for ourself, since we lose various advantages which stem from using two, or at the most, three category variables. One of these is the fact that tables are easily read with few categories, and as we increase the number we render the tables more confusing. Another advantage is that with dichotomous variables we conserve the number of cases on which our analysis is based. Obviously, if we were to employ three or four social class categories we would be reducing the number of respondents in each cell of our table. And, as pointed out several times, the more cases on which our statistics are based, the more accurate our portrayal of the population. As we refine our measures, then, we lose in the area of statistical significance. This whole problem of measurement of possibly contaminating variables need not arise in experimental research because here matching is typically carried out using randomization. This means that if three physicians' sons end up in the control group, three physicians' sons will probably end up in the experimental group—a refinement not possible with survey matching.

A further point in this regard is that in experimental research we are essentially matching on a host of variables at once (this due to randomization), while in survey research we can usually only match on one or two variables at a time. The one or two at a time limitation is again related to our limited number of respondents. When we break our two involvement groups down into manual and nonmanual families, we have four categories of individuals instead of the original two (involvement and noninvolvement). If we had still another dichotomous variable we wished to match on, we would have eight types of students. If we had a sample of one hundred students, we would quickly have percentages based on a very small and hence statistically shaky number of respondents. Because of this, plus the problem of making sense of a table with more than three variables in it, we typically match on only one or two variables at a time. Obviously this is not as precise a technique as matching on all variables simultaneously as we are able to do in experimental formats.

In light of this discussion, one could easily throw up one's hands and decide that survey research is too problematic to be worthwhile. Such a conclusion fails to note a major advantage of survey research over experimental research, however. This is the ability to generalize to a large population, a frequent deficiency in experimental work. In deciding on the appropriate research format this should be kept in mind, as well as the obvious point that one's hypotheses cannot always be tested *via* experiment. Such was the case with the high school plans example used in the preceding discussion. In any event, one must come to his own decision about research format, and this will be a decision which should be made within the limits set by the reality of the situation and the kind of research problem one has formulated.

As a concluding note here, the reader should be aware that there exist more sophisticated matching techniques with nominal variables, which somewhat alleviates the problems discussed above. For example, the necessity of "one at a time matching" created by the difficulty of making sense out of multicell tables is dealt with by Rosenberg, Coleman, and Labovitz. Rosenberg has applied a technique called "standardization" to survey data, which yields *one* summary effect measure of the original relationship with other variables matched. This means that it is not necessary to look at the original relationship within several subgroups and attempt to make sense out of these various comparisons. Coleman has developed a similar technique for nominal data which also produces one summary measure of the relationship. He contributes as well to the problem of percentages based on a small number of respondents by using a weighting technique. This issue is also dealt with by Labovitz, who discusses three strategies for minimizing the small sample problem: selecting only the two or three most important variables to match on; combining the matching variables into one summary index; and a technique termed "cell ordering and combination" (Rosenberg, 1962; Coleman, 1964; and Labovitz, 1965).

Analysis with Variables other than Nominal*

It has been suggested earlier that much of the research in sociology has been conducted with nominal variables rather than higher measurement level data. We should introduce one important qualification, however. Demography and ecology work almost exclusively with ratio variables. This is due in large extent to the fact that the unit which demographers and ecologists study is not the individual, but some larger collectivity such as the community, the city, or the nation. This allows the researchers to work with percentages as characteristics of the units. Data which might be nominal when individuals are studied are converted into ratio variables when collectivities are studied. (Percentages, obviously, have 0 points and ratio characteristics.) For example, religion at the individual level is a nominal variable. An individual is either Catholic or he is not—there is no 0 point, no continuum involved. The percentage of Catholics in a city, however, is a ratio variable, and we can carry out all the operations appropriate to this level of measurement.

It is in the fields of demography and ecology, then, that the bulk of the work with such variables has been carried out. This is not to say that it is not possible to find ratio variables at the individual level. A person's income and the number of years of university

---

*We illustrate non-nominal analysis with a ratio-level example. There are, of course, statistical measures, such as the Spearman rank order correlation (rho) which may be used on ordinal data and for which the calculative procedures are very straightforward.

education he has had are two examples. Generally, though, it is difficult to find more than a few individual-level variables for which ratio measures have been achieved.

To illustrate work with ratio data, then, we shall use an ecological problem. We should first point out that whether we are working with ordinal, interval, or ratio variables, the four phases of analysis discussed above remain the same, as well as the logic of causal analysis itself. The only difference concerns the type of measures of association used and hence the kinds of statistical significance tests employed.

Instead of working with percentage differences or measures like the Q coefficient, we work with some kind of *correlation coefficient*, the most common being the r measure. Suppose, for example, we have ten communities for which we have data on the mean length of residence of their immigrant members as well as the percent speaking English. The latter can be conceived of as a measure of assimilation into the community. We might set up our data for each community as follows:

TABLE 14–10 LENGTH OF RESIDENCE AND ENGLISH-SPEAKING DATA FOR IMMIGRANTS IN TEN COMMUNITIES

Community	Mean Years of Residence of Immigrants	Percent Immigrants Speaking English
A	3	8.0
B	1	10.0
C	8	20.0
D	6	30.0
E	2	14.0
F	7	35.0
G	9	55.0
H	1	12.0
I	3	18.0
J	5	25.0

A look at the table indicates that the percentage of people speaking English seems to increase with the mean year of residence. That is, there seems to be a positive correlation between the two variables. If we transform the data into graph form the correlation is more conspicuous:

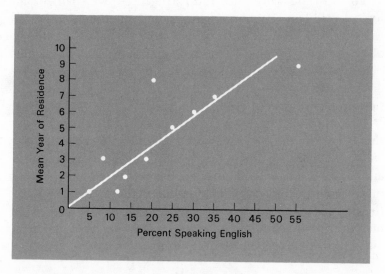

FIG. 14–3 THE DATA IN GRAPH FORM

The dots tend to go from bottom left to upper right—as mean year of residence increases so does percent speaking English. This figure is usually called a *scatter diagram*, because it indicates the scatter pattern of the dots formed by relating the two variables. The line in the figure is termed the *regression line*, and is that line which can be drawn closest to all the dots. There is one and only one such line for each scatter diagram. While we are not going to discuss exactly how one arrives at the regression line, we can see it as that line from which the average distance of the dots is a minimum. In fact, the correlation coefficient may be seen as a measure of the spread around the regression line. The smaller the spread the higher the correlation between the two variables. At the extreme, if all the dots are on the line the relationship is perfect ($+1$); if the dots are all over the place and the only line which can be drawn is a horizontal one, we have no relationship at all (see Figure 14–4.)

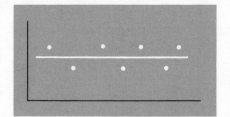

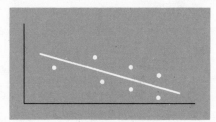

FIG. 14–4 0 RELATIONSHIP   FIG. 14–5 NEGATIVE RELATIONSHIP

We may also, of course, have negative relationships. If, in our example, we found something like Figure 14–5, we would have a correlation somewhere between 0 and −1; as the mean year of residence increases, the percentage of immigrants speaking English decreases. Like the Q coefficient, then, the r coefficient varies between −1 and +1. The formula for r, as well as significance tests for r, can be found in any statistics text. The purpose here is to convey a feel for the r measure rather than its concrete operationalization.

What do we do when we wish to introduce a third variable, however? Suppose we do find a positive correlation between the mean length of immigrant residence in a community and the percentage of immigrants speaking English. At one point in our analysis we would be interested in asking the questions: Why are the two variables related? What is it about mean length of residence that affects language acquisition? We may hypothesize that the intervening variable is that of community friendship patterns. That is, the longer the mean residence of immigrants in a community, the higher the proportion of their friends from the host community is likely to be. This in turn is expected to lead to a higher percent acquiring English. In order to test this we carry out essentially the same general matching operation as we did for nominal data—the principle is the same. We wish to match on community friendship patterns to see if this changes our original relationship between residence and percentage speaking English. Instead of using cross-tabulations, however, we use the interval-ratio data counterpart to this—partial correlation, or the correlation between two variables, given that there has been compensation for a third variable. We may see this measure as our original residence/language correlation computed within various percentage intervals of cross-ethnic friendships and then averaged across these intervals. This would produce the required correlation measure, assuming we have "matched" on friendship patterns. The result would then be compared to our original correlation. We might find, for example, that the original relationship before matching was +.60, a fairly high positive correlation. However, matching on friendship patterns might produce a partial correlation of only .20. We would then conclude that a major factor explaining our relationship is the percent of cross-ethnic friendships in the community.

To close the discussion of the analysis type and measurement, we might point out that there are measures of association that exist not only for nominal and higher level data, but for mixtures of these. We might, for example, be interested in the relationship between attending a private or public high school and one's total income after the first year on the job. Here we have a nominal variable related to a ratio variable, and there are special techniques for handling such a situation. Whatever the combination of levels of measurement, though, the fundamental logic of causal analysis remains the same. We have only to make the specific statistical procedures appropriate to the kind of variables with which we are working.

Problems of "Mixed-Unit" Analysis

Before concluding our discussion of explanatory strategies, we must deal with an interesting, though challenging type of analysis in sociology—what may be termed "mixed-unit" analysis. By this we mean the situation in which the variables we are working with characterize both groups and individuals. Figure 14–6 summarizes four logical types of two-variable analyses.

We may thus characterize both our independent and dependent variables according to whether they are properties of groups or of individuals. For example, the researcher may be working with the problem suggested above—that of relating the mean years of

Independent Variable

		Group Characteristic	Individual Characteristic
Dependent Variable	Group Characteristic	Ecology and Demography	Culture and Personality
	Individual Characteristic	Structural Effects Analysis	Standard Sociology Analysis

FIG. 14–6 TYPES OF TWO-VARIABLE ANALYSIS*

residence of immigrants in a community (the independent variable) to the percentage speaking English (the dependent variable). In this case both variables are community characteristics; they are thus attributes of groups as opposed to individuals. As the figure indicates, such work is most typical of demography and ecology. With one exception, no particular problems accrue from this kind of analysis. The logic of causal inference remains the same, although it is necessary to bear in mind the statistical tools appropriate for ratio level variables. One problem that might arise, however, is that the researcher may commit what has been termed the *ecological fallacy*. This was first discussed by Robinson (1950), who showed that correlations based on groups do not necessarily apply at the level of individuals. Robinson found a strong *negative* correlation between the percentage of foreign-born people in census areas and the proportion of illiterates in such areas. As the percentage of the foreign-born increased, the illiteracy rate decreased. Is it possible, though, to deduce from this that foreign-born *individuals* are more likely to be literate than native-born residents? The answer is clearly no. In fact, it may well be the case that foreign-born individuals are more likely to be illiterate than native people, because the group level correlation offers no guarantee that the *same* individuals who are foreign-born are also literate. They may very well be different individuals. Indeed, when Robinson later computed a correlation based on individuals, he found a *positive* relationship; that foreign-born inhabitants

*There are a number of typologies similar to the above—see for example, Riley, 1964.

are more likely to be illiterate than are native people. In short, we cannot infer from a group level correlation alone that a relationship is viable at the level of individuals.

A second type of two-variable analysis we term *standard analysis,* in that it represents perhaps the most common kind of relationship in sociology. This again is a situation in which both independent and dependent variables characterize the same unit —in this case the individual. A relationship between an individual's social class and his voting behavior would be an example. This is the most straightforward, least problematic kind of analysis represented in Figure 14–6.

It is when one is involved in analysis in the remaining two cells that certain difficulties arise—difficulties accruing from a mixing of group and individual level variables.

A very rare situation is exemplified in the case of attempting to explain a group characteristic by reference to individual level factors. The clearest example is provided by a body of studies in anthropology relating culture and personality. There are a number of positions as to what direction this relationship takes. One view is that the cultural features of a particular society (for example, religion, folklore) are expressions of the dominant personality attributes of its members. Relying heavily on Freudian concepts, researchers in this area gathered data from several societies in order to test this hypothesis (Kardiner, 1939; Whiting and Child, 1953). Because such studies have been criticized in detail elsewhere (Lindesmith and Strauss, 1950; Singer, 1961), and because they bear little relevance for contemporary sociological analysis, we shall not explore their deficiencies. Suffice it to say that two major problems of the approach concern the great difficulties of producing an argument which is noncircular and attaining relatively independent measures of the two variables being related.

A fourth type of mixed unit analysis relates to what have been termed variously in the literature *structural effects, contextual effects,* or *compositional effects* analysis. The attempt is to explain variation in an individual level variable by reference to a characteristic of groups. Two kinds of group characteristics may here be discerned; those which result from combining or aggregating individual characteristics into a group level characteristic, and those which are unaggregated measures. For example, if we were to count the number of middle-class students in a school and compute the percentage of the student body which was middle class, this percentage would be an aggregate group characteristic, since it is derived from the attributes of group members. On the other hand, if we were to classify schools as public or private, the measure would be *nonaggregate* in that it is independent of individual level factors.

Structural effects analysis is particularly important in sociology, since we are continuously concerned with the consequences for individuals of membership in different kinds of work groups, families, organizations, and communities. What is the effect on aspiration levels of being a student in a very bright class? How does being surrounded by high-productivity factory workers affect an individual's productivity? Or, as Durkheim asked, what is the effect on suicide of living in countries exhibiting high divorce rates (Durkheim, 1951)?

The methodological problems associated with this kind of question are quite extensive and can quickly become complicated. There are, however, two major problems with which we may deal, given the previous discussion. The first—the selection problem—applies to both nonaggregate and aggregate variables; the second—the matching problem—is associated most explicitly with aggregate measures.

PROBLEMS OF SELECTION. In Chapter 7 the example was given of a survey investigating the relationship between the presence of resource teaching in a school and the performance of students. We were thus relating a nonaggregate group characteristic to an individual level variable. At that time, the problem of selection was mentioned as a possible distorting factor. That is, what appears to be a relationship between resource teaching and performance might reflect only differences in the kinds of students attending the two types of schools. Let us elaborate somewhat more on this issue.

It is possible to discern three patterns of selection into any group—random, individual initiated, and group initiated. The first is the situation in which individuals appear in groups completely unsystematically. There is no reason whatsoever of suspecting any relationships between various characteristics of individuals and the particular groups they end up in. The composition of army units and prison cellblocks is usually arrived at randomly. And, of course, experimental situations in which researchers have complete control are likely to produce randomly constructed groups.

Obviously, however, this kind of situation is quite rare in non-laboratory environments. To the extent that some freedom of membership exists, individuals will choose groups that manifest desirable characteristics. We may term this *individual initiated* selection. Not only do individuals select groups, however, but groups in turn often place restrictions on the type of members they are willing to receive. Standards set by private clubs and fraternities are examples.

Turning to our school example, we must certainly investigate the selection hypothesis. How did students get into the resource and conventional schools? If we are to argue for a causal relationship between type of teaching and performance we must satisfy ourselves that the relationship does not come about either (1) because highly motivated and/or bright students *choose* to attend resource schools, or (2) because resource schools select only bright, motivated people to be involved in their programs.

Finding out about group-initiated selection (that is, in this case, the recruitment policies of schools) is relatively easy. If we do not find a selection process we may breathe easier; if we do, however, we must consider various strategies. We may briefly mention two of them (they are discussed in somewhat more detail in Chapter 7):

1. Carefully match on brightness and motivation, comparing only students in each school type similar on these two factors.
2. If the resources are available, construct a longitudinal format so that one can observe *change* in performance throughout the school years. If those initially low on some measures of performance have progressed positively, we have a much more convincing argument than one based simply on a cross-sectional format.

What about individual initiated selection? If the researcher is fortunate, he will find that students have little choice in the school they attend and are simply assigned on the basis of residence. Here, then, no possibility of direct selection exists. If this is not the case, though, he must again be suspicious, adopting either of the techniques listed above and any other strategies he can come up with. For example, one might actually ask students why they chose their school. This would shed a good deal of light on the extent to which their choice was based on teaching style as opposed to other factors. If choice could be shown *not* to be based on teaching style, the researcher is in a good position to argue that the relationship is uncontaminated by selection.

Even if students are allocated to schools by area of residence, there will probably be *indirect* selection operating. Communities are by no means randomly composed with respect to social class.

This might imply that resource schools differ in their class composition as well as in their teaching styles. We term this indirect selection, since we are not thinking of the case, say, of students high on motivation and brightness deliberately choosing resource schools. Rather, we have in mind the operation of ecological and demographic factors which produce a more subtle kind of selection. In this instance, differential class composition of communities could be the real reason for the school-type performance relationship. The strategy here, then, could be to match carefully on social class before seriously considering the original hypothesis.

Not only, of course, do individuals select themselves into groups, but they also differentially select themselves out. We must also ask when using group variables who, if anyone, has left the group, which would affect the relationship of interest.

In sum, then, whenever there are group-level factors as independent variables, attempts to disprove the alternative hypothesis of selection must be of central concern.

PROBLEMS OF MATCHING. We have already considered matching as a strategy for dealing with the selection problem. It assumes greater importance, however, when we are dealing with group level variables which are aggregated characteristics of individuals. Here the failure to adequately match on the individual level factor composing the aggregate measure leads to possibly serious misinterpretations of effects.

To illustrate the problem, let us take an often discussed relationship in the sociology of education—that between social class composition of school and aspiration level of students. Specifically, it is hypothesized that students in middle-class schools will have higher aspiration levels than those in lower-class schools, since the climate of achievement motivation extant in middle-class value systems is expected to foster a greater commitment to getting ahead. The argument, then, is that one is more likely to internalize such an ethic in middle-class as opposed to lower-class schools (Wilson, 1959). The question is how would one test this hypothesis? A first inclination is illustrated by the following table:

TABLE 14–11 COLLEGE ASPIRATIONS BY SCHOOL SOCIAL CLASS COMPOSITION

| | Schools with: | |
	50% or Over Middle-Class Students	Less Than 50% Middle-Class Students
Percent wanting to go to college	75.0	45.0

We thus count the number of middle-class individuals in each school (for example, students with fathers holding nonmanual jobs) and calculate the percentage of the student body this represents. We then divide the schools into two categories—those with 50 percent or more middle-class students and those with less than 50 percent middle-class students. The measure of aspiration level is the student's response to the question: Are you planning to attend college upon graduation from high school?

The table indicates a relationship between these two factors; that is, being in a school with 50 percent or more middle-class students seems to produce higher aspirations than being in a predominantly lower-class school (75 percent versus 45 percent plan to attend college). But is this really a structural effect? How do we know that the reason for the finding is not simply due to the fact that middle-class *individuals* are more likely to desire college than lower-class individuals? The relationship may not reflect a group influence at all, but only an individual level influence. That is, there is a greater percentage of middle-class students in the first school type. Further, middle-class students are known to have higher aspirations than lower-class students; hence the results of Table 14–11. There seems no reason to draw upon the more complex (although sociologically pleasing) interpretation of effects of social context. To demonstrate a structural effect, it is necessary to match on individual social class (Blau, 1960). Table 14–12 would be a start in this direction.

Table 14–12

	Schools with 50% or Over Middle-Class Students		Schools with Less Than 50% Middle-Class Students	
	middle-class students	lower-class students	middle-class students	lower-class students

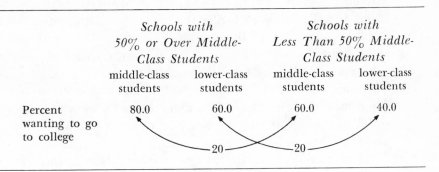

	80.0	60.0	60.0	40.0
Percent wanting to go to college				

The table now indicates that regardless of an individual's social class, he is more likely to want to go to college if he is in a school with a large percentage of middle-class students. For middle-class students, the difference due to the middle-class enrolment is 20 percent (80 percent versus 60 percent); while it is the same for lower-class individuals (60 percent versus 40 percent). Here, then, is an apparent effect over and above the individual's own position on the variable of interest, an effect of the social context in which he is embedded.

We say "apparent" because one may legitimately question the adequacy of our matching procedure. It has been argued that demonstrating a structural effect with an aggregate factor is problematic because of the stringent matching necessary on the individual level counterpart of the aggregate variable. To be more specific, are we really comparing students of equal social class in Table 14–12? As may be recalled, students with nonmanual fathers were termed "middle class," while those with manual fathers were described as "lower class." Within each category, however, there is considerable variation; nonmanual includes occupations as disparate as physician and clerk, while manual includes occupations such as street sweeper as well as highly trained electrician. Further, it might well be that in communities with a large population of middle-class inhabitants (columns 1 and 2 of Table 14–12), professional and business occupations would be the prevalent nonmanual occupations. Similarly, because of the high housing costs in such communities, electricians and other high-level manual workers would be more common than laborers and other unskilled workers. In short, it may well be that when we compare columns 1 and 3 of Table 14–12 rather than comparing students of equal social class, we are really comparing students from professional and business homes with those from clerical families. Further, columns 2 and 4 might well be comparing sons and daughters of craftsmen with those from laborer families. Far from having demonstrated a structural effect, then, we may have only a spurious relationship—one resulting from inadequate matching on our individual level variable.

What can one do, then, if his interest leads him to an investigation of effects of aggregate factors? In concluding this section, there are at least two solutions that we will briefly mention (Tannenbaum and Backman, 1964):

1. Utilize more than two categories of the individual level variable. In our example, rather than simply working with a nonmanual/manual break, it would be desirable to have four or five categories; for example, laborer, blue-collar worker, white-collar worker, business, professional. School comparisons within each of these categories would produce a much more conclusive analysis.

2. To the extent that it is possible, work with correlational and partial correlational methods as opposed to cross-tabulations. Such techniques can be shown to be more precise in terms of establishing true relationships between variables (Tannenbaum and Backman, 1964; Hauser, 1970).

CONCLUSION

Analysis in sociology is at best a tenuous business. We are typically in situations in which the ideal conditions of analysis have been only approximated. This is related to our preoccupation with behavior in the "real" world as opposed to laboratory experiments of behavior. We pay for this by constantly worrying about the extent to which the associations we are interested in are true reflections of reality or simply consequences of our inadequate control over the data. The good sociologist would seem to be one who is aware of the weaknesses of his analytical procedures and at the same time compensates for them by creative and imaginative strategies. Sociological research is thus a compromise between what we would like to do and what we can do; it is, in essence, the art of the possible.

REFERENCES

BLALOCK, HUBERT, JR., *Social Statistics.* New York: McGraw-Hill, 1960.

BLAU, PETER, "Structural Effects," *American Sociological Review,* 26 (1960), 178–93; reprinted in D. Forcese and S. Richer, eds., *Stages of Social Research: Contemporary Perspectives,* pp. 282–303. Englewood Cliffs, N.J.: Prentice-Hall, 1970.

BOOCOCK, S., "Toward a Sociology of Learning," *Sociology of Education,* 39 (1966), 1–45.

COLEMAN, JAMES, *Introduction to Mathematical Sociology.* New York: Free Press, 1964.

DURKHEIM, EMILE, *Suicide.* Glencoe, Ill.: Free Press, 1951.

FERGUSON, G. A., *Statistical Analysis in Psychology and Education.* New York: McGraw-Hill Book Co., 1959.

GREBENIK, E. AND C. MOSER, "Statistical Surveys," in Forcese and Richer, *Stages of Social Research.*

HAUSER, R. M., "Context and Consex: A Cautionary Tale," *American Journal of Sociology,* 75 (1970), 645–64.

HEERMAN, E. AND L. BRACKAMP, eds., *Readings in Statistics for the Behavioral Sciences.* Englewood Cliffs, N.J.: Prentice-Hall, 1970.

HOLLINGSHEAD, A., *Elmtown's Youth.* New York: John Wiley, 1949.

KARDINER, A., *The Individual and His Society.* New York: Columbia University Press, 1939.

LABOVITZ, SANFORD, "Methods for Control with Small Sample Size," *American Sociological Review,* Vol. 30 (1965), 243–49; reprinted in Forcese and Richer, *Stages of Social Research,* pp. 273–82.

LINDESMITH, A. R. AND A. L. STRAUSS, "A Critique of Culture-Personality Writings," *American Sociological Review,* 15 (1950), 587–600.

RILEY, M. W., "Sources and Types of Sociological Data," in R. C. Faris, ed., *Handbook of Modern Sociology,* pp. 1014–1020. Chicago: Rand McNally, 1964.

ROBINSON, W. S., "Ecological Correlations and the Behavior of Individuals," *American Sociological Review,* 15 (1950), 351–57.

ROSENBERG, MORRIS, "Test Factor Standardization as a Method of Interpretation," *Social Forces,* Vol. 41 (1962), 53–61; reprinted in Forcese and Richer, *Stages of Social Research,* pp. 261–73.

SELVIN, M. AND A. STUART, "Data-Dredging Procedures in Survey Analysis," *American Statistician* (June 1966), 20–23; reprinted in D. Forcese and Richer, *Stages of Social Research,* pp. 326–32.

SINGER, M. B., "A Survey of Culture and Personality Theory and Research," in B. Kaplan, ed., *Studying Personality Cross-Culturally,* pp. 9–90. New York: Harper & Row, 1961.

TANNENBAUM, A. S. AND J. G. BACKMAN, "Structural Versus Individual Effects," *American Journal of Sociology,* 69 (1964), 585–95; reprinted in Forcese and Richer, *Stages of Social Research,* pp. 303–15.

WHITING, J. W. M. AND I. R. CHILD, *Child Training and Personality.* New Haven: Yale University Press, 1953.

WILSON, A. B., "Residential Segregation of Social Classes and Aspirations of High School Boys," *American Sociological Review*, 24 (1959), 836–45.

ZEISEL, HANS, *Say it with Figures* (rev. 4th ed.). New York: Harper & Row, 1957.

SELECTED ADDITIONAL READINGS (ANNOTATED)

BLALOCK, HUBERT, JR., *Causal Inferences in Nonexperimental Research*. Chapel Hill: University of North Carolina Press, 1961. A pioneering attempt to suggest rules of causal inference in sociological analysis.

BLAU, PETER, "Structural Effects," *American Sociological Review*, Vol. 25 (1960), 178–93; reprinted in Forcese and Richer, *Stages of Social Research*, pp. 282–303. A good discussion of the use of group characteristics as independent variables—what Blau terms "Structural effects."

DOGAN, M. AND S. ROKKAN, eds., *Quantitative Ecological Analysis in the Social Sciences*. Cambridge: The MIT Press, 1969. An excellent collection of papers on ecological as well as mixed-unit analysis. The reader is especially referred to chapters 2, 4, and 6, which focus explicitly on analysis involving group and individual level variables.

FORBES, H. D. AND E. TUFTS, "A Note of Caution in Causal Modelling," *American Political Science Review*, Vol. 62 (1960), 258–64; reprinted in Forcese and Richer, *Stages of Social Research*, pp. 370–79. A formal treatment of the inferential or interpretive dimension of causal analysis.

HIRSCHI, T. AND M. SELVIN, "False Criteria of Causality in Delinquency Research," *Social Problems*, Vol. 13 (1966), 254–68; reprinted in Forcese and Richer, *Stages of Social Research*, pp. 335–52. The authors offer several errors in causal inference and suggest some general rules for causal interpretation.

HYMAN, HERBERT, *Survey Design and Analysis: Principles, Cases and Procedures*. New York, The Free Press, 1955. An excellent and thorough discussion of the entire survey research process. Part III is explicitly concerned with data analysis and the problems involved in establishing causality.

LABOVITZ, SANFORD, "Criteria for Selecting a Significance Level: A Note on the Sacredness of .05," *American Sociologist*, Vol. 3 (1968), 220–22; reprinted in Forcese and Richer, *Stages of Social Research*, pp. 322–26. Discussion of the implications of selecting a level of significance in examining hypotheses.

TANNENBAUM, A. AND I. BACKMAN, "Structural Versus Individual Effects," *American Journal of Sociology*, Vol. 69 (1964), 565–95; reprinted in Forcese and Richer, *Stages of Social Research*, pp. 303–15. This paper discusses the importance of controlling individual level variables when the researcher is intent upon considering the possibility of structural effects.

The Beginning
and
The End

The actual conduct of research is very dependent upon planning. Careful consideration of exactly *what* is to be done and *how* it will be done will avoid many of the errors and hasty compromises that might otherwise characterize a research project. At so many points through the course of research, it is necessary to make decisions, choosing among alternate strategies and techniques; every decision in this regard has consequences for subsequent decisions, limiting a researcher's freedom and range of discretion. Accordingly, to optimize the potential for full control over any research project, he should have from the outset as complete an understanding as is possible of the range of alternatives from which he may choose and of the implications of such choices.

Good and insightful advance planning is, of course, in part a function of the experience of a researcher and of his colleagues in the work. If he has experienced the actual conduct of research, encountered difficulties, and realized some solution to these difficulties, then he is better able to anticipate the problems that might be encountered in initiating another research project and carrying it to completion. Whether he draws upon his own experience, therefore, or that of someone else, prior planning, which consists of thinking out in advance the consequences and the interdependencies of each decision, is a prerequisite of any competent research.

Such planning is tangibly manifested in a thorough research proposal. There is certainly the attraction in a pragmatic approach to research wherein one chooses to muddle along and defer—sometimes forever—consideration of the obstacles which will have to be overcome in order to bring a research program to fruition. And certainly there will be opportunities enough to cover up research errors derivative of such a manner of research. But a careful proposal will serve to facilitate each stage of the research and will aid in the avoidance of error rather than require a belated cosmetic approach to the enquiry. In a very real sense, a research proposal is the first stage in the actual conduct of research.

A research proposal is a statement of research intention, both as to goal and to the means for the realization of that goal. Significantly, it is a statement subject to the careful study of the researcher himself and to the scrutiny of aides and colleagues. This examination occurs prior to any expensive and restrictive commitment to given data-collection orientations and procedures. Accordingly, refinements and corrections may be introduced from the outset at the most strategic and economical point.

A proposal, therefore, is a map of intended research wherein are specified the assumptions, concepts, and methods to be used through the conduct of the total research project. A proposal should contain at least the following:

1. A statement of research goal or hypotheses.
2. An outline of the preliminary literature survey, indicating (a) the theoretical bases of the research hypotheses, and (b) the methodological approaches which have been used in the prior examination of similar and/or related hypotheses.
3. A conceptual specification, both abstract and operational.
4. A declaration of research format.
5. A specification of how subjects or respondents will be selected.

6. A specification of the data collection tools which are to be employed, and how they are to be employed.
7. A specification of the anticipated analytical procedure(s), including the statistical measures which are to be used.
8. A cost projection, outlining anticipated allocations of money, time, and personnel.

Research Goal

It is usually easy for the researcher to indicate a broad interest in some area of research. He will have personal preferences and interests, and perhaps some prior professional or employee commitment. But necessarily, in order to effectively conduct research, an interest in some broad area will have to be broken down into researchable components. Failing this, a research effort is doomed to be so diffuse as to prove ineffectual.

Specification of research interest takes the form of hypotheses, whether descriptive or explanatory. The hypothesis provides a precise statement of a researcher's object of enquiry. As such, it guides the subsequent steps of research, for the nature of the hypothesis will affect the data needs of the researcher.

Literature Survey

The refinement of hypotheses will be realized through the course of a researcher's literature survey. Anyone contemplating research assumes a basic obligation to explore the published reports of related research. Such a search generally sensitizes a researcher to his area of enquiry, pointing up the findings, limitations, and difficulties associated with these reported findings. Consideration of the reported research will provide suggestions regarding suitable and practical conceptualizations, sampling and data-collection techniques, and similarly, appropriate techniques of data analysis.

Generally, the literature survey permits a researcher to place his work within the context of accumulated research findings and theory. Moreover, it permits him to draw upon the experiences of other researchers such that in the design of his own enquiry he can adapt to the virtues and the flaws of this prior work.

Conceptual Specification

Many research projects are ruined or seriously jeopardized before a researcher ever enters the field to collect his data. Quite simply, research is often handicapped by imprecise conceptualization. Failing to pin down his variables, a researcher is apt to tap such a broad range of meaning as to render his findings unintelligible. The meaning of the concepts used, their operational indicators, and the measurement procedures must be carefully spelled out so that any reader may be fully informed as to the specific intention of the researcher. In the research proposal, such conceptual specificity, and its perusal by colleagues permit a refinement of concepts and the avoidance of the idiosyncratic use of concepts.

Formal Sampling and Data Collection

A statement of the research format and the data-collection approach within the context of this format will also allow informed criticism and correction before a researcher actually incurs the costs of fieldwork. The research proposal should contain justification of the format proposed. Similarly, the precise research tool(s) and the manner in which subjects will be selected should be justified in terms of the nature of the research problem and in terms of the resources available to the researcher.

Information should also be included about the pretest that is to be conducted in order to assess the adequacy of the research design and tools adopted. Any data-collection approach should be pretested in order to expose hitherto undetected weaknesses, such as the ambiguous word or the unclear or misleading question. Such an investigation should be conducted using subjects as similar as possible to those actually dealt with in the research project proper.

In addition, therefore, to the simulated pretest represented by "picking the brains" of friends and colleagues, the application of the tools of research to some sample of persons such as are eventually to be studied is a crucial means of refining one's instruments.

Data Analysis

Not only should a research proposal project data-generation procedures but data analysis intentions also should be stated and justified. It is important to determine whether the researcher will in fact be collecting data appropriate to the intended analytical techniques. For example, he may blithely assume that the research data to be collected will be analyzed using some correlation model. Yet the proposed data collection may not yield data of a level of measurement appropriate to correlation analysis. If such a disparity is noted at the level of the proposal rather than after the data are in, an advantageous adjustment in data collection may well be made.

Cost Projection

A precise outline of anticipated research expenses is necessary for the efficient allocation of available resources. In a sense, this is necessary for the protection of the researcher and of any financial sponsor.

It is all too easy to elaborate a research approach which seems ideally desirable. Yet when some cost accounting is attempted, it often becomes clear that the ideal and the practical are not synonymous. A cost projection, as with every aspect of the research proposal, is part of the process of "putting all the cards on the table." Lacking such a cost projection, a research project may founder and wither permanently short of completion for want of funds.

The Research Report

When the collection of data and the subsequent analysis has been completed, research is still incomplete until the results are made public and disseminated to the community of scientists and others who are interested in the project. A research report, whether prepared for circulation within some wider research agency or administrative organization or to appear in book form or as a paper in some professional journal, should report the details of the conduct of the research. This report will be consistent with the sections of a research proposal insofar as it must outline the inception of the research, its theoretical basis and salience, the conceptualization, measurement, research format, sampling, data-collection tools, and the details of the analysis. It should include, for example, the reproduction of key questions in an interview or questionnaire, as well as details of the sampling, including the vital information concerning the rate of response.

In addition, the research report should include candid comment upon difficulties encountered; weaknesses the researcher has himself detected should be noted.

It is most vital, of course, that the research findings be specified, as clearly as possible. Elaborate comment upon the findings, including some speculation as to their significance, is not inappropriate. But the exact findings, as opposed to speculative interpretation, should be presented in such a manner that they will stand out from such comment. Tables and graphic aids should be as simple as possible so that the critical features of the data may be easily noted by the reader. Summary statistics should be employed to facilitate appreciation of the findings and to draw attention to the important characteristics of the data.

Finally, the complete research report should include, when feasible, suggestions for additional research. In initiating the research project, the researcher will have drawn upon the experience of others. Similarly, in suggesting additional research, a researcher will be drawing upon his recent experience in an area of enquiry in order to suggest the manner in which he believes subsequent research might most profitably proceed.

CONCLUSIONS

Any researcher is interested in maximizing the accuracy and adequacy of his data. The research proposal is invaluable in this regard, for it permits the scrutiny of intended research prior to the actual immersion in the project.

Yet even the most satisfactory data would fail to have their potential realized if they were not communicated, and communicated in the context of some larger tradition of research. The research report is the vehicle of such communication. Accordingly, it will incorporate any device that might suitably enhance, without oversimplification, the presentation of research results. Only at this point, with findings made public, is a research project in any sense completed.

ADDITIONAL READINGS (ANNOTATED)

BART, P. AND L. FRANKEL, *The Student Sociologist's Handbook*, Cambridge, Mass.: Schenkman Publishing Co., Inc., 1971. A succinct guide to published sources of information in sociology, and how to use them.

BATTEN, THELMA, *Reasoning and Research: A Guide for Social Science Methods.* Boston: Little, Brown, 1971. A good, lucid, and practical outline of how research is organized prior to, during, and after the data have been collected.

HAMMOND, PHILIP, (ed.), *Sociologists at Work.* New York: Basic Books, 1964. The several essays in this volume illustrate the less formal or "muddling through" aspect of research, as well as the manner in which the errors, deficiencies, and guesses of the behind-the-scenes project may be obscured in the "clean" report.

ZEISEL, HANS, *Say it with Figures* (Rev. 4th ed.). New York: Harper & Row, 1957. The best "how to do it" approach to data analysis and presentation, considering practical matters ranging from the construction of tables and the logic of causal analysis.

BIBLIOGRAPHY I: METHODS TEXTS AND REFERENCES

ACKOFF, R., *The Design of Social Research*. Chicago: University of Chicago Press, 1953.

BACKSTROM, C. M. AND G. HURSH, *Survey Research*. Evanston, Ill.: Northwestern University Press, 1963.

BART, P. AND L. FRANKEL, *The Student Sociologist's Handbook*. Cambridge, Mass.: Schenkman Publishing Co., 1971.

BALES, R. F., *Interaction Process Analysis: A Method for the Study of Small Groups*. Reading, Mass.: Addison-Wesley, 1950.

BLALOCK, H. M., *Causal Inferences in Non-experimental Research*. Chapel Hill: University of North Carolina Press, 1964.

————, *Social Statistics*. New York: McGraw-Hill, 1960.

————, *An Introduction to Social Research*. Englewood Cliffs, N.J.: Prentice-Hall, 1970.

BLALOCK, H. M. AND A. E. BLALOCK, eds., *Methodology in Social Research*. New York: McGraw-Hill, 1968.

BORGATTA, E. AND G. BOHRNSTEDT, eds., *Sociological Methodology 1969*. San Francisco: Jossey-Bass, 1969.

————, *Sociological Methodology 1970*. San Francisco: Jossey-Bass, 1970.

BRUYN, S. T. H., *The Human Perspective in Sociology*. Englewood Cliffs, N.J.: Prentice-Hall, 1966.

CAMPBELL, D. AND J. STANLEY, *Experimental and Quasi-Experimental Designs for Research*. Skokie: Rand McNally, 1963.

CICOUREL, A. U., *Method and Measurement in Sociology*. New York: The Free Press, 1964.

COCHRAN, WILLIAM, *Sampling Techniques* (2nd ed.). New York: John Wiley, 1963.

COLEMAN, J., A. ETZIONI, AND J. PORTER, *Macrosociology: Research and Theory.* Boston: Allyn & Bacon, 1970.

CONWAY, FREDA, *Sampling: An Introduction for Social Scientists.* London: Allen & Unwin, 1967.

COTTON, J. W., *Elementary Statistics.* New York: Pergamon, 1967.

DENZIN, NORMAN, *The Research Act: A Theoretical Introduction to Sociological Methods.* Chicago: Aldine, 1970.

DENZIN, NORMAN, (ed.), *Sociological Methods: A Source Book.* Chicago: Aldine, 1970.

DIRENZO, GORDON, *Concepts, Theory and Explanation in the Behavioral Sciences.* New York: Random House, 1969.

DOGAN, M. AND S. ROKKAN, eds., *Quantitative Ecological Analysis in the Social Sciences.* Cambridge, Mass.: M.I.T. Press, 1969.

DORNBUSCH, S. M., AND C. F. SCHMID, *Primer of Social Statistics.* New York: McGraw-Hill, 1955.

DUVERGER, MAURICE, *An Introduction to the Social Sciences.* New York: Praeger, 1964.

EDWARDS, A. L., *Techniques of Attitude Scale Construction.* New York: Appleton-Century-Crofts, 1957.

ETZIONI, A. AND F. DUBOW, eds., *Comparative Perspectives: Theories and Methods.* Boston: Little, Brown, 1970.

FALLDING, H., *The Sociological Task.* Englewood Cliffs, N.J.: Prentice-Hall, 1968.

FILSTEAD, W., ed., *Qualitative Methodology.* Chicago: Markham Publishing Co., 1970.

FISHBEIN, MARTIN, ed., *Readings in Attitude Theory and Measurement.* New York: John Wiley, 1967.

FORCESE, D. AND S. RICHER, eds., *Stages of Social Research: Contemporary Perspectives.* Englewood Cliffs, N.J.: Prentice-Hall, 1970.

FRANKEL, MARTIN, *Inference from Survey Samples: An Empirical Investigation.* Ann Arbor: University of Michigan Institute for Social Research, 1971.

FRANKLIN, B. AND H. OSBORNE, *Research Methods: Issues and Insights.* Belmont, Calif.: Wadsworth, 1971.

FRANZBLAU, A. N., *A Primer of Statistics for Non-Statisticians.* New York: Harcourt Brace Jovanovich, 1958.

GALTUNG, JOHAN, *Theory and Methods of Social Research.* New York: Columbia University Press, 1967.

GOODE, W. AND P. HATT, *Methods of Social Research.* New York: McGraw-Hill, 1952.

GREENWOOD, ERNEST, *Experimental Sociology: A Study in Method.* New York: King's Crown Press, 1949.

GREER, SCOTT, *The Logic of Social Inquiry.* Chicago: Aldine, 1969.

HABENSTEIN, ROBERT, *Pathways to Data: Field Methods for Studying Ongoing Social Organizations.* Chicago: Aldine-Atherton, 1971.

HAMMOND, P. E., ed., *Sociologists at Work.* New York: Basic Books, 1964.

HAYS, WILLIAM, *Statistics.* New York: Holt, Rinehart & Winston, 1963.

HAYS, WILLIAM AND ROBERT WINKLER, *Statistics: Probability, Inference, and Decision.* New York: Holt, Rinehart & Winston, 1971.

HEMPEL, C. G., *Fundamentals of Concept Formation in Empirical Science.* Chicago: University of Chicago Press, 1952.

HOPE, K., *Elementary Statistics.* New York: Pergamon, 1967.

HOROWITZ, IRVING L., ed., *The Rise and Fall of Project Camelot.* Cambridge, Mass.: M.I.T. Press, 1967.

HUMPHREY, G. AND MICHAEL ARGYLE, eds., *Social Psychology Through Experiment.* New York: John Wiley, 1960.

HYMAN, H., *Survey Design and Analysis.* New York: Free Press, 1955.

HYMAN, HERBERT et al., *Interviewing in Social Research.* Chicago: University of Chicago Press, 1954.

JUNKER, BUFORD, *Field Work: An Introduction to the Social Sciences.* Chicago: University of Chicago Press, 1960.

KAPLAN, ABRAHAM, *The Conduct of Inquiry: Methodology for Behavioral Science.* San Francisco: Chandler, 1964.

KELMAN, HERBERT, *A Time to Speak: On Human Values and Social Research.* San Francisco: Jossey-Bass, Inc., 1968.

KERLINGER, F. N., *Foundations of Behavioral Research: Educational and Psychological Inquiry.* New York: Holt, Rinehart & Winston, 1964.

KISH, LESLIE, *Survey Sampling.* New York: John Wiley, 1965.

LABOVITZ, S. AND R. HAGEDORN, *Introduction to Social Research.* New York: McGraw-Hill, 1971.

LASTRUCCI, C. L., *The Scientific Approach.* Cambridge, Mass.: Schenkman, 1963.

LAZARSFELD, P. F. AND MORRIS ROSENBERG, *The Language of Social Research* (rev. ed.). New York: Free Press, 1971.

LINDZEY, G. AND E. ARONSON, *Revised Handbook of Social Psychology*, Vol. 2. Reading, Mass.: Addison-Wesley, 1968.

LIPSET, S. M. AND R. HOFSTADTER, *Sociology and History: Methods.* New York: Basic Books, 1968.

MADGE, J. H., *The Tools of Social Science.* London: Longmans & Green, 1953.

MANN, PETER, *Methods of Sociological Enquiry.* Oxford: Basil Black-well & Mott, 1968.

MARSH, R. M., *Comparative Sociology: A Codification of Cross-Sectional Analysis.* New York: Harcourt Brace Jovanovich, 1967.

MAXWELL, A. E., *Analyzing Qualitative Data.* London: Methuen, 1961.

McCALL, G. AND J. SIMMONS, *Issues in Participant Observation: A Text and Reader.* Reading, Mass.: Addison-Wesley, 1962.

MERRITT, R. L. AND S. ROKKAN, eds., *Comparing Nations.* New Haven: Yale University Press, 1966.

MILLER, D. C., *Handbook of Research Design and Social Measurement.* New York: McKay, 1964.

MILLS, C. W., *The Sociological Imagination.* New York: Oxford University Press, 1959.

MOORE, F. W., ed., *Readings in Cross-Cultural Methodology.* New Haven: HRAF Press, 1966.

MOSER, C. A., *Survey Methods in Social Investigation.* London: Heinemann Educational Books, Ltd., 1968.

NAGEL, ERNEST, *The Structure of Science: Problems in the Logic of Scientific Explanation.* New York: Harcourt Brace Jovanovich, 1961.

NETTLER, G. WYNN, *Explanations.* New York: McGraw-Hill, 1970.

NORTHROP, FILMER, *The Logic of the Sciences and the Humanities.* New York: Macmillan, 1949.

PHILLIPS, E. S., *Social Research: Strategy and Tactics.* New York: Macmillan, 1966.

PLUTCHIK, R., *Foundations of Behavioral Research.* New York: Harper & Row, 1968.

PRZEWORSKI, A. AND H. TEONE, *The Logic of Comparative Social Inquiry.* New York: John Wiley & Sons, Inc., 1970.

RICKMAN, H., *Understanding and the Human Studies.* London: Heinemann Educational Books, Ltd., 1967.

RILEY, M. W., *Sociological Research.* New York: Harcourt Brace Jovanovich, 1963.

ROKKAN, STEIN, ed., *Data Archives for the Social Sciences.* Paris: Mouton Press, 1966.

ROKKAN, STEIN, *Comparative Research across Cultures and Nations.* Paris: Mouton Press, 1968.

ROKKAN, S. AND J. VIET, eds., *Comparative Survey Analysis,* Paris: Mouton Press, 1969.

ROSE, ARNOLD, *Theory and Method in the Social Sciences.* Minneapolis: University of Minnesota Press, 1954.

ROSENTHAL, R. AND R. ROSNOW, *Artifact in Behavioral Research.* New York: Academic Press, 1970.

RUDNER, R. S., *Philosophy of Social Science.* Englewood Cliffs, N.J.: Prentice-Hall, 1966.

SCHUESSLER, KARL, *Analyzing Social Data: A Statistical Orientation.* Boston: Houghton Mifflin, 1971.

SELLITZ, CLAIRE et al., *Research Methods in Social Relations* (rev. ed.). New York: Holt, Rinehart & Winston, 1961.

SIEGEL, SIDNEY, *Non-parametric Statistics for the Behavioral Sciences.* New York: McGraw-Hill, 1956.

SIMON, J., *Basic Research Methods in Social Science.* New York: Random House, 1969.

SJOBERG, GIDEON, ed., *Ethics, Politics, and Social Research.* Cambridge, Mass.: Schenkman, 1967.

SJOBERG, G. AND R. NETT, *A Methodology for Social Research.* New York: Harper & Row, 1968.

DESOLA POOL, ITHIEL, ed., *Trends in Content Analysis.* Urbana, Ill.: University of Illinois Press, 1959.

STEPHAN, F. F., AND P. J. MCCARTHY, *Sampling Opinions: An Analysis of Survey Procedure.* New York: Wiley, 1958.

STOUFFER, SAMUEL, et al., *The American Soldier.* Princeton: Princeton University Press, 1951.

STOUFFER, SAMUEL, et al., *Measurement and Prediction.* New York: John Wiley, 1966.

SUDMAN, SEYMOUR, *Reducing the Cost of Surveys.* Chicago: Aldine, 1968.

TAYLOR, C. L., ed., *Aggregate Data Analysis.* Paris: Mouton Press, 1968.

THOMLINSON, RALPH, *Sociological Concepts and Research.* New York: Random House, 1965.

Toma, Elias, *Economic History and the Social Sciences: Problems of Methodology.* Berkeley: University of California Press, 1971.

Torgerson, W. S., *Theory and Methods of Scaling.* New York: Wiley, 1958.

Vallier, Ivan, *Comparative Methods in Sociology.* Berkeley: University of California Press, 1971.

Wakeford, John, *The Strategy of Social Inquiry: A New Programme in Methods and Measurement for the Student of Sociology.* London: Macmillan, 1968.

Wall, W. D. and H. L. Williams, *Longitudinal Studies and the Social Sciences.* London: Heinemann Educational Books, 1970.

Wallace, Walter, *The Logic of Science in Sociology.* Chicago: Aldine-Atherton, 1971.

Wartofsky, M., *Conceptual Foundation of Scientific Thought.* New York: Macmillan, 1968.

Webb, Eugene et al., *Unobtrusive Measures: Nonreactive Research in the Social Sciences.* Chicago: Rand McNally, 1966.

Whyte, W. F., *Street Corner Society: The Social Structure of an Italian Slum* (enl. 2nd ed.). Chicago: University of Chicago Press, 1955.

Wilson, E. Bright, Jr., *An Introduction to Scientific Research.* New York: McGraw-Hill, 1957.

Zeisel, Hans, *Say it With Figures.* New York: Harper & Row, 1957.

Zetterberg, Hans, *On Theory and Verification in Sociology* (3rd ed.). Totowa, N.J.: Bedminister Press, 1965.

BIBLIOGRAPHY II: METHODS WORKBOOKS

Batten, Thelma, *Reasoning and Research: A Guide for Social Science Methods.* Boston: Little, Brown, 1971.

Dean, D. and P. Valdes, *Experiments in Sociology* (2 volumes: Student's Manual and Instructor's Manual). New York: Appleton-Century-Crofts, 1967.

Larsen, O. and W. Catton, Jr., *Conceptual Sociology.* New York: Harcourt Brace Jovanovich, 1963.

Straus, M. and J. Nelson, *Sociological Analysis: An Empirical Approach Through Replication.* New York: Harper & Row, 1968.

Wiseman, J. and M. Aron, *Field Projects for Sociology Students.* Cambridge, Mass.: Schenkman, 1970.

INDEX

Abstraction, 27, 28, 29, 30, 31–32, 33, 34, 35, 37, 38, 45, 53, 54
  and communication, 28
  and models, 38, 115
  and operationalization, 30, 33, 34
  of phenomena, 27, 30, 32, 37
Analysis:
  in causal survey, 221–48
  in descriptive case study, 196–200
  in descriptive survey, 200–212
  in experiment, 218–20
  and level of measurement, 73–74, 201, 207–8, 210, 244–45, 248
Aristotle, 43
Arkin, M., and Cult, 125, 136
Aron, Raymond, 17, 25
Artificiality, 96–97, 101, 108
  and generalization, 156
  in observation, 143–44, 153, 156
  and validity, 101
Association, measure of, 221, 222–28, 245–47

Backman, J. G., Tannenbaum and, 256–57, 258, 260
Bacon, F., 3, 42–43
Bales, Robert, 59, 74, 153, 154, 155, 157, 218
Ball, John, 174–75, 176
Barber, B., and Fox, 21, 25, 43, 50
Bart, P., and Frankel, 267
Batten, Thelma, 267
Becker, Howard, 151, 152, 157
Berelson, B., 190
  with Lazarsfeld, and Gaudet, 88
  and Steiner, 4, 12
Bisco, R., 188–89, 190
Blalock, A., and Blalock, 75
Blalock, H. Jr., 136, 214, 232, 257, 258
  and Blalock, 75
Blau, Peter, 35, 84, 87, 255, 257
Blishen, Bernard, 32–33, 34
Boguslaw, Robert, 120
Boocock, S. S., 236, 257
  and Coleman, 120

Brackamp, L., Heerman and, 229, 258
Breuer, J., and Freud, 82, 88
Brown, C., Colman, Smallwood and, 214
Burgess, R., and Bushell, 109
Bushell, D., Jr., Burgess and, 109
Butterfield, Herbert, 12, 43, 50

Campbell, Donald, 96, 99, 108
  and Stanley, 109
Campbell, D., with Webb, Schwartz, and Sechrest, 85, 88, 157
Causation, 7–8, 9, 11–12, 43, 78, 100–101, 102, 103, 105, 259
  and analysis, 105, 220–23, 225–32, 236–38, 245, 248–49, 253
  causal variable, 90, 106, 200, 220
  and hypotheses, 194
  and selection problem, 252
  by third factors, 242
  time order and, 106, 233–36, 241
  (see also Explanation, Matching)
Child, I. R., Whiting and, 250, 258
Cochran, Mosteller and Tukey, 128, 134, 136
Coleman, James, 74, 214, 243–44, 257
  Boocock and, 120
  Lipset, Trow and, 82, 88, 183
Colman, H., Smallwood and Brown, 214
Communication, 28–29
Comte, August, 4
Concepts, 29, 30, 32, 33, 34, 35, 37, 38, 39, 40, 43, 44, 45, 47, 48, 49, 50, 53, 54, 75
  critical concepts defined, 30
  defined as abstractions, 37
  and models, 115
  and observation, 151
  and operationalization, 31, 33, 34, 186, 264
  and questionnaire construction, 165
  and research proposal, 264
Confidence interval, 128–29, 132, 133
Content analysis, 185–86, 190
  defined, 186
Copernicus, 3

275